A
Conspiracy
of Goodness

A
Conspiracy
of Goodness

Contemporary Images of Christian Mission

DONALD E. MESSER

2 b

Abingdon Press
Nashville

A CONSPIRACY OF GOODNESS:
CONTEMPORARY IMAGES OF CHRISTIAN MISSION

Copyright © 1992 by Abingdon Press

This book is printed on recycled, acid-free paper.

Library of Congress Cataloging-in-Publication Data

MESSER, DONALD E.
    A conspiracy of goodness: contemporary images of Christian mission/Donald E. Messer.
        p.   cm.
    Companion volume to: Contemporary images of Christian Ministry c1989. ·
    Includes bibliographical references and index.
    ISBN 0-687-09484-4 (alk. paper)
    1. Mission of the Church. 2. Church—Unity. I. Title.
BV601.8.M448   1992
226—dc20   91-38562
                                                                                        CIP

Scripture quotations, unless otherwise noted, are from the New Revised Standard Version of the Bible, copyright 1989 by the Division of Christian Education of the National Council of Churches of Christ in the USA. Used by permission.

Those noted GNB are from the *Good News Bible*—Old Testament: Copyright © American Bible Society 1976; New Testament: Copyright © American Bible Society 1966, 1971, 1976. Used by permission.

Those noted KJV are from the King James Version of the Bible.

Those noted REB are from *The Revised English Bible.* Copyright © 1989 by The Delegates of the Oxford University Press and The Syndics of the Cambridge University Press. Reprinted by permission.

Those noted RSV are from the Revised Standard Version of the Bible, copyright 1946, 1952, 1971 by the Division of Christian Education of the National Council of Churches of Christ in the USA. Used by permission.

Excerpt from *You! Jonah!* by Thomas J. Carlisle on page 75 is used by permission of Wm. B. Eerdmans Publishing Company, Grand Rapids, Michigan.

95 96 97 98 99 00 01 02 03 04 — 10 9 8 7 6 5 4 3

TO

GRANDMA FOLTZ

*whose love was so inclusive
that all her grandchildren thought
they were her favorite!*

Contents

Foreword

A Conspiracy of Goodness is such an unfashionable book that it verges on being embarrassing.

Where has Donald E. Messer been during these recent years of revolutionary thinking about ministry? He has certainly traveled and read and experienced and taught enough to be aware of fashions, but where does that awareness show?

For instance, the biggest trend in prescription for the future of the church is to engage in market analysis and then adjust to satisfy what the potential consumer wants. On the face of things, it may seem strange for the church to do this market analysis of the "unredeemed world" and take the signals from its desires. Yet letting the consumer world call the tune works: act upon it and you can go "Mega." Bring up the cost of discipleship and the cross later, if at all.

Messer brings them up sooner: a sure recipe for disaster. Yet speaking of discipleship, cross, and mission, does not mean that this author is crabby (and, remember, crabbiness is in fashion these days, too!). I see here something of the spirit of Jesus' market analysis in the Marcan version of the story of "The Rich Young Ruler." Jesus had a way of diagnosing what kept and would continue to keep one from the sweep of the kingdom and then to confront that right off. In this case, riches were the barriers. "Jesus, looking at him, *loved him* and said, 'You lack one thing; . . .' And the young ruler was 'shocked and went away grieving,' " for what he already had kept him from being open to what Jesus could demand and give. My act of italicizing two words from Mark 10:21 should be accompanied by the conventional insertion of "*[Emphasis mine]*," but I think it was the emphasis of Mark. Matthew and Luke do not include the words.

11

Donald E. Messer lets us see that he loves the world, the created and jeopardized sphere, the redeemed and wayward sphere, the potentially holy but self-profaning sphere. Because he loves them, he sets out to diagnose need, to see what keeps each from being realized. But in these chapters we see little market analysis. Instead, Messer reaches elsewhere for what he thinks the Christian community and gospel have to offer: to the sources of that gospel and community themselves.

That, I have said, is an unfashionable thing to do, and I can picture the kind of reviews this book would get if the fashionables would take it on. In its own way it is liberal in an era when "L" is to be expunged from vocabularies. It also dares to speak well of "compassion" in a time when the cynics have said that that biblical notion is, like so many biblical notions, sentimental, too soft to help one survive in the era of the self-help market. Messer's heroines and heroes are the often discredited self-sacrificers who did not know the first rule of life, of Christian life, in our time: be fashionably self-centered and let the overflow of your consequent goodness trickle down to the less fortunate.

As if his general cultural stance did not buy Messer enough trouble, he takes on more when he then turns in the other direction and reaches for concepts which the conventionally late-liberal crowd ignores or disdains. For example, "mission"—it is astonishing to find this quintessential mainstream Protestant risking association with evangelicals by speaking well of evangelism and even taking some lessons from missionaries, a long written-off breed. Further, he adds to the risk by envisioning kinds of ecumenical-evangelical ententes which would represent not compromises, but mutual enrichments. While many other liberals are romantic about a Christianity that can survive and serve apart from institutions, he is an institutional church freak, paying attention to the daily life of ordinary believers who, in faith, would live extraordinary lives.

How does he do it? How does he sustain himself and lure all but the cynics and fashionable with his vision of mission?

For one thing, he does it through a refreshing alertness. I used Messer's earlier *Contemporary Images of Christian Ministry* in a course on "Introduction to the Study of Ministry," and found it inspiring many questions about the author. Many of these could be reduced to: shouldn't the Board of Iliff School of Theology investigate this seminary president? How can anyone read so widely, absorb so much, and put so much energy into teaching and envisioning, when the tasks of administration ought to be bearing down on him? Is there not some danger that he may be making a contribution to ministry? Messer, in my view, models effective leadership, exemplifying the need to be attentive to duties but not to be confined by them; the ability to reflect the larger world, and then test it closest to home.

The second feature that I find refreshing has to do with the author's use of sources. These years some of us are studying fundamentalisms in world religions. We find that they engage in "selective retrieval" (paraphrasing Karl Rahner) of real or presumed basics inherited from the past. Selective retrieval is too good an idea to let the fundamentalists monopolize it. They do not all like the notion anyhow, arguing that they are not selective but simply comprehensive about fundamentals. Messer is selective, since he is drawn chiefly to the dynamic elements of tradition, but he is engaging in retrieval. He takes notions from the biblical, early Christian, reformed, Wesleyan, evangelical, and ecumenical pasts, and projects them into futures. How, he seems to ask, would things look if we took these traditional elements and tried to grasp their momentum as if for the first time?

This is a thoroughly ecumenical book, but it betrays its Wesleyan heritage. That's intended as a compliment. In the 200th year of organized Methodism in America seven years ago, I was asked, on the spot, to give a fifteen-minute lecture on the Wesleyan situation. The summary matched some of the *Ur*-themes of *A Conspiracy of Goodness*. I argued that the John Wesley genius and package combined three elements. First was some sort of experience of the warmed heart. Second was attentiveness to "care structures," the details of community. Third was the positive virus to effect change, to transform the world ("spread scriptural holiness," and all that). Not: back to Wesley, but selectively retrieve these Wesleyan themes and grow into them.

The thesis continued: most Wesleyans and Methodists can get any two of these into their act, but rarely three. The people with a warmed heart and good care structures are not good at world-transforming. The care structure and world-transforming sorts are often ill at ease with the warmed heart.

Albert Outler, the notable senior United Methodist historian of theology stood by, having just previously given his asked-for fifteen-minute impromptu lecture on Luther in that year of Luther's 500th, a theme I was addressing. After I spoke Outler told the audience that in one short extempore speech I had lost all credibility as a historian of American religion: I had been naive enough to think that American Methodism had somehow been influenced by John Wesley. Not being close enough to the scene I cannot know whether in his smiling cynicism he was right about the empirical reality. But there are reasons to be confident about the sources, about what Wesley grasped from the larger Christian tradition and projected. Messer revisits those sources, without needing to keep citing chapter and verse from an eighteenth-century church leader. If a contemporary South African politician, a Calcutta nun, or a novelist says something congruent with or analogous to this threefold tradition, he quotes it confidently.

I called this an ecumenical book, which it is. Messer offers many types in it, including that of the "fence mover." That one suits him best, as he removed fences between the past called "tradition" and "contemporary life"; between "lay" and "professional" ministry; between "ecumenicals" and "evangelicals," and more. There is something convenient and comforting about fences which stay put, which rule some people in and others out. I pass on to you, then, an inconvenient and discomforting book dedicated to the higher comfort. Comfort: $con + fortare =$ to strengthen. This is strong stuff.

Martin E. Marty
The University of Chicago

Introduction

Those who dance are thought mad by those who don't hear the music.
ANONYMOUS, CITED IN JONATHAN COLEMAN, *Exit the Rainmaker*

Since his release from prison, South Africa's Nelson Mandela has traveled the globe denouncing the sin of apartheid and preaching a gospel of justice. After twenty-seven years in prison, he emerged to proclaim a new day for his people and country. Instead of expressing animosity about his long imprisonment, he offered symbolic olive branches of reconciliation to all people, regardless of race. He entered into dialogue with President Frederik de Klerk, during which both men indicated respect and trust for each other, even when they disagreed on basic policies and the pace of progress. Besieged on many fronts as he struggles to bring justice and peace, he constantly pushes to work harder and harder, though he is already more than 70 years old. He responds to friends and family who press him to slow down, "I've got no time to waste. I'm on a mission."[1]

Mandela epitomizes what it means for Christians to embrace the apostolic or missional character of ministry in our time. As a Methodist layman, his vocational ministry has been politics but his vision of mission has been God's loving liberation of his people and nation. While nurtured spiritually in the church, his primary arena for service has been in the ambiguous world of politics. In contrast, his friend Anglican Archbishop Desmond Tutu has shared the same vision of mission but has acted out his ministry in the world primarily through the church. Both men are part of the *laos*—the people of God, lay and clergy, who are called to participate in the *missio Dei*, i.e., God's mission in the world.

Mandela and Tutu illustrate Martin Luther's concept of the "priesthood of all believers." Though usually understood as "the ministry of the laity," why should one not speak also of "the mission of the laity"? Mission is more enveloping and more encompassing, and less individualistic than ministry. Mission is the vocation of the entire community of faith; every Christian receives the call to be in mission as apostles of the one Body of Christ.

Both Mandela and Tutu are present-day apostles of Jesus Christ. The English translation of the Greek work for apostle means literally "one who is sent out." Thus, an apostle is a personal messenger or ambassador, commissioned to share the message. Beginning with the original disciples of Jesus, the apostles of every generation have had to authenticate and to incarnate Christ's mission of love and liberation in the world. As Robert Neville observed: "An apostolic minister is an agent of the universal church, ancient in history and global in compass, bringing the grace in that church to a local context."[2]

To speak of Mandela as an apostle may be disconcerting for some persons. In fact, identifying any politician as an apostle may seem incongruous, since those who seek or hold power often act in complex, compromising contexts. Mandela acknowledges that he is neither a "messiah" nor superhuman.[3] "Dirty hands" seem inevitable because of involvement in tragic dimensions of life and death. Moral purity is impossible in politics, yet faithful Christians are called to responsible leadership in the public domain. There is no escape from living in the world, being touched by a mixture of good and evil in all of our actions or inactions.[4] To suggest that Mandela lives out his Christian discipleship through politics as the missional leader of his people is not to endorse every policy he proposes or statement he has made. Rather it is to accept his self-understanding as a Christian layperson participating in a mission greater than himself.

Recovering the Apostolic Character of Ministry

This book, however, is an essay in practical theology, not political ethics. Mandela and Tutu dramatically exemplify what it means when Christians, laity and clergy, seek to identify and participate in God's mission in the world. Most Christians, however, live out their lives in faithful obedience and discipleship far from the television cameras and newspaper headlines. Their witness and work, though, is no less significant in the economy and grace of God.

The recovering of our apostolic ministry may not sound very futuristic. However, I am convinced that the most dynamic models of ministry in the next millennium will be those that struggle seriously with our biblical and theological heritage as well as the critical contexts in which we live. The apostolic imagery, a cherished tradition with powerful meanings, should be reappropriated for today's church and ministry. The vision of the church in Antioch (Acts 11-13), where the apostles of the church first responded to the call to cross new frontiers in mission must be reclaimed. Missional metaphors introduced in this book—such as a company of star throwers, a covenant of global gardeners, a community of fence movers, and a collegiality of bridge builders—seek to be faithful to apostolic understandings, though using more modern language and images.

The reclaiming of the apostolic or missionary character of ministry is not necessarily synonymous with the "laying on of hands" or even the apostolic succession of the bishops. Rather it underscores the grace and authority that comes to all baptized Christians, lay and clergy, who affirm their church's ministry. The ordained ministry, however, clearly is based on a missionary foundation. "The ordained minister," asserts Orlando E. Costas, "is a gift of grace that the church received in mission." Clergy represent resources that "the Spirit gives to the church to enable it to participate in mission."[5]

In general, contemporary theological education has been oriented primarily toward the pastoral care of congregations, not the church's mission to the world. As attention to "foreign missions" faded in some quarters, the understanding of mission has often been overshadowed by internal church reorganization, counseling concerns, management matters, church growth techniques, and similar concerns. Missiology disappeared from the seminary curriculum, and professors in the field are an endangered species. Overreacting to the problems and prejudices of "missions" in the past, some theological educators express hostility to the very idea of mission. Thus the missional character of the church's ministry has often been overlooked or understated. This book seeks to reawaken the church and theological seminaries to the pressing missional dimensions of the church and its ministry.[6] This book consciously seeks to appropriate the missional insights of global Christianity for Christian ministry and to root them in an understanding of the minister as apostle.

Discerning God's Loving and Liberating Initiatives

Surprisingly, the word mission, a derivative from the Latin mitto and from the Greek apostello ("to send"), never appears in the Bible. Just as Jesus was sent from God, so Jesus sent his apostles to others. By the end of the seventeenth century references to "missions" and "missionary" pertained almost exclusively to Christian work outside Europe among nonevangelized "foreign" people. For the most part, the language of mission has been confined to the Christian religion, until recently when some other faiths began to adopt it.

In this book, "mission" and "missional" are not synonymous with "foreign missions." Mission means the Christian church and its ministers, lay and clergy, discerning and responding to God's loving and liberating initiatives in the world. The "salinization of mission" (i.e., "traveling over salt water") is not required.[7] God's mission exists on everyone's doorstep, not only in distant places.[8]

Mission represents more than proclamation or witness or evangelization or service or church growth. The witness (*martys*) of New Testament apostles was often sealed in suffering martyrdom. This witness manifests itself in proclamation (*kerygma*), fellowship (*koinonia*), and service (*diakonia*). These three dimensions relate integrally to one another. Christian witness and service are like the two blades of a pair of scissors, operating in unison, but held together by the axle of the church's fellowship.[9]

Mission is essential to the meaning of church, not just another task assumed by the church. "Mission is the fundamental reality of our Christian life," writes Emilio Castro. "Our life in this world is life in mission."[10] Or in the often quoted words of Emil Brunner: "The Church exists by mission, just as a fire exists by burning."[11] Church is mission, ministry is missional, and every Christian is a missionary.

This book explores the missional character of ministry, but it is not reduced to a single meaning. Expressing the mission of the church for the twenty-first century cannot be captured in a simple slogan such as "the evangelization of the world in this generation." Christians embody more diversity in their thinking and theology today, and the world is far more complex, than when John R. Mott popularized that logo.[12] However, the task of identifying or articulating God's mission remains imperative, lest the church become nothing more than a collection of service ministries rather than a community in mission.

This book, therefore, is not a mission manifesto, but rather an exploration of the perils and possibilities that exist for the church and its ministers. Designed for laity and pastors, as well as seminarians, the author hopes that this book will stimulate imaginative thinking and inspired actions. As a companion volume to the author's *Contemporary Images of Christian Ministry*, this work underscores the integral relationship of mission and ministry presented.

Ministry Flows from Mission

The false dichotomy often posited between mission and ministry must be rejected. The mission of God has always defined and described the ministry of Christ's disciples. Ministry flows from mission. Bridging the contemporary gap becomes essential if the church of Jesus Christ intends to recover its apostolic nature and address the perplexing problems of the modern world.

The gap between mission and ministry appears in how approaches to the ministry have been classified and developed in recent decades. Lynn N. Rhodes has identified four types of overlapping ministerial models.[13] *First are those that focus on the arts and skills of professional church leadership.* Epitomized by books promoting the pastor as a professional, these understandings of ministry tend to describe what clergy do and how they can do this more effectively. This model, which many seminaries embraced in the 1970s, attempted to upgrade both the professional performance and the social status of the cleric. It underscored ministry as a career with concern expressed for salaries, pensions, benefits, office hours, and so forth. The professional model sometimes promotes the service of persons to the church structure rather than God's mission. Contemporary crises, says Kennon L. Callahan, call for a new understanding of clergy as missionary pastors.[14]

Christ's ministry can never be reduced to a functionalist definition. Moving away from the professional model does not mean abandoning the need for professional competence and ethical standards, but it does insist that ministry is more than applying good skills to life's problems. A passion for soul-saving and earth-keeping requires professional competence but not a professional mind-set. Jesus was never a "professional," but rather the suffering servant of God.

A second model primarily focuses on the personhood of ministry. The essence of ministry is not defined as skill development but in terms of relationships. The pastoral care movement of the 1960s and beyond illustrates this model. The minister as therapist dominates, along with the idea of the church as a giant support group for the pastor and others.

While counseling remains exceedingly valuable and important, it is not the prime work of the ordained ministry. When individualism reigns supreme and persons "hang out their shingle" and make pastoral counseling a private profession, then ministry as a gift to the whole people of God is forgotten. Clergy are never just private practitioners. Instead, the "office" or role belongs to the whole church and symbolically conveys meaning beyond the action of the personality cloaked in its garments or bearing its titles.

The healing dimensions of person-centered ministry dare not be discounted. The caring spirit of the counseling emphasis can be manifest in groups designed for isolated military families, persons struggling with addictions, those recently divorced or widowed, and so on. Sponsoring support programs enables people, both inside and outside of the congregation, to overcome pain and brokenness and potentially become more concerned about others and the world.

The personhood model, at its best, reminds us of the mystery of ministry. The personal qualities of the religious leader are intrinsic to the office. The personal piety and charisma of the preacher do make a difference. People perceive clergy as representatives of God's grace. Fortunately, God works through the "office" of priest or pastor, despite the limitations of the "person" possessing or holding it.[15]

A third model stresses the ministry of office and order. The sacraments and the representative ministry of the ordained become the focus of attention. The biblical and historical foundations of the office of clergy receive emphasis. Especially evident among Roman Catholics and Episcopalians, it is a part of most rationales regarding ordination.

The process of ordination, however, is not equivalent to professional licensing procedures. Ordination is always a communitarian act, as the church authenticates God's call and authorizes the persons called by God. Clergy who think of themselves primarily as "enablers" or "facilitators" need to rethink the meaning of ordination and the authority of the clergy.

The purpose of theological education is to develop a learned clergy and laity who can give leadership to the church and to the world in Christ's name. James Forbes of Riverside Church in New York points out that the African American pastor seldom suffers all the pangs of guilt over authority that plague the white pastor. Forbes contends that unless the clergy claim authority appropriate to the ministry of office and order, then the community of faith loses its sense of purpose and direction.[16]

The fourth type of model emphasizes how a church's vision of mission impacts its notion of ministry. Ministry is organized contextually and defined by its mission. Discernment of God's mission within a particular context decisively shapes one's model of ministry. In the 1960s Colin Williams and George Webber pioneered these perspectives.[17] During the 1980s feminist and Two-Thirds World theologians have contributed significantly to understanding ministry in a new form.

Without diminishing the importance or necessity of the other three models that underscore professional skills, personal care, and the office of the ministry, I advocate and foresee the prime significance of the fourth type in the 1990s and the next millennium. The church and its ministry face stagnancy and sterility in a global, ecological, nuclear age unless mission re-enters our vocabulary and re-energizes our vocation. Our discernment of God's mission must inform our understandings of needed pastoral skills, pastoral care, and the clergy office.

Overcoming Our Allergies to Mission

In order to recover the apostolic character of ministry, we must overcome our stereotypical allergies to mission. Adverse reactions to the excesses of the missionary movement of past centuries, when Western values and imperialistic objectives often merged inextricably with Christian faith and humanitarian goals, have resulted in the terms "mission," "missions," and "missionary" to fall into disuse, disfavor, and derision.

Clever cartoonists regularly satirize and stereotype missionaries in popular publications. Noted novelists tend to portray missionaries as incredibly insensitive to the cultural traditions of other people. If one's passport identifies a person as a missionary, the probability of being denied a visa to many countries increases. To speak of someone having "missionary zeal" usually conveys negative connotations. One missionary lamented: "In my father's day coming home was a kind of triumph. The missionary was a hero. Today he is an anti-hero. Even in Christian churches I am eyed askance as a throw-back to a more primitive era."[18]

Many today, both outside the church and among liberal and mainline Christians, scorn the image of a missionary.[19] Due to the excessive criticisms leveled against missionaries, this designation may be a "dead metaphor" unable to convey to the contemporary age a positive power and meaning. Yet this title endures because it has been applied equally to lay and clergy, without distinction. Most other traditional images of ministry have been clericized.

This author shares in the criticism of past and present missionary practices that betray cross-cultural insensitivity and ignorance. However, I am humbled by, and appreciative of, the Christian commitment, courage, and sacrificial service of persons commissioned as missionaries of the church. None of us would have heard the gospel ourselves without those who accepted God's call to go to new and often difficult places. I have visited missionaries throughout the world, lived in their homes, heard their stories, witnessed their work, and learned firsthand from people in those places how much missionaries have contributed and are appreciated. Missionaries have much to teach us about the apostolic character of ministry in a global village.

Identifying Dysfunctional Theologies

In order to recover apostolic ministry, we must identify and discard dysfunctional theologies. Those theologies, more concerned about the inner life and system of a bureaucratic church than mission, develop a dysfunctional community of faith unresponsive to caring for the future of God's creation. Ministry detached from God's mission in the world is heretical.

Instead of mission shaping the church and its ministry, management and maintenance predominate. Sociologists speak of this phenomenon as "professional deformation," since members and leaders become "increasingly unaware of the world in which the organization exists and they undermine the viability of the organization they so desperately serve."[20] The dysfunctional church, oriented to its own perpetuation and support, neglects its responsibility for being the people of God serving in the world.

When the essence of the church and its ministry is no longer mission, euthanasia of the ecclesia occurs inevitably. Churches born in mission are preoccupied now with management and maintenance. As church memberships plummet, priority goals shift from service to survival. "The world is our parish" becomes "the parish is our world" when concern for maintenance overshadows the concern for service. Once this happens, Gregory Baum notes, "a dialectic begins to operate according to which the excessive concern for maintenance becomes dysfunctional and undermines the institution's well being."[21]

Dysfunctional theologies promote an individualistic ministry—one person responding to God's love with little regard for the community of faith. Theologically, Christian ministry is communitarian—an expression of the gift of God given via the church to the individual, however, lay people and clergy understand ministry as self-expression and self-fulfillment.

A dysfunctional theology of ministry also tends to be extremely clericalized. When persons speak of "ministers" of the church, they mean the ordained "pastors" of the congregation. In contrast, "missionary" has been a term used both for lay and clergy. Often one loses the idea of the *laos*—all the people of God, both lay and clergy. Sometimes the personal and professional needs of the clergy so dominate church thinking that mission is scuttled. However, the needs of the professionalized clergy dare not take precedence over the missional priorities of the church.

Lest I be misunderstood, this is not an anti-clerical treatise, but an argument for revitalizing the missional dimension of all ministries. The attitude of pastors toward the missional outreach of a local congregation often determines the attitude of that church to missional causes and concerns. If the clergy appear apathetic to Christ's mission in the world, then it is exceedingly difficult to mobilize the laity for service beyond the local church.

Ending the Ecumenical/Evangelical Cold War

The disgrace of disunity in the Body of Christ becomes especially painful and poignant when perceived against the imperative of engaging the whole human community to meet the crises of the twenty-first century. How are Christians to reach out to persons of other faiths and/or no faith when denominational walls keep Christians from communicating and working together?

When I was twenty years old, I studied in India and during the Christmas holidays I stayed in the Muslim home of a college friend in Sri Lanka. One night as we left an Anglican service of worship, Ali turned to me and asked, "What is the difference between a Methodist and an Anglican?" What irony! At a moment when I wanted to share my faith in Christ, I stood instead amid Buddhist and Hindu temples telling my Muslim friend about an eighteenth-century dispute and division that had absolutely no relevance or meaning in this cultural context. This incident reinforced my commitment to ecumenism and the world mission of the church. Denominationalism is a scandal to the world and a sin before God.

Unfortunately, Protestant mission literature and debate usually represent one of two theological camps: ecumenical or evangelical. The former generally refers to persons who are in some way affiliated with, or affirm, the World Council of Churches. Evangelicals often associate with each other through the Lausanne Conference, or distinguish themselves by a degree of antipathy to the World Council of Churches. Obviously, such broad categories do not do justice to the diversity within the spectrum of mission thinking. Evangelical ecumenists and ecumenical evangelicals exist, as well as critics of the World Council of Churches, who also criticize the evangelical movement. However, overall, these two theological streams contend for the minds and hearts of Protestants.

Though I have never been a participant in any of the major ecumenical conferences or decisions, I personally would identify myself with this conciliar tradition. In writing this book, I am deeply indebted to the ecumenical movement for its pathfinding efforts at revisioning mission and ministry. Every attempt, however, has been made to faithfully present the perspectives and criticisms made by evangelicals. I pray that this book might be a small step in the process of ending the "Cold War" that for too long has absorbed needlessly the energies and resources of Christians, conservative and liberal.

Since I identify with the ecumenical tradition, special effort has been made to identify evangelical authors and contributions. In a way, this seems biased and artificial, since not every person cited is identified by their theological perspective. Likewise persons outside North America and Europe are often identified by their home country. This too has its limitations as it appears they are exceptions to the norm. Be assured that this is not the intent, but to assist the reader in appreciating the pluralistic global, as well as theological, perspectives that are contributing to this discussion on the mission of ministry.

Finding positive, nonperjorative language often proves problematic. For example, *Third World* designations are widely used but often resented. The term *Third World* evolved in the language of politics and economics since 1949, supplanting the phrase "underdeveloped nations," and used in contrast to highly industrialized countries. Some nations now have a high per capita income and therefore are not viewed as "developing" economically, but they still relate politically to countries who have historically experienced colonialism, imperialism, or neo-colonialism. Since *Third World* terminology has perjorative implications, *Two-Thirds World* is used in this book to express the majority status of the people under consideration. However, since language reflects cultural and personal imperfections, every term is, to a certain degree, prejudicial. Overall, the effort is to be inclusive in every way, though admittedly this does not always prove to be possible.

A Synoptic Overview

The opening chapters explore key theological perspectives relating mission and ministry and focus on the necessary dialogue between biblical texts and contemporary contexts. The challenge of avoiding world havoc and creating a world house is underscored as a central task of apostolic ministry in our time.

Humanity is poised over the epicenter of a global earthquake, but remains oblivious to the damage being inflicted to God's creation and obtuse to the danger of the extinction of all life. When the ground trembles beneath San Francisco or Armenia, people around the world respond with compassionate alacrity. But when the rain forests burn in the Amazon, an ozone hole opens in the atmosphere, or nuclear weapons proliferate among the nations, complacent apathy prevails. This radically unprecedented context and crisis calls the church to rethink mission and ministry for the twenty-first century. Theology, mission, and ministry must move beyond rigid past boundaries and help shape a global environment for future generations.

Revisioning the missional character of ministry requires a radical rephrasing of Jesus' question: what does it profit persons to gain their own souls and lose the whole world? Mission and ministry in the past have often been defined exclusively as "soul saving," disparaging the world as either inferior or secondary. Rabbi Abraham Heschel once complained that too many Christians were more concerned about their personal salvation than about joining God in God's work in the world. Now this solitary understanding is being challenged. What value is soul saving if life itself becomes extinct? How can religion remain so ego-oriented when the ecosystem is threatened? How does salvation for the individual relate to macro questions about the salvation of the globe itself? Under the umbrella of earth keeping, soul saving takes on a new dimension and priority.

Recovering the apostolic character of ministry requires articulating new metaphors for understanding the role of the church in the decades ahead, images faithful to biblical and theological perspectives and models of ministry that can motivate Christians toward greater faithfulness and action in this global context. Chapters four, five, six, and seven introduce four images or metaphors for missional ministry. Each of these—a covenant of global gardeners, a collegiality of bridge builders, a company of star throwers, and a community of fence movers—seeks to use contemporary idioms to express theological ideas appropriated from the church's tradition and experience.

In the final chapter, the witness and experience of Christian rescuers who engaged in "a conspiracy of goodness" during the European holocaust of World War II is analyzed as a model of mission and ministry appropriate for our own time. Facing incredible obstacles and dangers, these Christians dared to do good amid evil. They illustrate what it means to tend global gardens, to build bridges, to throw stars, and to move fences. Their loving and liberating activities incarnate an apostolic or missional ministry that offers a vision of a revitalized church for our own time.

Acknowledgments

The sociology of knowledge teaches that all of us are culture-bound and time-limited. While this book seeks to be ecumenical and inclusive and not a denominational essay, it also reflects my United Methodist roots and commitments. Abstractly, I can never escape the fact that I am a United Methodist pastor who has served the past twenty-one years as a college and seminary president. Autobiographical bias may emerge even when the personal pronoun is absent. I am deeply indebted to my particular religious heritage, in more ways than I can perceive or acknowledge.

In writing a book, the best one can ever do is to indicate via footnotes the sources of one's ideas and quotations. Yet this is never enough because one's thought is shaped by countless sources of information and insight. Absent from those endnotes are those many professors and friends over the years who have helped shape one's thinking and stimulated one's reflections.

Special gratitude is extended to Delwin Brown, Sara Myers, Sheila Davaney, Betty Thompson, and Paul Murphy who critically read all or portions of this manuscript in the preparation stage. The entire Iliff

School of Theology faculty joined in critiquing one chapter. David Nieda, Kent Messer, Paul Sears, Scott Daniels, Christine Gallagher, Darrell Reeck, Walter G. Muelder, Alberta Smith, Annabel and Robert Clark provided valuable research assistance.

These ideas and themes were shared and tested at various lectureships and conferences across the country. The occasions included the Stark Lectures at Dakota Wesleyan University, the Week of Lectures at The Iliff School of Theology, the Issues Forum of the United Methodist General Council on Ministries in Atlanta, Georgia, the National Conference of United Methodist Lay Leaders in Nashville, Tennessee, the Conference on the Future in Oklahoma City, Oklahoma, The United Methodist Board of Global Ministries in New York City, First United Methodist Church in Sioux Falls, South Dakota, United Methodist district meetings in Tucson, Arizona, Bishop/Cabinet Retreat in Cedar Rapids, Iowa, Ecumenical Clergy/Laity Seminar in Grand Junction, Colorado, as well as the Iliff-at-Aspen Summer School. In each place I benefited from the cross fire and criticism of discussion.

Specifically, I want to thank the Trustees of The Iliff School of Theology for a three-month study leave in 1989 and my administrative colleagues at Iliff (Jane I. Smith, Thomas K. Craine, James W. McGillivray, and Virginia M. Dorjahn) who bore extra heavy administrative responsibilities in my absence. As Executive Secretary to the President, Virginia M. Dorjahn carried double duties as she faithfully typed and edited this manuscript. The librarians at Iliff and Cambridge University generously extended their professional services. My editor at Abingdon Press, Paul Franklyn, has been exceedingly helpful and encouraging.

Above all, I owe a great debt of gratitude to my wife, Bonnie, our children, Kent and Christine, and our son-in-law Gordon Gallagher, who have challenged my thinking and made my life worth living!

CHAPTER ONE

The Mission of Ministry

You cannot take Jesus to India. You cannot take Jesus to Africa. The call to take Jesus to the heathen is ridiculous. We cannot take Jesus anywhere. He is already in Africa. He is already beside the mother in the hut in India. He is already there loving and healing and ministering.

D. T. NILES

A distinguished contemporary American author, John Hersey, has written an intriguing novel, *The Call*, with the subtitle *An American Missionary in China*. Though fictionalized, this historical novel reflects the story of his own father, whose spiritual odyssey combined the evangelical impulse of Christianity with the humanitarian spirit of wanting to help other persons. Answering the call of God, his father committed his life at the beginning of the twentieth century to saving souls in China. The book weaves a fascinating tale of challenge and complexity as one person sought to make the world a better place for the Chinese people.

The call of God is the major motif of Hersey's novel. What fascinates the Yale University novelist is that despite overwhelming odds, great fears and frustrations, times of triumph and lost hopes, what sustained his father and rekindled his vision and spirit was his sense of having been summoned by God for a lifetime of Christian service.

A revival in 1903 at Syracuse University changed his father's life. He heard a Scottish rugby player utter three quiet sentences embedded with a Bible quotation: "Rejoice, O young man, in thy youth. Remember now thy Creator in the days of thy youth. For many are called, but few are chosen" (Ecclesiastes 11:9*a*, 12:1*a*; Matthew 22:14, KJV). After hearing those words, his father reported years later:

At that moment the miracle happened. I "knew." I had surrendered myself. I saw a blinding light. My heart pounded with joy. I was shriven. The tons of my

27

sins were off-loaded from my aching bones. And from that moment to this I have
been verily on top of the world.[1]

The Call to the Mission of Ministry

Experiencing the call of God has always been at the heart of Christian
understandings of the missional character of the church's ministry. The
call experienced by John Hersey's father replicates the story of countless
other Christians who have embraced the apostolic or missional
dimension of ministry throughout the globe.

Apostles served as ambassadors, persons who were called and "sent
out" to serve and share the gospel. A missional ministry is a calling, not a
career. Literally, ministry means "to serve." Thus it is not just another
job, occupation, or profession but a vocation one accepts in response to a
summons from a loving God. The church needs a laity and clergy who are
willing to think, live, and die the life of an apostle of Jesus Christ.
According to Bishop Dan E. Solomon, the church requires a "leadership
that is missional and not just functional."[2]

The call came to Moses while he was doing the respectable thing,
minding his own business, leading an ordinary shepherd's life, tending
to his in-law's sheep in the obscurity of the wilderness. Imagine his
surprise and his shock as he confronted a burning bush and an angel
appeared. He must have wondered if he was hallucinating, or if he had
been sucking for too long on a strange weed! But in a response to the call,
"Moses, Moses!" he responded, saying "Here I am" (Exodus 3:4).

Skeptics might question whether the event at the burning bush ever
took place. After all, no independent on-site verifications occurred, no
secondary witnesses testified, and no scientific observations of flaming
plants existed. What we do have, however, is the faith history of the
Hebrew people, who never questioned the reality that God spoke to a
simple shepherd, commissioned him to be their prophetic leader, and
subsequently led them out of the oppression of the Egyptians into the
promised land. Neither do we have any evidence that Moses ever
doubted he had been duly called by the Divine, nor that God
accompanied him in his missional ministry no matter how deep the
difficulty or torturous the trial.

The fiery drama of Moses' call contrasts with the biblical account of how
Jesus recruited his first disciples. Passing the corner of Market and Main,
along the Sea of Galilee, Jesus saw some ordinary fishermen named
Simon Peter and Andrew. He said to them, "Follow me, and I will make
you fish for people." No questions asked! No requests for a job
description or a personnel handbook! Why, not even an explanation of
the pension plan! Instead Scripture simply says: "Immediately they left

their nets and followed him." A short distance away, perhaps at the corner of Sin and Decadence, Jesus again stopped and seeing the son of Zebedee, and John, his brother, called to them, asking that they quit mending their nets and join in a different type of fishing expedition. No blazing bushes! No angelic voices! Just the authoritative call to adventure in the mission of ministry (Matthew 4:18-22).

Since the time when Jesus called the earliest disciples to drop their work and follow him, the church has asked of its leadership the nature and meaning of their call. For Paul, the decision to enter the ministry was not a choice among professions but a response to God's command on the Damascus road. Saul had a career, Paul had a calling. That call motivated, sustained, and empowered Paul in his missionary travels, despite persecution, imprisonment, controversy, and setbacks.

The call comes to laity and clergy, sometimes for a lifetime of full-time professional church work, sometimes for lay vocational service in the world. God calls persons, not just into the priesthood but into all of life's noble vocations and avocations. The dominant biblical understanding of the idea of calling is an urgent invitation or summons from God to enter into a life of service. Martin Luther emphasized that every vocation was sacred; we can make out of any work a calling of honor to God. Johann Sebastian Bach wrote the initials—S.D.G., *Soli Deo Gloria*, "to the glory of God alone" and J.J., *Jesu juva*, "Help me, Jesus"—at the top of each composition he wrote. The vocation of every man and woman, noted Albert Schweitzer, is to serve other people.

The summons to Moses, the invitation of Jesus, and the rugby player's call to Hersey's father represent but a handful of illustrations. God's call can be traced through the Scriptures from the experience of Abraham and Jeremiah to Mary and Paul. It can be substantiated in history with the call experienced by Augustine or John Wesley or Martin Luther King, Jr., or Mother Teresa. In addition, consider the individual stories of Christians who over the centuries have quietly lived out their lives in humble service, and we can see that the church universal truly connotes a community of the called.

God's request often requires a struggle of the soul, since the divine command may be contrary to our human desire for comfort, success, and wealth. In John Wesley's terms, accepting the call means being "ready to do anything, to lose anything, to suffer anything." No wonder we often pretend not to hear!

Sometimes people misunderstand what God tries to tell them. There is an old story about a farmer who thought he had received a call to be ordained because he had seen in the clouds the letters "P C," which he interpreted to mean, "preach Christ." After many frustrating and fumbling attempts to preach, he realized he was really called to "plow corn." Today God calls persons not only to "preach Christ" but to "program computers" and to do "professional counseling."

God's call to mission and ministry comes in many different ways and at various times. It may be as dramatic as a burning bush to a shepherd, or as dynamic as the invitation of Jesus to some fishing folk, or as dry as the quiet words of a rugby player to a college student. When one experiences the call, and responds, inevitably lives change and history is transformed. The status quo is upset and revolutions are unleashed.

One significant phenomenon currently is that so many second-career persons are leaving the security of their secular professions to become Christian pastors. Lawyers are walking away from lucrative careers. Clinical psychologists are training to be preachers. Journalists are choosing to proclaim the Word. Homemakers are discovering there is life and ministry after age forty! Seminaries now attract mature Christian persons who come to offer the church and humanity insights from their rich life experiences and knowledge. A similar phenomenon also occurs in reverse, with persons moving away from ordained ministries and taking on the yoke of service inherent in business and professional vocations.

Everyone can be a vessel of God's loving and liberating mission in the world. God needs business persons willing to commit their lives to integrity and public service. God needs professionals ready to serve not only individual human needs but also to ensure that their professions meet the highest ethical standards. God needs students willing to surrender their lives to the full-time service of church and humanity. Whatever the circumstances of life, God has a calling for the mission of ministry. A person confined to bed in a nursing home can still write letters on behalf of Amnesty International to protest torture and other global violations of human rights. The manifold possibilities for fighting world hunger and the madness of the arms race exist. God calls people to tasks, both great and small, long-term and of shorter duration.

A sixty-year-old man who recently accompanied a short-term volunteer mission team to the South Pacific illustrates what one person can accomplish. He had been affiliated with the church primarily because he thought it was good for his wife and children.

In Tonga he visited a boys' school that owned a herd of cows to provide milk for the students and to provide revenue to support the school. In the course of conversation, he learned about the school's erratic electrical supply, which often failed at milking time. An electrical engineer by profession, he naturally asked, "Well, why don't you get a standby generator?" The director of the school replied that they had had one for twenty years "but nobody knows how to make it work."

Early the next morning, after a sleepless night, he knocked on the mission leader's door and announced he was going back to the school to fix their generator. She replied, "Well, Brother, the Holy Spirit has got ahold of you. You are being called to fix that generator."

He decided to take another month off from his business to return to Tonga, where with the help of the students, he built a platform for the generator and got it working. His postcard back home read: "August 3—6:30 P.M. Engine started."

Local newspapers reported the event and the King and Queen of Tonga visited the site. What had happened to this man, however, proved more significant: for the first time in his life he knew what it meant to serve other people in the name of Jesus Christ. Recently he reported his plans to return to Tonga, saying, "They have another job for me to do."[3]

God has many engines that need to be restarted in this world, if the divine vision of justice, peace, and the integrity of creation is to be realized. If we allow the Holy Spirit to teach us, we can each find a calling for our talents and resources. The call for the mission of ministry is for new Christian apostles in a nuclear, global, and ecological age. Needed are more respondents saying "Here am I. Send me."

The Dialogue Between Text and Context

The relationship and tension between biblical texts and particular contexts is essential for shaping an understanding of the call to a missional ministry. Clearly many persons respond and act based on their commitments to scriptural mandates for mission. Others react, not so much to the primacy of Scripture, but to the desperate cry they hear from humanity and the planet earth. Creative and critical dialogue between text and context helps keep both in perspective in our search for truth and our quest to be of service.

Mission and ministry are never abstract exercises; context and crisis give meaning to concrete historical and cultural situations. God's liberating and loving struggle for freedom, justice, and peace is global. Contexts and circumstances, however, differ, so the communication of the gospel likewise varies. John W. DeGruchy argues that:

> Contextuality does not exclude but requires and makes universality meaningful. The ministries of both black and white pastors in South Africa should relate integrally to each other in terms of the mission of the church even though they may minister in different ways. . . . To minister in any one place requires an awareness of the universal mission of the church; and yet, at the same time, that task has to be grounded in each specific situation.[4]

Theological reflection is not an art reserved for the seminary academician or the church hierarchy. Theology reflects both the biblical texts and the context and crisis mission faces. The tension between orthodoxy ("right doctrine") and orthopraxy ("right practice") cannot be dismissed by simply choosing one over the other. Both are required. "Yet I am impelled to ask," questions Phillip Berryman:

Who is more likely to understand the situation of the Brazilian peas-ant . . . theologically and pastorally—an individual who supervises a doctrinal watchdog agency in the Vatican or a theologian who teaches half the year in a Brazilian university and spends the other half trekking into roadless sections of the Amazon basin, as does Clodovis Boff? . . . Sipping espresso in a Roman piazza, Ratzinger might come to an insight that eludes Boff as he slogs through the jungle with blistered feet and infected mosquito bites. In the ordinary run of things, however, Boff's pastoral practice will have a positive impact on his intellectual work.[5]

Contextualization ought not to be confused with contextualism. The latter accommodates to the context or culture, saying or doing anything as long as it fits comfortably in the circumstances. For instance, what if President Dwight D. Eisenhower with all of his popular charisma had personally walked hand-in-hand with an African American child up the school steps when government authorities blocked the entrance?[6] In contrast, what a difference it made when First Lady Barbara Bush embraced a baby with AIDS (Acquired Immune Deficiency Syndrome). In one purposeful missional act, she struck a blow against prejudice and fear by contextualizing God's liberating love on every newscast and newspaper in the United States. Imagine what might happen if Catholic cardinals listened to abused women in shelters and family planning centers such as Planned Parenthood! Think of Episcopal prelates spending a night sleeping with the homeless, or Southern Baptist leaders stopping a train carrying nuclear weapons, or United Methodist bishops running errands for homosexual persons who suffer from AIDS!

Contextualizing the gospel—bringing the Bible and context into dialogue—involves risk and invites controversy. Charles H. Kraft has suggested that perhaps half of the "heresies" condemned by various historic church councils were not really distortions of the universal Christian truth but attempts to contextualize the gospel for people in particular cultures and times. These attempts at contextualization ran contrary to the established doctrinal opinion of the time and were deemed heretical. Mentioning Kraft's thesis is not necessarily to concur with him, but rather to note the dangers and difficulties of relating the gospel to new situations. Minority perspectives are often subject to anathema because the majority writes the rules and history![7]

The idea of indigenization relates to contextualization. Beginning in the nineteenth century, church leaders proposed the goal of establishing self-supporting, self-governing, and self-propagating churches, free and independent from the umbilical cord of mission agencies. Only after the communist revolution in China isolated that church from the rest of the world did the Chinese "Three-Self" movement flourish and succeed. The indigenous Chinese Protestant Church increased from seven hundred thousand members at the time the missionaries left, to nearly five million today.

Contextualization adds a "Fourth Self": self-theologizing. Text and context in dialogue may free Christian theology from the chains of Aristotelian, Latin, and Teutonic thought prisons. Hans Küng once declared that the old assimilation method of missions aimed at making persons into Europeans before inviting them to be Christians![8] The new attitudinal mode of mission consciously criticizes Christianity's connection with Western culture and power. The Sri Lankan Jesuit, Aloysius Pieris, contends that today's missional church "must step into the baptismal waters of Asian religion and pass through passion and death on the cross of Asian poverty."[9] Likewise today's missional ministry in the United States needs to step into the baptismal waters of secular culture and new age religion and feel the cross of contemporary poverty and pain, before the church can know the experience of resurrection and new life.

Biblical Mandates for Mission

Today's context for mission and ministry inspires awe, in light of the perils and possibilities of a nuclear, global, and ecological age. Succeeding chapters address those challenges. What makes Christian witness and involvement distinctive, however, is the motivating and sustaining power of the biblical text. The Bible tells the story of the mission of God (*missio Dei*). The drama of God's loving and liberating initiative for all creation flows from Genesis to Revelation. The biblical record documents God's work in human history as well as the divine call for human participation in God's mission.

The metaphor of a good and giving God punctuates the opening biblical chapters of Genesis and permeates both the Old and New Testaments. The temptation for *all* Christians has been to proof text mission by citing one passage of Scripture almost to the exclusion of others. A theology of mission and ministry must include the total scriptural picture. As one evangelical writer, Arthur F. Glasser, noted:

In our day, evangelicals are finding that the biblical base for mission is far broader and more complex than any previous generation of missiologists appeared to have realized. Gone are the narrow presuppositions of the early

Pietists whose missionary understanding had but a single focus: an overwhelming concern for the spiritual condition of "the heathen" living outside the pale of *corpus Christianum*.[10]

Highlighting certain key biblical themes does not deny the existence of other valuable and valid passages and perspectives worthy of exploration. Rather it illustrates the fundamental biblical basis for recovering the apostolic or missional nature of ministry.

Old Testament Themes

Five Hebrew Bible or Old Testament motifs for mission at least can be identified.[11] *First is the global theme of universality.* The book of Genesis states that God (Yahweh) is the God of all peoples, nations, and nature. The scripture record portrays God's election of Israel not as a strictly private relationship but rather as a special public responsibility for the Jewish people. The calling of Israel was to be the *pars pro toto*, a minority called to serve the majority.[12]

Whenever the Jewish people forgot or distorted this universal theme, prophets like Amos, Jeremiah, and Isaiah emerged to condemn ethnocentric pretension and the subversion of God's loving and liberating intentions for all. During the experiences of the exile, Jeremiah, Ezekiel, and Second Isaiah envisioned an expanding horizon of God's universal intent.

The emphasis on global or universal perspectives in mission and ministry now echo in every denomination and seminary. The image of a global village has become almost a cliché, as people begin to realize the interdependency of the world.

Globalization or universalism, however, does not mean the same thing for all Christians. Seminaries tend to stress certain dimensions more than others. Don S. Browning notes four perspectives on its meaning. First is the emphasis on evangelism, carrying the gospel to all people in all nations. A second stresses ecumenism, which encourages greater cooperation and understanding among churches and people with different Christian theologies. Interreligious dialogue, the third dimension, emphasizes bridging the gaps between the world's religions. The fourth interpretation focuses on social justice or human development issues, that is, seeking to improve the welfare of suffering people around the world.[13] This book embraces all four emphases as basic to a missional understanding of church and ministry.

A second thematic motif emphasizes rescue and liberation. Yahweh saved Israel from slavery and delivered the Jewish people to freedom. As a result, Israel's prophets proposed that Yahweh was the redeemer of all nations. Illustrative are the servant songs of Isaiah 40–55, which describe the spread of salvation around the globe. As a missionary *par excellence*, the Servant epitomizes how God can work in and through persons. God's Servant brings deliverance not only to humanity but to nature: "unfailingly he will establish justice. He will never falter or be crushed until he sets justice on earth, while coasts and islands await his teaching" (Isaiah 42:3*a*, 4, REB). The Servant of the Lord is described as a substitute, accepting the judgment of God that belonged not only to Israel but to all peoples and nations (Isaiah 53). By walking the path of suffering and death, the Servant rescues and liberates everyone. Thus not surprisingly Paul justifies his worldwide mission to the Gentiles by citing these Servant Songs, declaring: "For so the Lord has commanded us, saying, 'I have set you to be a light for the Gentiles, so that you may bring salvation to the ends of the earth' " (Acts 13:47).

Oppressed Christians around the globe write theologies of liberation and emancipation. Powerful perspectives have emerged from the Two-Thirds World, emphasizing both the need for individual conversion and political transformation. Evangelism and social justice are integrated in a concern both for those who sin and those who are "sinned against." In particular, the concerns of persons of color and/or feminists offer needed insight as Christians seek to cope with contemporary contexts, both locally and globally.

The third missionary motif relates closely to the first two themes. Yahweh, a missionary God, calls Israel to share God's love and liberation with all nations. Repeatedly the prophets remind Israel that their selection by God involves the whole of creation. God declares: "I shall appoint you a light to the nations, so that my salvation may reach earth's farthest bounds" (Isaiah 49:6*b*, REB).

Chosen by God as recipients of justice and mercy, the Israelites received the command to be the people of God amid others in order that God's grace, mercy, and justice might be made manifest. The prophets encouraged a missionary strategy of presence, urging Israel to be present as a witness of Yahweh among the nations. Additionally, Yahweh attracted a striking number of individuals through the active missionary witness of word and deed. J. Verkuyl notes: "The stories of Melchizedek, Ruth, Job, the people of Nineveh described in the book of Jonah, and many others in the Old Testament are windows, as it were, through which we may look out on the vast expanse of people outside the nation of Israel and hear the faint strains of the missionary call to all people already sounding forth."[14]

The missionary of the future will represent more of the global nature of Christianity. When the twentieth century began, 85 percent of all Christians lived in the West. When the twenty-first century dawns, 58 percent of all Christians will be living in the Two-Thirds World. In 1900, 3 percent of Africa's population (or 9 million persons) were Christian; by the year 2000, nearly 50 percent (or 324 million persons) will be Christians. In Latin America, there were 62 million Christians in 1900 and 555 million expected in 2000. In South and East Asia there were 19 million in 1900 and 225 million anticipated in 2000.[15] Christianity has proved more successful in winning adherents in the Two-Thirds World than in retaining them in Europe. In Great Britain, only one person in ten attends church each Sunday. In Scandinavia 90 percent of the population claims Lutheran church membership, but only 5 percent enter churches on Sunday.

Nearly 90 percent of all the world's missionaries for the past two hundred years have come from Europe and North America (80 percent from the English-speaking world). Today Two-Thirds World churches send over twenty thousand missionaries to other peoples. Larry Pate of Overseas Crusade has estimated that at the current rate of growth the non-Western missionary force will number one hundred thousand by the year 2000. Others project that by the year 2025, churches of the southern hemisphere will send 50 percent of the global missionary community.[16] International missionaries are now coming to the United States. For instance, Korean missionaries have helped Korean communities of faith grow dramatically in the USA. Placement of missionaries varies significantly. Some estimates indicate more missionaries located in Alaska (population 585,000) than in the entire Muslim world of 900 million people.

The fourth theme recognizes the antagonism against God's loving and liberating initiatives. The Hebrew Bible contains many stories of conflict between the powers that would destroy God's intent for creation and those that would preserve and enhance life. The battles against false gods which humans have fashioned (the Baals and the Ashtaroth) and the struggles against social injustice illustrate the antagonism to God's love and liberation. Grand visions of a coming realm of God ("a new heaven and a new earth") are projected, when all relationships will be perfectly restored and all of creation—people, plants, animals, and the total environment—will exist in proper accord with God's intentions and initiatives (see Isaiah 2 and 65 and Micah 4). The goal of revisioning mission and ministry amid threats to life and creation reiterates Micah's dream that:

They shall beat their swords into plowshares, and their spears into pruning hooks; nation shall not lift up sword against nation, neither shall they learn war any more; but they shall all sit under their own vines and under their own fig trees, and no one shall make them afraid. (Micah 4:3a-4)

Participation in God's mission usually means a ministry full of conflict and costs. The consequences of seeking to live and serve and die as an apostle can be very high. One finds antagonism to God's mission of justice, peace, and the integrity of creation not only within the culture and the churches, but also in one's own family or oneself.

Matching missional profession with missional performance proves challenging and complex. The idealism of answering the call to service must be matched by the integrity of the character and competence of the missionary. Not all who believe they have experienced Christ's call are suited to be representatives of the church in complex and cross-cultural situations. The church must always test this call to verify if persons have the faith and the fruits of the faith in their own lives, as well as evidence of the gifts and of graces necessary for the immense tasks.

Vatican II ("*Ad gentes*") described the high calling of a missionary. "By a truly evangelical life, in much patience, in long-suffering, in kindness, in unaffected love," the missionary will suffer, if need be, even death, as an ambassador of Christ.[17] Louis J. Luzbetak speaks of the missionary's spirituality as requiring "a deep, living faith, . . . with God as the very heart and center of their lives" along with a "selfless dedication to the needs of others." Missionaries must combine this with "a deep appreciation for the contribution that human knowledge and skill can make toward more effective mission policies and practices."[18]

Committed to the poor and oppressed, Sheila Cassidy yielded her life to Christ and went to Chile as a missionary doctor. The authorities imprisoned her after she treated a revolutionary leader. From her prison cell she wrote *Audacity to Believe*, some of which I have paraphrased here:

> You offered yourself freely, did you not? No one forced you?
> *Of course!*
> Well then? Now your offer's been accepted.
> *But I didn't think it would mean this.*
> What did you think, then?
> *I don't know. I thought it might mean being a famous missionary doctor.*
> Perhaps Christ doesn't want you to be a missionary. Not yet, anyway.
> *But why?*
> Who knows! Perhaps He wants you here among these prisoners. To be a presence, to be a Christ for them.
> *But for five years?*
> So what. You offered yourself. Was it only a short-term offer?
> *No, no! It was for always, anywhere!*
> Well, what are you worried about, then . . .[19]

A fifth Hebrew Bible theme underscores God's compassion for the poor, the oppressed, the weak, and the outcast. Israel was not chosen because of its higher ethical standards or practices, but because of God's free grace.

Compassion for the unworthy remains the cornerstone of Jewish faith and the distinguishing mark of Yahweh. God is described as the "father of the fatherless, and protector of widows" who gives the friendless a home and brings out the prisoner safe and sound (Psalm 68:5-6, RSV). David J. Bosch notes that:

> Whereas the gods of the predominantly hierophantic religions stressed order, harmony, integration and the maintenance of the status quo, the violation of which would provoke their fury, Yahweh revealed himself as the God of change, the God who comes to the rescue of the poor and the needy.[20]

The centrality of compassion to the faith mandates a missionary religion. Hosea and Jeremiah anguished for the hurt of the marginalized. In Hosea's words, "my heart recoils within me; my compassion grows warm and tender" (Hosea 11:8b). Micah links justice, compassion, and humility as the requirements of God (Micah 6:8). The Book of Jonah stresses the supremacy of compassion. Abraham J. Heschel claims God rejoices in doing kindness and offering compassion.[21]

The Jewishness of Jesus is epitomized by his compassion for the poor, the oppressed, the weak, and the outcast. Jesus embodied the pain of the marginalized in his own life and ministry. Repeatedly Scripture reports "he had compassion on them" and healed them (Matthew 14:14), or fed them (Mark 8:2), or taught them (Mark 6:34), or mourned with them (Luke 7:12-13). His two best-known parables—the Good Samaritan and the Prodigal Son—underscore compassion.

This compassion motif energizes mission. Christians may be divided on issues of evangelism or interfaith dialogue, but are more unified in relief efforts and social service outreach that emphasize feeding the hungry, caring for refugees and orphans, providing clothing and shelter for the poor, and so forth. Ecumenical and denominational agencies like Church World Service and the United Methodist Committee on Relief provide millions of dollars yearly for compassionate care of persons in distress without regard to their religion, nationality, race, or any other status.

The human need continues to escalate. Within the United States the homeless represent an alarming challenge, as their numbers increase in an affluent land. In fact, people generally are so well-fixed economically that almost every home hoards pennies. An organization in New York, Common Cents, has discovered almost every household has $13.00 in coins forgotten in pockets, containers, and drawers. Collecting them, they have provided meals and rent subsidies for the homeless, housing for AIDS patients, and summer camp for children from welfare hotels and shelters.

Missionary organizations worldwide reach out in compassion. Responding to natural disasters and persistent human needs, Christians seek to express God's love for the oppressed. The cries for help, however, overwhelm the capacity of the church to respond. For example, forty million children in South America, Central America, and the Caribbean have made the streets their home. Some twenty-eight million live in Brazil alone. One day a street child wandered into a Brazilian church. Watching intently as the bread for communion was broken, he asked, "will there be enough for me?"

New Testament Themes

The New Testament itself is a product of the missionary work of the early church. Its writings testify to the church in mission. Each book could be highlighted for its importance in mission understanding, but only eight key themes or messages will be accented. They occupy a central place in reclaiming the apostolic nature of ministry.

The Kingdom or Reign of God represents the overriding missional perspective of the New Testament. These eight key themes are all related to the vision of God's reign on earth. The Kingdom of God was central to the preaching of Jesus and the apostles. Proclamation and incarnation of God's liberating love undergirds and motivates all mission and ministry. God's kingdom extends beyond the church to all creation. People who do not even know the name of Jesus often are advocates or champions of God's love on earth. Their lives witness to the beauty and power of God's spirit on earth. Christians testify in prayer and action to the hope of "Thy Kingdom come, Thy will be done, on earth as it is in heaven."

First and foremost is the understanding of Jesus the Christ as Savior of the world. The Old Testament motifs of universality, rescue and liberation, missionary, antagonistic powers, and compassion are all reflected in the life, teachings, death, and resurrection of Jesus. Christ exemplifies the experience of God's coming kingdom or realm of love and liberation on earth. Jesus' definition of his mission expresses this new epoch: "The Spirit of the Lord is upon me, because he has anointed me to bring good news to the poor. He has sent me to proclaim release to the captives and recovery of sight to the blind, to let the oppressed go free, to proclaim the year of the Lord's favor" (Luke 4:18-19).

Significantly, Jesus omitted from Isaiah 61 the reference to the "day of the vengeance of our God." Two biblical scholars, Joachim Jeremias and Walter Grundmann, argue that the storm of protest engendered by Jesus' actions probably resulted because Jesus selectively stressed grace rather than vengeance.[22] Thrice Jesus quotes Isaiah pericopes (Isaiah 29:18-20, 35:5-6, and 61:1-2), intentionally eliminating the escatalogical day of vengeance. As David J. Bosch has noted: salvation is not what people expected—"God's compassion on the poor and outcast has superseded divine vengeance!"[23]

Oppressed persons everywhere identify with this loving and liberating pronouncement of Jesus. Embedded in these words lies the key scriptural paradigm highlighted by Christians in the Two-Thirds World. In this mandate for mission and ministry, contemporary Christians see themselves in community with Jesus the liberating Christ.

The second theme expressed the mission mandate of the Great Commission to proclaim the gospel to the whole world. Each of the Gospels expresses a version of this imperative, but the most quoted is Jesus' affirmation in Matthew to all nations and peoples. Jesus declared the missionary mandate of the risen Christ: "Go therefore and make disciples of all nations, baptizing them in the name of the Father and of the Son and of the Holy Spirit, and teaching them to obey everything that I have commanded you. And remember, I am with you always, to the end of the age" (Matthew 28:19-20). No single passage of Scripture has exercised more power or influence in the missionary thrust of the church.

Biblical scholars and missiologists continue to dissect the language of this saying. Controversy surrounds the phrase "all nations" *(panta ta ethne)* as to whether it means "ethnic units" or "people groups" since "nations" is a relatively modern political term meaning sovereign state.[24] Basically it refers to all human beings wherever they live.

Critics of the decline in mainline church memberships and of ecumenical missionary policies often cite the Great Commission. Lamenting his own United Methodism, Gerald Anderson argues that:

Over the last decade or so, something has happened in our church that undercut our Wesleyan tradition and diminished our response to the Great Commission. Obviously you can't give what you don't have. And what we no longer seem to have in some quarters of our church today is an abiding conviction about the necessity of personal faith in Jesus Christ for salvation. How else can we account for the loss of more than a million members, closing 3,000 churches, 900 fewer missionaries over the last fifteen years or so?[25]

The third theme of mission in the New Testament is manifest in the Great Commandment. Jesus asserted that the greatest commandment is to "love the Lord your God with all your heart, and with all your soul, and with all your mind, and with all your strength," and "your neighbor as yourself" (Mark 12:30-31). The motif of love in all three Synoptic Gospels has provided a powerful impetus for Christian mission and ministry, motivating persons to share their lives and resources in generous and sacrificial ways.

Sometimes, however, the Great Commandment conflicts with the

Great Commission, especially in regard to questions of evangelism and other world religions. Does love of neighbor mean denigrating another's faith? Does love permit uplifting one's own faith while at the same time respectfully acknowledging another's? Perhaps Billy Graham best overcame the inevitable tension when he declared that "the uniqueness of Jesus Christ stands on its own authority without castigating other religions and ideologies. It does not need to be propped up by opposing things we don't like or don't agree with."[26]

Fourth, the parables of Jesus constitute a unique message of mission in the New Testament. Nothing touches the conscious and the subconscious levels of motivation more deeply than the power of an evocative story. Jesus' parables are extended metaphors that use familiar people or events to convey unfamiliar or unexpected images such as the kingdom or reign of God. Subversive by intent, the parables grasp the attention of the listener, twist acceptable cultural standards upside down, and destabilize traditional religious teachings.

Biblical commissions and commandments have motivating authority for the already converted, but the parables have an evangelistic authenticity that prompts persons to engage in ministries for justice and mercy. Ever startling is the oxymoronic story of a despised person from an ostracized class being called the "Good Samaritan" by Jesus because he had compassion and crossed barriers to minister to a person in need. The story of a feast given for outcasts because prominent guests refused to come provides another example. And who can forget the haunting portrait of the Last Judgment when we learn that because we did not feed the hungry, clothe the naked, visit the imprisoned, and so forth, we failed to encounter the incognito Christ.

Theologian Sallie McFague has suggested that Jesus himself represents a parabolic event of the kingdom or reign of God. Jesus' practice of dining with "tax collectors and sinners" that so shocked his contemporaries illustrates this possibility.[27] This radical inclusiveness, says Elisabeth Schüssler Fiorenza, affirms that "not the holiness of the elect but the wholeness of *all* is the central vision of Jesus."[28]

Fifth, the cross and resurrection are thematic symbols without parallel in the New Testament. Discipleship did not mean primarily studying the teachings of Jesus, but entering into Christ's suffering. Paul's second letter to the Corinthians rejects equating mission with demonstrable success and triumphalism (II Corinthians 2:17), but rather glories in weakness (II Corinthians 12:9). The apostle anticipates suffering and affliction, stumbling stones to those who expect only success. In II Corinthians mission is identified with the cross—not only Christ's but also the apostle's.

Bishop Anastasios of Androussa reminds Christians of the centrality of the cross and resurrection in the church's mission, lest it be a mere shadow or phantasy. He proclaims:

What our brothers and sisters in the isolated corners of Africa and Asia or in the outskirts of our large and rich cities long for, in their depression and loneliness, is not vague words of consolation, a few material goods or crumbs of civilization. They yearn, secretly or consciously, for human dignity, hope, to transcend death. In the end they are searching for the living Christ, the perfect God-man, the way, the truth and the life. All, of whatever age and class, rich or poor, obscure or famous, illiterate or learned, in their heart of hearts long to celebrate the resurrection and the celestification of life. In this the prospect of a mission "in Christ's way" reaches its culmination.[29]

The resurrection is an event of history because it epitomized an experience of revolutionary hope. Something did happen in Jerusalem a few days after the Crucifixion. We know the disciples underwent a life-changing experience of hope on that first Easter. Thus the cross and resurrection must be at the center of a church's mission and ministry. Christians are Easter people, not Good Friday disciples. Christ was alive! Death had been conquered! The promises of God had been fulfilled and could be trusted. Propelled by that faith, Peter, Paul, and the other early Christians sacrificed themselves unstintingly in missionary service. Instead of declaring in despair, "Look what the world has come to," they proclaimed "Look what has come to the world!"[30]

A sixth distinctive feature of the New Testament is the accent on the Holy Spirit. A risen Christ uttered missional commands, accompanied by an understanding that the Holy Spirit empowers disciples to respond in obedience and service. Without the work of the Holy Spirit, the church could not effectively fulfill Christ's mission.

Generally, Christians situated in a particular context or crisis provide the best interpretation of the work of the Holy Spirit in that place and time. The temptation is particularly keen for Christians in North America and Europe to presume superior theological insight and seek to bypass local Christian communities of faith in reaching decisions about mission resources, institutions, personnel, and theology. The same temptation often manifests itself when suburban Christians seek to dictate to inner-city people or when urban churches attempt to control rural congregations. Paternalism rather than partnership triumphs.[31]

It is the Spirit that calls persons into Christian ministry. Persons are asked to make vocational life choices in order to undertake special tasks within the mission of God. The ordained ministry is not a career one chooses because it appears to be interesting work or because one does not know what else to do with one's life. In the words of Orlando E. Costas, one enters the mission of ministry because of: "The holy conviction that

God has chosen one to do a particular task and has given one the necessary gifts to fulfill it. Ultimately, the ministry is obedience to the internal witness of the spirit."[32]

The seventh motif of the New Testament is of a community of faith in mission. All of the images of the church envisioned in the New Testament focus on mission; none are self-contained. "When the church ceases to be in mission," claims Lesslie Newbigin, then it "ceases to have any rights to the titles by which she is adorned in the New Testament."[33] Mission manifested itself in the lives and deaths of early Christians. Paul epitomized this missionary commitment. As the great apostle to the Gentiles, he continued to advance the gospel's proclamation on a broken front, establishing churches and writing epistles to scattered Christians.

Biblical records are incomplete, but according to legend Paul was beheaded and Peter was crucified upside down in Rome. Contrary to biblical portraits defaming Thomas as the "doubting disciple," traditions in India report that he died a martyr near Madras after planting a church that still exists there today. Their martyrdoms were not that of isolated individuals but representative of the community's suffering in each and every place. The martyrs gave their blood generously for the sake of God's mission in the world through the church.

The eschatological dimension is the eighth characteristic of mission. A nonbiblical term, echatology refers to the end or last period of existence. How one envisions the end makes a substantial difference in how one understands the present. Anglican Archbishop Robert Runcie recalls that his mother had a fondness for first reading the last page of detective mystery stories so she would know how all the clues fit together! He suggests Bible reading that begins with the Book of Revelation's vision of a new heaven and a new earth: "Here is God's disclosure of the unity of the whole human family. . . . *And the gates of the City shall not be shut.* (Rev. 21:22-27) Exclusiveness is not a characteristic of the City of God. . . . Neither the Church nor the world 'sets the agenda': God has his agenda of shalom, unity and communion."[34]

Often Revelation has been interpreted loosely as a collection of predictions about the future. Popular supermarket books give detailed descriptions linking "the beast" with unpopular figures as diverse as the Pope, Saddam Hussein, and the Sandinistas. Media preachers may identify the "plagues" with humanism, communism, feminism, or whatever else can be fashionably denounced. Elisabeth Schüssler Fiorenza claims this is a fundamentalist media misuse of Revelation because it neither proclaims "the apocalyptic promise of justice and salvation to the poor and to the oppressed" nor does it "challenge the complacency and security of the relatively well-to-do."[35]

experienced by early Christians living in the Roman Empire. A writing of prophetic eschatology, it revisions the church's mission in an apocalyptic context of justice and salvation for the poor and oppressed. By taking a "perspective from below," Revelation has expressed the yearnings of the powerless and the poor to participate in the justice of God's loving and liberating initiatives. Mortimer Arias in *Announcing the Reign of God* notes that John, the writer of Revelation, was imprisoned and in exile when he wrote his visions. Arias reminds us:

> We should not forget that the hopeful message of the coming kingdom has been proclaimed not in times of peace and freedom but in times of unrest, oppression, and persecution. The apocalyptic literature was born out of oppression and marginalization for the people of God. It was not written to threaten or to frighten people but to raise their hope.[36]

We live at a great moment in history. The perils and possibilities appear enormous. Liberation, justice, and peace for all peoples can be more than a dream of a new heaven and a new earth dancing in our heads. We, too, can see holy cities, new Jerusalems, descending from heaven. We, too, can envision a God who will wipe away every tear and conquer death. We, too, can be apostles of hope, each in our own place and each in our own way.

Neither the world nor the church sets the agenda or the demands for Christian ministry, lay and clergy. On the contrary, God calls us to leadership and the gospel must shape our response.

CHAPTER TWO

World Havoc or World House?

Only the kingdom of heaven runs on righteousness. . . . The kingdoms of the earth run on oil. . . . It seems that all of life itself is wrapped up in those lines. All of us . . . people . . . nations . . . live by need and not by truth.

LEON URIS, *Exodus*

Just prior to his assassination, Martin Luther King, Jr., envisioned what he called a "world house." He imagined a disparate and diverse family inheriting a home in which all must live together. King's vision was the great new problem of humanity. We have inherited a "world house," said King, "in which we have to live together—black and white, Easterner and Westerner, Gentile and Jew, Catholic and Protestant, Moslem and Hindu—a family unduly separated in ideas, culture and interest, who, because we can never again live apart, must learn somehow to live with each other in peace."[1] Unless we transform this worldwide neighborhood into a global community, learning to live together as sisters and brothers, "together we will be forced to perish as fools."[2]

The tide of human history since King's death has not only underscored this portrait of a global village house, but has also reaffirmed his perception of an urgent need to create new human relationships lest humanity destroy all of God's creation. Nuclear annihilation and human extinction may be "the fate of the earth," genetic engineering may remake creation in humanity's image, and environmental destruction may already have prompted "the end of nature."[3] Desperate poverty and dehumanizing starvation stalk the globe.

According to the *World Development Forum*, if our world were a house of one thousand people: "there would be 564 Asians, 210 Europeans, 86 Africans, 80 South Americans, and 60 North Americans. In the village would be 300 Christians

45

(183 Catholics, 84 Protestants, 33 Orthodox), 175 Muslims, 128 Hindus, 55 Buddhists, 47 Animists, 85 from other religious groups, and 210 atheists. Of these people, 60 would control half the total income, 500 would be hungry, 600 would live in shantytowns and 700 would be illiterate."[4]

Lest we "perish as fools," the urgent imperative, in the words of philosopher Alfred North Whitehead, is for persons to shift their "basic outlook" and experience "a major turning point in history where the pre-suppositions on which society is structured are being analyzed, sharply challenged, and profoundly changed."[5]

An episode symbolizing this shift in "basic outlook" occurred on October 27, 1986, when representatives of twelve major religions gathered, at the invitation of Pope John Paul II, in Assisi, Italy to pray for world peace. This unprecedented event recognized a new world reality and planetary threat necessitating a new religious response. In contrast to previous Christian hostility toward other religions, or insistence that Christianity fulfills the partial truths taught by other religions, the occasion signaled a new era of respect, understanding, dialogue, and cooperation and the emergence of a unique "universal ecumenical mentality."[6]

In this new global context and crisis, revisioning Christian mission and ministry for the twenty-first century is not just an option or an opportunity but an obligation of faithful obedience. Believing "the earth is the Lord's, and the fullness thereof" (Psalm 24:1a, KJV) and empowered by a commitment to God's love in Jesus Christ, Christians are called to a new missionary era for the salvation of the earth and its inhabitants. Gordon D. Kaufman, reflecting on the forces threatening human existence and the planet, remarks that:

> Throughout the world there appears to be a growing passion to reconstruct the present order into one more truly humane. That is the great aspiration of our time—underlying much of the unrest of our world—whether we are Christians or Buddhists, Americans or members of the so-called third world, communists or adherents to Western-style democracy. How shall we build a new and more humane world for all of the peoples of the world? That is our most important question.[7]

Major Threats to Existence

Throughout human history, Halley's Comet has appeared every seventy-five years without fail. Each time it creates a new excitement among the peoples of the earth. It serves as a natural reminder of the rhythms of responsibility we share as inhabitants of the planet earth. Now for the first time, however, we can contemplate the possibility that when Halley's Comet returns again in 2061, life as we know it will not exist. Catastrophe will result neither from natural calamity, nor from comets crashing to the earth, but from a failure of humanity to preserve creation.

The threat we fear the most, and often feel the least capable of combating, is the possibility of nuclear annihilation. The militarization of the earth has transformed a potentially peaceful planet into an armed camp with neighbor armed against neighbor. The proliferation of nuclear weapons to more and more nations of the world and the potential for nuclear terrorists are haunting prospects.

The global escalation of the arms race has been so dramatic in recent years that it has surpassed the comprehension of most ordinary mortals. Global military spending is now about $1 trillion per year. Every minute $1.8 million is spent; $2.7 billion is the cost of one day of spending. In a few hours that equals what the United Nations spends in one year!

As nuclear weapons now numbering fifty-five thousand proliferate among the nations of the world, the potential for accidental, terrorist, or purposeful use increases. As the republics formerly composing the Soviet Union broke away in the early 1990s, and as anarchy threatened, concern intensified about who controlled these weapons. When war engulfed the Middle East in 1991, advocates for using nuclear weapons emerged. Among the first targets attacked in Iraq were plants apparently within a few years of manufacturing nuclear weapons.

By some sheer miracle nuclear war has not yet been unleashed, and *The Bulletin of the Atomic Scientists* has reset the dial on the Doomsday Clock of nuclear annihilation to "seventeen minutes before midnight."[8] Prior to the initial breakthroughs in negotiations between the Soviet Union and the United States, they had edged the dial superimposed on a world globe to "three minutes before midnight." Both relationships between the military superpowers and drastic reductions in nuclear weapons must be priority concerns of Christians in the twenty-first century. The issue of curbing the proliferation of nuclear weapons, with The Nuclear Non-Proliferation Treaty scheduled for renewal in 1995, represents a more immediate problem. Failure to do so could have catastrophic consequences.

Second to the specter of nuclear war, global warming caused by worldwide industrial expansion may be the most serious threat to humankind. Scientists fear that society is altering the chemical balance of the earth's atmosphere and changing climates worldwide more rapidly than previously predicted. The year 1990 registered the highest global temperature in the last century or so. As living standards around the globe improve through agricultural advancements and industrial development, permanent damage to the environment occurs.

The "greenhouse effect," that is, the gradual warming of the earth due to carbon dioxide buildup in the atmosphere, could have radical consequences. The possible climatic implications include melting of the polar ice caps and raising the level of world oceans from ten inches to four feet. Huge amounts of carbon dioxide released into the atmosphere by the burning of fossil fuels cause global warming. Additionally, mounting evidence suggests that other gases—including fluorocarbons from aerosol sprays, nitrous oxides from fertilizers and even methane from underground coal mines and mass cattle production facilities—also play a major role. Released into the atmosphere, these gases soak up the infrared rays of the sun. The atmosphere retains this radiation as heat, in much the same way a greenhouse does. Gradually temperatures increase.

The United States, with only 2 percent of the world's population currently, uses 24 percent of its energy. China, with 10 percent of the population, uses 9 percent. If China achieved the same rate of energy consumption as the United States, this would almost double world consumption. Since China depends on burning coal, there would be a vast increase of carbon dioxide and sulfur dioxide.[9] Many persons believe that the United States declared war over Kuwait, partially, in order to ensure easy access to oil. By continuing to encourage overuse, the United States remains the world's greatest producer of greenhouse gases.

The prescriptions for solving these problems remain highly problematic. Banning the use of fossil fuels is almost unimaginable. Halting industrial progress could trigger tragedies of tremendous proportion. No easy answers or solutions exist. To resurrect the old axiom of H. G. Wells, life is a "race between education and catastrophe." The church's recommitment to an intellectual mission of education and research leading to wisdom are urgently needed. To be avoided is the temptation to turn questions immediately into moral issues, asking what we should do before we ask what we should know.

The complex mechanisms that control the earth's temperature have evolved over a period of more than 4.5 billion years. The question now is whether we will have polluted our own nests to the point of destroying earth's biosphere within the next seventy-five years? When Halley's Comet comes again, will earth be as inhospitable as Venus?

Integrally related to global warming is *a third threat: the world crisis in food production, deforestation, disease, and population growth.* E. F. Schumacher shocked us into a new consciousness when he declared civilization "has marched across the earth and left a desert."[10] Famines in Africa, which have evoked admirable outpourings of generosity in terms of food relief, exemplify an aberration in the world's economy, but a frightening foretaste of humanity's future. The world's population numbers more than 5 billion people. At a compounded growth rate of 3 percent a year, it will exceed 10 billion by the year 2012, or 80 billion by the end of the twenty-first century. Furthermore, with 24 billion fewer tons of topsoil each year, the farmers of the world attempt to feed 86 million more people each year.

Disease persists as a most destructive force in the world today. Most of the five hundred thousand women who die annually from childbirth-related causes would have lived if they had had the family planning help they desired. Forty thousand children die every day, 14.6 million each year. Most would live if they were treated with ten cents in oral rehydration salts or $1.00 in antibiotics or $1.50 in preventative vaccine. Measles, neonatal tetanus, diarrhea, and respiratory infections cause two-thirds of the deaths of children. An extra $2.5 billion would keep most of these children alive and healthy. The entire world spends $2.5 billion on the military every day. United States' companies spend $2.5 billion each year to advertise cigarettes, and the former Soviet Union had been spending that much each month on vodka.

The World Health Organization claims that many of the 40 million deaths each year in the Two-Thirds World could be prevented by shifting a small amount of money to health care, but their military expenditures and crushing debt payments (now three times more than what Two-Thirds World countries receive in foreign aid) actually result in declining health spending per person.[11]

Especially alarming is the global threat of AIDS (Acquired Immune Deficiency Syndrome). As of June, 1990, the World Health Organization estimated one in every four hundred adults in the world is infected. Over 126,000 have died in the United States. In Africa alone it is estimated that one-quarter to one-half of black Africans, aged twenty to forty years old, may die of the disease in the 1990s. Five to six million Ugandan children are expected to become orphans by 2010 because their parents will die of AIDS. To date, no cure exists and those with AIDS often receive little care.[12]

C. Dean Freudenberger sketches an awesome threat in *Food For Tomorrow?* He claims that one-half of the food-producing soil has disappeared and one-third of the remaining soil will be lost by the year 2000. Deserts are expanding on every continent, adding land the size of Luxembourg each year. By the year 2000 when the population will exceed 6 billion, less then 5 percent of the earth's surface will be arable. Thirty million farmers have left the land in the United States in the past thirty years. The crop yield in the United States peaked in 1975; prior to the year 2050 crop yields will have declined from 15 to 30 percent.[13]

Additionally, the World Resources Institute reports 40 to 50 million acres of tropical forest, an area the size of Washington State, vanish each year as trees are cut for timber and cleared for agriculture and other development. Forests are disappearing at an acre and a half per second. A 40 percent reduction of the 1980's forests in the Two-Thirds World can be expected by the year 2000.[14] Deforestation results in a dramatic decline in songbirds. In Palestine in 1939, W. C. Lowdermilk proposed an "Eleventh Commandment." Fearful of what suicidal agriculture was doing to the planet, he suggested Moses would have been inspired to add that:

> Thou shalt inherit the Holy Earth as a faithful steward, conserving its resources and productivity from generation to generation. Thou shalt safeguard thy fields from soil erosion, thy living waters from drying up, thy forests from desolation, and protect thy hills from overgrazing by thy herds, that thy descendants may have abundance forever. If any shall fail in this stewardship of the land, thy fruitful fields shall become sterile, stony ground and wasting gullies, and thy descendants shall decrease and live in poverty or perish from off the face of the earth.[15]

When the United Nations celebrated its 40th anniversary, Japan's prime minister, Yasuhiro Nakasone, warned in his address against human-made monsters confronting the world's flora and fauna. He noted that:

> Our generation is recklessly destroying the natural environment which has evolved over the course of millions of years and is essential for our survival. Our soil, water, air, flora and fauna are being subjected to the most barbaric attacks since the Earth was created. This folly can only be called suicidal.[16]

As prime minister he sometimes retreated to a small temple in Tokyo to practice *zazen*, a form of Buddhist meditation. In appealing for new levels of international cooperation, he recited a haiku he had written to underscore the philosophical view that persons are "born by the grace of the great universe." He then pleaded that the nations of the world:

> work together so that, in the middle of the next century, when Halley's comet completes another orbit . . . and once again sweeps by our planet, our children and grandchildren. . . . , will be able to look up at it and report that the Earth is one.[17]

Genetic engineering is a fourth major threat to human existence. We live in a new epoch in the evolution of humanity—a time when humanity has the potential power to manipulate nature—the created becoming Creator—unleashing frightening new possibilities that may prove beyond control. Bioengineering introduces a new technology that could be as dangerous to human existence as nuclear annihilation.

Scientists as early as 1981 successfully transferred a gene from one animal species to another. The gene that produced hemoglobin in a rabbit was transferred into the fertilized egg of a mouse. The newborn mouse, and its descendants, differed uniquely from any other mice in history because they then produced hemoglobin as effectively as did rabbits. A new rabbit-mouse had been created!

Of course, the scientific intent was not to populate the world with rabbit-mice, but rather to engineer incredible breakthroughs that will revolutionize life on this planet. The potential for advances in medical care and the treatment of human suffering appears enormous. "Harmful" genetic characteristics could be eliminated in fetuses before birth. Some dream of the day genes can be inserted into humans, helping facilitate or retard growth, regenerate limbs, and so forth. A whole new world of antibiotics, enzymes, antibodies, vaccines, and hormones might be created. The revolution in human gene therapy has already begun in the United States with experiments to treat cancer and an immune disorder by inserting new genes into cells.[18] The United States government has launched the Human Genome Project which seeks to identify "all human chromosomes at their highest level of resolution, listing the whole encyclopedia-length recipe for making a human being."[19]

The potential for biotechnology offsetting threats to world agriculture and destruction of the environment by industry must also be underscored. Experiments in the energy industry may lead to substitutes for fossil fuels. Bioengineering may someday replace petrochemical farming. The field of animal husbandry could be transformed, for example, as genetic transplants create cattle that can grow as well on cheap grass or hay as on high-priced grains. Through the use of cloning, higher quality meats could be produced. Already a new biotechnical drug called Bovine Growth Hormone (BGH) promises to increase a cow's milk output by 20 to 40 percent.[20] If safe for human consumption, imagine how many more children in the world might receive needed milk.

Algeny, the underlying philosophy of biotechnology, posits that organisms are not final discrete entities but temporary sets of relationships. All living things can be reduced to base biological material, DNA, which in turn can be extracted, manipulated, and reorganized— creating new, perfected organisms. These new creations are more efficient than the old. Nature is not a given into which we are born but an option we can program. Theologically, we are talking about molding humanity in our own image!

Just as we once rejoiced at the prospect of "atoms for peace" and hailed nuclear energy as humanity's great new savior, we have reason to fear the advent of genetic engineering. Genophobia is not necessarily paranoia. A rebirth of the ethics of eugenics should prompt us to remember the sterilization measures earlier this century and the Nazi nightmare of the Holocaust, when the "ideal" human was viewed as being a blond-haired, blue-eyed, Aryan heterosexual. Once set in motion, the engineering that eliminates genital defects eventually might be used to improve looks, eliminate skin color, reduce our emotional tendency to cry, or make us all left-handed heterosexuals!

A new age has dawned. What limits will be placed upon those who tamper with the structure of life? Who will exercise such power? What happens if terrorists gain control and unleash genetic illnesses or new creations upon the planet? Truth again becomes stranger than fiction, as science fiction is rapidly being transformed into our scientific future. The choices and decisions made in the coming years will determine in a startling way whether we have a world house or world havoc.

These challenges—nuclear proliferation, the greenhouse effect, world hunger, and genetic engineering—create a new context for revisioning mission and ministry in the twenty-first century. Other challenges could be cited. For example, the persistence of inequitable economic opportunity around the globe certainly undermines the possibilities for a just and peaceful world house. As East-West political tensions decline, North-South conflicts may escalate as the gap between the rich and the poor widens. Christians dare not look uncritically at their mission theology, strategies, and resources. "New occasions teach new duties" and the time seems ripe for reconsidering the past and reconceiving the future.

Renaissance in Creation Theology

Critics have argued that the Hebraic-Christian tradition has provided a theoretical or theological framework justifying the "mastery" of the earth to the point of its ruination. According to them, our spiritual tradition persuaded the world that humankind is in charge of the natural world and can do what it pleases. The Genesis image of humanity having dominion and going forth to multiply has propelled life toward cliffs of destruction. By claiming humanity's superiority over the natural world, we have evolved an insensitivity to the ecology of God's creation.

This criticism is too extreme. Historian Barbara Tuchman argued that governments frequently follow policies contrary to their self-interest. While there has been a theological tendency to buttress the thinking of destructive forces, I suspect that with or without such thin theological support humanity would have joined this march of folly. Our myopic selfishness, and our almost magical belief in scientific panaceas, make it difficult for humanity to ever make the long-term sacrifices necessary for preservation's sake.

A renaissance of interest in creation theology and ethics offers an encouraging new sign, however, in the Christian community. We worship a God of both nature and history. Until recently the fuller meanings of Christian stewardship have been slighted. Stewardship is now being viewed as an end in itself, not just a means to some other end. Within the life of most Christian congregations, stewardship still refers to the acquisition and management of ecclesiastical properties and monies. Functionally, we seek to be good stewards of those resources in order to accomplish our mission and ministry, forgetting that stewardship itself is a metaphor representing "a kind of summing-up of the meaning of the Christian life."[21] Stewardship for our religious foreparents represented more than a religious campaign to fill the church's coffers in order to make sure that the heating bill and the pastor's salary were paid. It was a profound concept that dealt not simply with tithing but also with one's total philosophical and theological outlook.

The church must recover the many rich nuances of the biblical concept of stewardship. The Bible makes twenty-six direct references to "steward" and "stewardship." In the Hebrew Scriptures a steward is a type of servant, not one who simply takes orders but rather one who supervises or manages what belongs to someone else. In Hebrew society this steward-servant usually worked for a royal personage. Thus when the analogy was transferred to Scripture, the steward-servant was accountable to God, who is the owner. The Gospel of Luke (12:42ff.) uses steward and servant interchangeably in the teaching of Jesus and concludes: "From everyone to whom much has been given, much will be required; and from the one to whom much has been entrusted, even more will be demanded."

The Pauline and other epistles further expand the concept of stewardship. Christians are called to be stewards of "the mysteries of God" and reference is made to "the stewardship of God's grace." The Greek word usually translated into English as "steward" is *oikonomos*, a term with a broader meaning than the English implies. It suggests a responsibility for the planning and administrating of a household, with connotations of the terms "economics" and "ecumenics." Douglas John Hall notes that: "Reflecting upon the word picture as such, we might say that stewardship has not only to do with money, budgeting, and finances but with the whole ordering of our life, our corporate deployment of God's 'varied grace' in the life of the world."[22]

Christians understand that humanity does not own the earth but only manages creation. "The earth is the Lord's and all that is in it" (Psalm 24:1). The right to property cannot be considered an absolute; we are never free to do whatever we will. God exists as the ultimate owner of the household earth; we are called to be steward-servants, caring and preserving creation. In doing so, we are reminded of the question asked and the answer given by Rabbi Joshua ben Qarehah:

"Why of all things did God choose the humble thornbush as the place from which to speak with Moses?" The Rabbi replied: "If God has chosen a carob tree or a mulberry tree, you would have asked me the same question. . . . God chose the humble thornbush—to teach you that there is no place on earth bereft of the Divine Presence, not even a thornbush."[23]

Renunciation of Exclusiveness and Superiority

Past relationships, however, complicate peaceful living and cooperation in the new world house that King envisioned. Historically, Christian missions have too often been associated with political domination, economic exploitation, military conquest, and racism. Christian claims of exclusiveness, claiming superiority over the spiritual and ethical systems that have sustained millions of people over thousands of years add to the difficulty of uniting the family of God. As Stanley J. Samartha realizes: "The relentless stream of negative judgments passed on the cherished beliefs and practices of people who have their own scriptures, hermeneutics, philosophies and theologies, their own cultures, social structures and civilization has left deep wounds on the soul of many neighbours of other faiths."[24] The past, however, need not be a prison. Samartha notes that many world religions exist because of mission and conversion. If we can avoid the imperialism and insensitivity of former times, then "there is no reason why the profound possibilities of mission and conversion cannot become a source of mutual enrichment and genuine renewal. Without the practice of mission and the possibility of conversion, there can be no renewal, no springtime in human life."[25]

The myopic human tendency is to see the best in one's own country and only the worst in another. While spending my junior year of college abroad in 1960–61 as a student at Madras Christian College, Tambaram, India, I was tempted to criticize the excesses seemingly tolerated by Hinduism: the caste system, arranged marriages, and magnificent temples amid poverty. But my Hindu friends quickly pressed me to explain why Christians accommodated to racism, segregation, militarism, high divorce rates, and crime. Many missionaries, lacking cross-cultural experiences and education, have had, says Kenneth Cracknell,

a tendency to see everything overseas in terms of spiritual darkness. They were, so to speak, programmed to see the darkest and basest side of the religions and cultures among which they ministered. Nor were they immune from that profoundly human temptation to compare the best in one's own culture and beliefs with the worst in that of other people. Like us they confused the ideal for the reality in their praise of Christian modes of believing and took the degradation and moral failure of communities among whom they worked as evidence of the inadequacy of other religions' inspiration.[26]

Too few North Americans possess the cross-cultural expertise necessary for communicating the gospel. Many remain unaware of their own social "baggage," unable to separate cultural mores from Christian morals, and unwilling to acknowledge their own complicity in evil social structures. Even those who do not view themselves as evangelists and who go with specializations in education, medicine, or other technical areas need preparation in understanding other cultures and countries, and engagement in critical self-examination of their own values and life-styles. The questions they face must be addressed to all of us who claim to be Christian. Can we truly renounce our luxuries and embrace poverty? Can we truly respect the religious heritage and hopes of others when they differ from our own? How are we entrapped in a way of life that bears little resemblance to that of the carpenter of Galilee? To what degree can we suffer with our sisters and brothers in Christ?

The Holocaust and Hiroshima changed Christian theological reflection forever. A half-century has elapsed since these two catastrophic events occurred, but Christians have been slow to grapple theologically with their meaning in terms of the mission of the church. These cataclysmic events cannot be simply dismissed as aberrations of war, for they rubbed raw the sores of anti-Semitism and racism which have plagued Christian mission. They call the church to be converted from its claims of exclusiveness and superiority.

Anti-Semitism, nourished by Christian thinking and communities, helped create a cultural and religious milieu that enabled Hitler to rise to power and to seek systematically to destroy the Jewish people. When a predominantly white "Christian" nation was responsible for detonating the first atomic bombs on largely civilian, non-Christian populations in Japan, an era ended when Christians could dare to presume their religious and ethical superiority.

Groups like Jews for Jesus spend millions each year attempting to convert Jews to Christianity. Individual Jews may choose to convert to Christianity, but a mission aimed at the conversion of Judaism is theologically problematic. Proselytizing that involves deceptive, psychologically manipulative tactics is particularly reprehensible. "Saving the Jews" sometimes means focusing primarily on high school and college students who know so little about Judaism they do not comprehend the subversive intent and distortions.[27] As Karl Barth so eloquently said:

The Gentile Christian community of every age and every land is a guest in the house of Israel. It assumes the election and calling of Israel. It lives in fellowship with the King of Israel. How, then, can we try to hold missions to Israel? It is not the Swiss or the German or the Indian or the Japanese awakened to faith in Jesus Christ, but the Jew, even the unbelieving Jew, so miraculously preserved, as we must say, through the many calamities of his history, who as such is the natural historical monument to the love and faithfulness of God, who in concrete form is the epitome of the man freely chosen and blessed by God, who as a living commentary on the Old Testament is the only convincing proof of God outside the Bible. What have we to teach him that he does not already know, that we have not rather to learn from him.[28]

To claim ethical superiority for Christianity over Judaism or Buddhism discounts too quickly the lessons of the Holocaust or Hiroshima. Christians must renounce such theological and ethical ethnocentricity and meet our global neighbors of every faith and no faith as repentant sinners, kneeling as servants both to experience God's grace and to wash the feet of all our sisters and brothers.

Recently I walked where the devil walked. I saw in Dachau the face of the demonic and I toured the torture chambers of Hell. As I wandered through the grounds and the museum, and looked at the crowded barracks, killing grounds, and gas chamber, I could still hear the cries of those who suffered and died there during its twelve years of operation.

The exact number of persons who were persecuted at Dachau is unknown. Records show more than 206,000 prisoners registered, but many other persons passed through to the hundreds of other concentration camps established all across Europe. Lists in the museum categorize the Jews, the political opponents, the clergy, the homosexual persons, and the other so-called "undesirable elements" who were imprisoned and killed as enemies of the Nazi government.

Statistics are cold and impersonal; more than one hundred thousand persons died by a single atomic blast in Hiroshima. Of the city's 150 doctors, 65 were killed and the rest were badly wounded; of the 1,780 nurses, 1,654 were dead or injured too severely to serve. Writer John Hersey traveled to Japan while the ashes were still warm and personalized this almost incomprehensible tragedy by describing the lives of survivors and their families. His stories of Terufumi Sasaki and Kiyoshi Tanimoto dare not be forgotten since they personify what otherwise might be lost in statistical categories.

A young surgeon, Dr. Terufumi Sasaki, discovered he was the only uninjured doctor in a six-hundred-bed Red Cross hospital. Seeing only partially through glasses borrowed from a wounded nurse, he confronted thousands of severely wounded patients streaming in the doors, lining the steps, lying under the porte cochere, and extending out into the streets for blocks in every direction. He could barely move as he sought to bandage the wounded, stepped over the dead and dying, and tried to save those who seemed to have a chance to live.

A few other doctors, along with ten nurses, finally joined him as they sought to care for ten thousand people. Blood and vomit and cries of pain permeated the hospital; hundreds of patients were dead but no one was available to carry away the corpses amid the atomic holocaust. During the first three days he slept only one hour. Even then the wounded awakened him shouting, "Doctors! Help us! How can you sleep?"[29]

Reverend Kiyoshi Tanimoto, pastor of the Hiroshima Methodist Church emerges from the rubble. Through his eyes we see unspeakable horror, as the flesh pulls off the arms of the people he tries to rescue. We watch his endless energy as he tirelessly struggles to save people, by using a bamboo pole to propel a small punt as he rescues people from the raging fires enveloping the city. We sense his compassion as he walks amid the dying, offering cups of water to people crying for non-existent medicine. We feel a shepherd's love when he forgives a man who accused him of being an American spy. The man dies in his arms, as he reads from Psalm 90: "Lord, thou hast been our dwelling place in all generations" (KJV).

Tanimoto incarnated the missional character of ministry as he reached out to people in need without making distinctions. The white blast of the nuclear age obliterated dogmatic barriers that separated the suffering. Tanimoto cared for all the hungry, the homeless, and the hurt, without regard to their religious or ideological commitments. He labored beside Jesuits and Catholic seminarians and when he fell, ill and exhausted, his friend, a Buddhist priest, ministered to him with healing herbs.

The lessons of the Holocaust and Hiroshima dare not be sidestepped in revisioning mission and ministry for the twenty-first century. They transcend time and teach theological truths that must not be forgotten. Exclusiveness and superiority are alien to the mind of Christ.

Today a Catholic chapel, a Jewish synagogue, and a Protestant church have been erected at Dachau in memorial of those who suffered during the Holocaust. The words emblazened in four languages on the Dachau wall have special poignancy: *"Never Again."* The same should appear at Hiroshima and Nagasaki.

The choice of those two words, "Never Again," were not accidental. They deliberately echo the promise of God embedded in the Hebrew Bible in the Book of Genesis. As symbolized by the wonderful story of the Flood, Noah and the Ark, and the Rainbow, we predicate our faith on God's promise "never again" to destroy all living beings.

The "good news" of the flood story is that God decided against completely destroying the earth. Noah and his family survived as a remnant. Then after the flood God entered into a covenant with humanity that "never again" would the divine destroy the human. This is the great promise of God. As Krister Stendahl has noted: "God's will is clear. So clear that this covenant—the rainbow covenant with all life on earth—is the only unconditional covenant in the Bible."[30]

The Holocaust and Hiroshima epitomize the terrible tendency of humanity to destroy other living beings. What frightens us is not that God will destroy the earth in the future but that humanity will annihilate every living being. Instead of naming a woman or man of the year, *Time* magazine recently honored the earth as "Planet of the Year," underscoring the dire threat to existence. The promise of God is clear and sure: "Never again." What we need is humanity's concomitant commitment: *"never again" shall we seek to destroy the peoples, the planet, and all the living things God has created.*

The Genesis story places great responsibility on fairly ordinary human beings. Noah claimed no expertise on rain, ships, animals, or anything. He was a righteous, faithful person who cared about creation and who obeyed the commands of God. "The Noah story teaches us a different lesson. It teaches that any of us who regard ourselves as simply reasonably decent people are obligated to act."[31]

Historically, the church has often adopted the ark as its symbol. The church has always believed it has a responsibility for preserving creation. God has called the church to be an ark, exercising stewardship for the global good. God declared "Never again shall the waters become a flood to destroy all living creatures." An Australian biologist, Charles Birch, speaking to the church about the stewardship and preservation of the environment, said:

We have been warned as Noah was warned. Skeptics laughed and ridiculed then as they do now. The skeptics drowned and Noah, the original prophet of ecological doom, survived. We are warned that a flood of problems now threatens the persistence of our industrial society. But this time the ark cannot be built of wood and caulking. Its foundations will be a new awareness of the meaning of life, of the life of all creatures, both great and small. Its name will be the ecologically sustainable and socially just society. If this ark cannot be made watertight in time, industrial society will sink, dragging under prophets of doom as well as skeptics and critics.[32]

And then he added an incredibly important word of hope—a message all of us must repeat: "We do not have to be victims of circumstance. In the ecological view the future is not predetermined. It is radically open.

Through its openness to the lure of God, the self becomes freed from total pre-occupation with itself. Its concern becomes the world. That is still possible for each one of us."[33]

Hiroshima teaches that the imperative of mercy is never enough. When tens of thousands are dying all around us, and triage medical ethics alone seem possible, then the Christian call to preventive social and political action becomes clear. A mission of mercy must always be accompanied by a mission dedicated to justice, peace, and the integrity of creation.

Henri J. M. Nouwen reports he was only thirteen years old when World War II ended. Years later when he was an adult he learned of the Holocaust and often asked himself why Christians did not resist the persecution and destruction of the Jewish people. Why were there no massive Christian uprisings and marches protesting the genocide? Why did religious people not invade the camps and tear down the gas chambers and ovens? Why did those who were worshiping nearby not go out of the church buildings and resist the powers of evil so visible in their own land?

Today I am an adult living only a few miles from the place where Trident submarines are being built, weapons able to destroy in one minute more people than were gassed in Nazi Germany . . . Today I am a well-informed person fully aware of the genocide in Guatemala and the murderous terror in El Salvador. Today I am a well-educated teacher who is able to show clearly and convincingly that the costly arms race between the superpowers means starvation for millions of people all over the globe. . . . Today I am asking myself the question: "Does my prayer, my communion with the God of life become visible in acts of resistance against the power of death surrounding me?" Or will those who are 13 years old today raise the same questions about me 40 years from now that I am raising about the adult Christians of my youth. I have to realize that my silence or apathy may make it impossible for anyone to raise any questions 40 years from now, because what is being prepared is not a holocaust to extinguish a whole people but a holocaust that puts an end to humanity itself.[34]

The Holocaust and Hiroshima remind us that in the conflagrations of life and death, Christ calls us to transcend human divisions and to embrace all of God's children and creation. By failing to protect Jews, homosexual persons, and other "enemies" of the state, Christians lost any possible legitimacy to claims of superiority. When nuclear bombs explode, no safe places exist—even the green parks of Hiroshima burned, the potatoes baked under the earth, and the radiation warped the genes of the unborn. If the church intends to address the major threats to existence in the twenty-first century it must learn from history and recant its past claims of exclusiveness and superiority.

Reappropriation of the Rainbow Symbol

Christians need to reappropriate the symbol of the rainbow as a reminder of God's promise of life. Whether we are persuaded by the evidence of a literal flood or not, we are captivated by the parabolic story of Noah building an ark, the neighbors belittling him, and the animals parading aboard two-by-two. Then comes the spectacular climax when the flood recedes, a dove flies forth, and God makes a solemn covenant with Noah and every living thing, saying ". . . that never again shall all flesh be cut off by the waters of a flood, and never again shall there be a flood to destroy the earth" (Genesis 9:11). The appearance of a rainbow seals the covenant.

What is crucial to our faith is not the parable but the promise of life implicit in it. It is an everlasting and unconditional agreement. As one Jewish scholar interprets it, the rainbow is both "a sign of God's rulership over the natural order and as God's permanent signature to His promise. The rainbow is thought to remind God of this promise and to remind man of the grace and the forbearance of his Creator."[35] This promise affirms God is working to preserve earth and the human race. Our call is to join the Divine in "making human life more human" and averting catastrophe.

Despite the major threats to existence, not all is doom and gloom. Everywhere people are reaching for rainbows, seeking to become faithful caretakers of God's earth and hoping to transform the present world condition. As the Talmud directs, when a funeral procession intersects with a wedding march, the mourners must give way. Radiance and joy challenge the darkness. It is a time not for optimism but for hope. The time has come for reappropriating the rainbow as a central religious symbol for all humanity.

Among the signs of hope, as persons reach for rainbows, let me succinctly cite six. *First, there are signs of sanity—the drift toward nuclear annihilation is not inevitable.* Recent breakthroughs evident in the relationship between the United States and the former Soviet Union were unthinkable just a few years ago. The walls have crumbled in Europe. Organizations like the Physicians for Social Responsibility are convincing other persons in all walks of life that no one wins in a nuclear holocaust.

Second, a new wave of environmental concern is sweeping the earth. Pollution is a global phenomenon. Averting "the end of nature" requires global cooperation. People are rediscovering that they, too, are critical parts of the ecosystem of the universe and they are demanding that leaders and politicians address the problems of rain forests, ozone holes, acid rain, and so forth.

The Chernobyl nuclear reactor catastrophe symbolizes ecological disaster. Once a prosperous place of fifty thousand, Chernobyl exploded into a radioactive "ghost town." Tens of thousands of persons were irradiated. Nature was contaminated. Yuri Stscherbak recalls that in the Apocalypse we read: "And there fell a great star from heaven . . . and the name of the star is called Wormwood: . . . and the waters became wormwood; and many men died of the waters, because they were made bitter" (Revelation 8:10, 11, KJV). Ironically the Ukrainian word for wormwood is Chernobyl. The fallen star named Wormwood indeed represents an apocalyptic warning and motivation for a global environmental movement.[36]

Third, some Christians are beginning to acknowledge the special Christian responsibility for the poor. What Latin Americans call a "preferential option for the poor" is a biblically based assertion of outrage against injustice. God does not love the victims of society more than others, but because Yahweh is a righteous God, divine concern extends out especially to persons, classes, races, and nations in need. Rich persons are not excluded from God's Kingdom, for they too are often victims of systems that trap and dehumanize them. The wealthy can experience conversion and provide an option for the poor by engaging in mission for justice, for social transformation, and for political systems that will offer social alternatives in order to eliminate disparities between the rich and the poor, and encourage a society of people who do justice and love mercy.

By revisioning mission, the church can make this option for the poor more evident in its own life. Most mainline congregations give an average of 1 to 3 percent for mission, with evangelical communities giving 3 to 5 percent. Of the $1.8 trillion that American church members earn each year, they keep 98 percent and donate the other 2 percent, or $38 million, to Christian causes. Only 20 percent of the $38 million goes to ministries that target those in need in the United States or other countries. Churches spend most of the money on buildings, professional staff and overhead costs rather than mission. The mission challenge is to get more persons and congregations to reach for this rainbow.

A fourth rainbow sign has been worldwide manifestations of assistance in times of famine and other disasters. Temporary relief efforts are indispensable, if people are to survive and become productive persons again. Everyone knows the "band-aid" dimension to all relief efforts. Yet simultaneously one must also acknowledge the urgent mobilization of concern that swept the earth in response to famines in Africa, earthquakes in Mexico and the Soviet Union, and refugee crises in Asia and elsewhere. Organizations like Bread for the World, CROP, and others are making a difference. Lest we dismiss too quickly the involvement of popular recording artists, let us remember that the youth of the world from China to Kenya joined in singing Michael Jackson's and Lionel Ritchie's "We Are the World." Calling for a new unity among the people of the earth, they sang about God's global family and the universal need to love. A new consciousness about human rights and suffering is emerging despite drastically different cultures and political systems. Music transcends geographical and religious boundaries.

Another rainbow sign emerges out of the South African scene and the debate over investment and disinvestment. People are asking stewardship-type questions about how they should use their money for social value as well as for profit. The need for South African disinvestment may disappear, but socially responsible investing has grown to encompass other issues. From 1984 to 1990 ethical investments in pension funds, mutual funds, and municipal and private portfolios increased from $40 billion to over $500 billion. Business ethics need no longer be an oxymoron!

The development of interest in social responsibility investments is certainly a welcome new sign on the horizon. A first step for investors might be to contact the Social Investment Forum in Minneapolis, which won't make recommendations but will acquaint one with the options available. For example, the Clavert Social Investment Fund does not invest in issues primarily engaged in production of nuclear energy, or in businesses invested in South Africa, or manufacturers of weapons systems. The Dreyfus Third Century Fund seeks general "enhancement of life in America" but does not consider overseas involvement or exclude defense contractors or liquor producers. The Pax World Fund avoids the securities of companies engaged in military activities or in the gambling, liquor and tobacco industries. It invests in companies producing life-supporting goods and services. Some investment advisors like the Franklin Research and Development Corporation and Progressive Securities Financial Services Corporation are dedicated to meeting ethical and strategic as well as financial objectives of the responsible investor. Overall, the goal is to make financially sound investments consistent with an ethical commitment to justice, peace, and the integrity of creation.

A sixth sign of hope is the growing number of individuals who are making their own personal witness, joining in God's mission to the world. Many scholars and scientists are utilizing their talents to search for solutions to the most perplexing human problems facing humankind. Those, for example, related to *The Bulletin of the Atomic Scientists* are exploring new solutions to war and trying to mobilize public concern for changing dangerous public policies. Agronomists are seeking answers for the world crisis in agriculture. Governments are moving to restrict bioengineering. Environmental degradation including the "greenhouse effect" is gaining front-page attention and inspiring international conferences such as the United Nations' "Earth Summit" in Brazil leading to a Magna Carta for the globe.

Within the life of the church there are countless persons who are witnessing to their faith. A Seattle couple has moved beyond the tithe principle, not satisfied with the 10 percent standard. By using public transportation and simplifying their life-style, they reserved 32 percent from one income. They used that 32 percent to pay the salary of an agriculturalist laboring to help ten thousand people become agriculturally self-reliant in rural Haiti. One California church has set a goal of designating more than 50 percent of its income for international mission. Another congregation meets in the homes of members rather than invest in more buildings and gives 60 percent to mission callings.[37] Rainbow signs like this confirm in a positive way Dietrich Bonhoeffer's assertion that "unless the church is the church for others, it is not the church at all."

Beyond "No-Fault" Theologies

Admitting personal or societal wrongdoing and acknowledging individual or corporate sin is neither easy nor popular. We commonly deny our responsibility for our own faults. "No-fault" insurance and "no-fault" divorce are ideas come of age. No one accepts blame; things just happen. No attempt is made to assess blame, guilt, or responsibility. The merit in this perspective should not be dismissed categorically, but when carried to an extreme it becomes subversive to human character.

The phenomenon of a "no-fault" view of history increasingly concerns historians. A history professor at Cornell was astonished to discover his students uniformly and readily accepted a perspective that endorsed terrorism as the only option available to certain oppressed groups. Harvard historian, Richard Hunt, was alarmed to discover students accepting Nazi Germany as an inevitable result of economic and social conditions of the time. Hunt concluded that his students held "depressingly fatalistic conclusions about major moral dilemmas facing the German people at their particular time and place in history." His larger concern was the societal trend "toward a no-fault, guilt-free society" since "the virtues of responsible choice, paying the penalty, taking the consequence all appear at low ebb today."[38]

Individual Christians likewise are tempted to adopt popular "no-fault theologies." One "no-fault" theology that people prefer is "the devil made me do it." The new age gospel of the occult and interest in exorcism seems to hold an incredible interest for contemporary persons. In close company are the apocalyptics who seem to be saying "Why worry about preserving

the environment—we soon will be experiencing the Second Coming!"
Grace Halsell documents in *Prophecy and Politics* how apocalyptic
preachers appeal to self-righteous nationalists who see the sins of other
nations but not their own. They use the Bible to justify their belief in the
inevitability and the rightness of an imminent global cataclysm.[39]
Whether one blames one's own wrongdoing, or the world's problems, on
God—or the devil—it simply provides another way of evading
responsibility for one's own action.

A second "no-fault" theology suggests that "society forced me." Enmeshed in
the cultural and political structures of our societies, we cannot even
imagine the possibility that God might have another plan for humanity.
We are locked into our patriotic nationalism and fail to envision new
patterns of world order. Because others exploit the world's natural
resources and enjoy the fruits of pollution, we have difficulty visualizing
how our individual decisions to adopt simpler life-styles can help. We
tend to surrender to the inevitability and high finances of biotechnology
without even waging a battle.

*A third "no-fault" theology transfers responsibility to someone else for what has
gone wrong.* We are victims of heredity and environment. "My parents
messed me up!" "It's Ronald Reagan's fault!" Blame the "liberals" or the
oil companies. We lack control over our own moral destinies. This has
prompted Anna Russell's sardonic verse in which she notes that because
she had ambivalent feelings toward her brother, "naturally" she
poisoned her lovers. From this she has learned the lesson

> That everything I do that's wrong
> Is someone else's fault.

The fallacy of this thinking is that we do not inherit the world from our
parents but rather we borrow it from our children. In fact, we bear
responsibility for building military machines, flooding the landfills with
our garbage, polluting the rivers, running the risk of genetic engineering,
and mortgaging the futures of our children and grandchildren with
astronomical national debts.

*A fourth "no-fault" theology excuses wrongdoing because "I was just
following orders!"* Reflecting on the atrocity of the crucifixion of Jesus, its
inhumanity and miscarriage of justice, we experience feelings of
outrage. Surely some sensitive souls with authority and power could
have intervened. Many of those who could have helped, however,
acted "under orders," having surrendered their consciences to others.

"Following orders" continues to be a popular "no-fault" policy. A jury
of his military peers found Lt. William Calley guilty because he had

slaughtered helpless Vietnamese women and children. However, many spoke in his defense, saying he had performed a glorious, patriotic deed. Today many persons working in nuclear plants and other industries that tamper with the future of human existence refuse to say "No," either for personal economic reasons or because they believe they must follow specific orders.

A fifth "no-fault" theology against sin is "I don't want to get involved." I once heard about a man who crawled from a car accident, bloodied and bruised. Asked what he was doing, he responded, "I don't want to get involved." Patently ridiculous in such a case, it is likewise absurd for us to try to crawl away from the nuclear arms race, the environmental crisis, genetic engineering, or world poverty. We are involved and called to be globally responsible.

When these five popular "no-fault" theologies link arms with "no-fault," "guilt-free" philosophies of history, the time clock on the future of humanity and the earth is ticking closer and closer to doomsday. When Christians begin to believe that contemporary problems are somebody else's responsibility and no alternative policy choices exist, then we teeter on the tightrope of catastrophe.

Accountability and hope are integral elements of a Christian understanding of stewardship or trusteeship of the earth. Christian faith is neither a "no-fault" theology nor a "pull-yourself-up-by-your-boot-straps" ethic. God invites us to join in loving and liberating initiatives in the world that seek justice, peace, and the integrity of creation. Though we are sinners, unable to pull ourselves up to God by our bootstrap efforts—the Good News of the gospel proclaims that God was in Jesus the Christ reconciling the world, not counting our trespasses against us. If we repent and seek new ways, we become not just guilty sinners, but forgiven sinners. The atonement of Jesus empowers us to be forgiven sinners, entrusted with a missional ministry of justice and mercy, bringing reconciliation or "at-one-ment" with and for the earth and the whole human family.

Nonexistence or Coexistence

The choice between nonexistence or coexistence (world havoc or world house) is fundamental to understanding the missional character of ministry in the twenty-first century. Humanity lives perilously above a fault line that could cause a global earthquake. The church possesses neither the answers nor the power sufficient for resolving these threats to existence, but it can be a significant partner with others in creating new understandings and mobilizing persons and governments to action.

Mission theology in the past has focused primarily on salvation history rather than emphasizing creation theology. A renaissance of interest in creation theology, a reappropriation of the rainbow symbol, a renunciation of exclusiveness and superiority, and a rejection of "no-fault" theologies will assist in shifting the basic outlook of humanity and move the world toward a more humane future.

Already hopeful signs of a new outlook and a new openness for religious people to work together to address the challenges of creating a world house abound. In Canada the Council of Muslim Communities and the Council of Churches jointly wrote to the Muslims and Christians of the Sudan urging them to help resolve tragic issues dividing their country. Along with the Canadian Jewish Congress, these two groups have sought to create more just and humane refugee and immigration policies. In Thailand Christians and Buddhists are fighting together against tourist-funded prostitution, as "Christian" men from North America and Europe exploit "Buddhist" women. In Liberia calls for a cease-fire in the civil war were issued jointly by the Liberian Council of Churches and the National Muslim Council of Liberia. Christians and Buddhists from nine Asian countries met recently in Seoul, Korea, and expressed opposition to using the Pacific as a nuclear dumping ground. Scientist Carl Sagan at a world conference noted that the ozone hole does not have a Christian, Buddhist, Muslim, Jewish, or Hindu solution; all people of faith must be committed to its resolution. The United States and other superpowers cannot launch a preventive military attack to stop the "greenhouse effect."[40]

As Pope John Paul's interfaith prayers at Assisi demonstrated, questions of freedom, justice, and peace necessitate revisioning Christian mission and ministry. Existence depends upon coexistence and cooperation by all peoples of all faiths. Future missionary endeavors must radiate a new theological perspective and understanding. They must restructure relationships around the globe to ensure not only a more hopeful future, but even the possibility of a future for God's creation.

CHAPTER THREE

The World as God's Body

Earth's crammed with heaven, And every common bush afire with God; But only those who see take off their shoes . . . The rest sit round it and pluck blackberries, And daub their natural faces unawares.

ELIZABETH BARRETT BROWNING, *Aurora Leigh*

An ecological, nuclear age evokes new images of God. Much traditional God-language tends to be distant, dualistic, hierarchical, and triumphalistic, shifting responsibility for the world from humanity to divinity. God is perceived as one in total control, invulnerable, and impassible. Monarchical, royalist, and patriarchal concepts of God discourage a theology which takes seriously the need for mutuality, co-creation, and relationship. Breaking through to new levels of consciousness and perception, Christian theologians are envisioning new ways of thinking and relating the Divine to a global age.

By experimenting with a new language for God and new metaphors to describe the relationship between God and the universe, we may better face the needs of a world threatened by extinction. Theologian Sallie McFague envisions a God both of justice and care that links us and our earth.

We can no longer see ourselves as namers of and rulers over nature but must think of ourselves as gardeners, caretakers, mothers and fathers, stewards, trustees, lovers, priests, co-creators and friends of a world that, while giving us life and sustenance, also depends increasingly on us in order to continue both for itself and for us.[1]

Over the centuries Christians have imaged God in distinctly different ways in an effort to express in word pictures the salvific love of God. In light of the potentially catastrophic context and exigencies of our time, it is imperative that Christians think in bold and imaginative ways about

67

the mission and ministry of God. In the past, says Dorothee Söelle, authoritarian religion that imagined God solely as a dominating power contributed to those who were passively obedient to the Nazis and to Christian participation in the Jewish Holocaust.[2]

Many Christians, of course, profess no need for reconceiving God or revisioning mission. For them the traditional language and expectations seem sufficient. Repetition of time-tested creeds and reaffirmation of traditional credos suffice for the church to be renewed and re-energized for mission.

"Every naming of God," contends Brian Wren, "is a borrowing from human experience." As Gordon Kaufman has noted in *Theology for a Nuclear Age,* images of God do make a difference. One group of Christians tends to think of God as a king who will fight on the side of "his" chosen ones, the Americans, in the Armageddon with the communists. Another Christian group passively waits for an all-powerful divine father to handle the situation.[3]

Other Christians believe that exclusivistic models must surrender to more inclusivistic perspectives. A new vision of mission draws on the paradigm of Jesus. Jesus "epitomizes the scandal of inclusiveness" for:

> What is proclaimed in Luke 4 as the heart of Jesus' ministry—good news to the poor, release to the captive, liberty for the oppressed—and what is manifested as well by his healings of the sick is pushed to an extreme in his invitation to the ritually unclean to eat with him. Jesus offended by inviting the outsiders to come in, to join with him not merely as needy outcasts but as his friends in joyful feasting. The central symbol of the new vision of life, the kingdom of God, is a community joined together in a festive meal where the bread that sustains life and the joy that sustains the spirit are shared with all.[4]

The monarchical model of God as King ruling over the earth, distantly related to all creation, impassive to the needs of "his" subjects, demanding repentance and service encouraged exclusiveness. Admittedly, this description borders on caricature, but such royal imagery was better understood and perhaps appreciated in earlier ages when monarchs thrived and authoritarianism reigned. In an age of "perestroika" and "glasnost," however, when communist and other dictatorial totalitarians are crumbling to the forces of democracy, these metaphors sound curiously like remote linguistic dinosaurs for expressing the salvific love of God for both the human and the nonhuman life of the universe.

Thinking of the World as God's Body

Instead of imagining the world simply as the kingly realm of God, Grace Jantzen and Sallie McFague propose thinking of the world as God's body. The world is the dwelling place of God. Instead of a passive divine being, the incarnate God is at risk. When the earth is harmed, God is wounded. Using this metaphor we envision not a distant, invisible God, but a God "liable to bodily contingencies."[5] God could presumably create a new body if the earth exploded, but this proposed imagery enables us to see how God cherishes creation. McFague says the world as God's body may be a way to restate

the inclusive, suffering love of the cross of Jesus of Nazareth. In both instances, God is at risk in human hands; just as once . . . human beings killed their God in the body of a man, so now we once again have that power, but . . . we would kill our God in the body of the world. Could we actually do this? To believe in the resurrection means we could not. God is not in our power to destroy, but the incarnate God is the God at risk: we have been given central responsibility to care for God's body, our world.[6]

All metaphors have limitations and it would be absurd to push this analogy too far. Metaphors are not descriptions but imaginative constructions. Expressing the metaphor of the universe as God's body should not be equated with endorsing pantheism. God cannot be reduced to the world or become synonymous with the world anymore than we can become totally identified by our bodies. Just as we can distance ourselves from our bodies, so God transcends the world. Yet Christians have always asserted that all reality flows from God. As Grace Jantzen notes: "the world, ourselves included, is God's deliberate and loving self-expression. The universe cannot be utterly alien, impersonal and meaningless, but the personal and significant self-expression of God. Thinking in this way about the universe already removes much of the sting of pantheism."[7]

Imagining the world as God's body is not to describe God but to think of God's creation in a fresh way. The universe becomes sacramental with the presence of an invisible God. Instead of thinking of salvation as something that solely concerns the spirit without regard to the body, salvation can be understood as social, political, and spiritual. By visualizing the globe as God's body we begin to recover something of the insight of the Native Americans who have always understood the world as sacred ground, to be treasured and protected, not damaged and destroyed. In Bishop Anastasios of Androussa's language:

Reverence for the animal and the vegetable kingdoms, the correct use of nature, thought for the conservation of the ecological balance, the fight to prevent nuclear catastrophe and to preserve the integrity of creation, have become more important in the list of immediate concerns for the churches. This is not a deviation, as asserted by some who see Christ as saving souls by choice and his church as a traditional religious private concern of certain people. The whole world, not only humankind but the entire universe, has been called to share in the restoration that was accomplished by the redeeming work of Christ.[8]

Affirming the Missio Dei

When the twentieth century dawned, the conversion of "pagan" peoples provided the primary motivation for mission. The "Copernican revolution in missions" occurred with the re-introduction of "missio Dei" into mission theology, and talk shifted from "our mission" and "the church's mission" to the mission of the Triune God. "Missio Dei" is the term typically used to define mission as an activity of God. Christians are called to join in God's loving and liberating initiatives for the redemption and restoration of creation.[9]

A trinitarian approach to the theology of mission has characterized "missio Dei." For centuries the concept was employed to refer to the mission of the Son by the Father, and of the Holy Spirit by the Father and the Son. After the sixteenth century its modern connotation of the church being sent into the world was developed. The two dimensions were united in 1952 at the International Missionary Council in Willigen, Germany.[10]

Discernment of God's initiatives in the world is always problematic, especially when God's action is understood to transcend the work of the church in the world. It is especially difficult to know what is truly the divine movement of grace in the hidden ways and the incognito persons of history. Amid ambiguities one can never be absolutely certain whether or not one has appropriately discerned God's will. There are no guarantees of success and a high probability of failure. A congregation and its ministers must be intentionally missional in order to discover God's mission. "To know what God is doing in history," observed Eugene L. Stockwell, "there is no short cut around a willing dive into the history into which God, whether we like it or not, has already thrown us."[11]

When people suggest that God may be acting in the revolutionary political movements of our time, many conservative Christians object to "the Trojan horse" of mixing evangelism and politics within "the well-guarded walls of the ecumenical theology of mission."[12] The ideas that God might be at work beyond the life of the church, or that humanization might be the goal of mission, stimulate controversy.[13]

An alternate concept developed by evangelicals has been "missio Christus" which argues that mission flows out of the person and work of Christ in the world. Christ's coming, his cross, and his commission (Matthew 28) have been offered as the incentive, message, and agenda for missions. Calling persons to repentance and conversion has received priority, though clearly evangelicals have been actively engaged in various projects providing food, medical care, education, and development services. However, in recent years evangelicals have increasingly shown a concern for social justice questions and the gap between "missio Dei" and "missio Christus" understandings has narrowed. A framer of the Lausanne Covenant has acknowledged that the Great Commission cannot be held in isolation from the Great Commandment. Thus John R. W. Stott would argue that "evangelization and sociopolitical action are partners in mission with the former having a certain priority."[14]

In this time of unparalleled threat to all of existence, the idea of a solely church-centered approach to mission seems parochial and self-defeating. The *missio Dei* proves greater than the limits of vision and resources of Christ's church. Resolution of the crises of a nuclear, ecological age necessitates the participation of the global family of God. To suggest that God's loving and liberating initiatives are not restricted to the church is not to downgrade the value or importance of the community of faith, but to summon the church to a new level of leadership for the sake of all life.

Imaging God in Surprising Ways

Christians often speak of joining the mission of God and affirming a missionary God who "sent" Jesus Christ to earth. One's understanding of God thus has a determinative influence on ascertaining the nature of the church's mission and ministry. Missiologists in endorsing the "missio Dei" underscore a trinitarian understanding of God.

An innovative and surprising proposal by theologian Sallie McFague is her attempt to image God as mother (or father), lover and friend. While not likely to be widely embraced, her personalized models for God do provoke us to think more creatively about the mission of God for our time. The temptation will be to rapidly dismiss these metaphors for God, but if we can hold them at least long enough to imagine their possibilities and implications, their shock value may open us to fresh insights into God's will for our time. What would it mean if we heard God calling us to mother, love, and befriend the universe?

The monarchical model is based primarily on the biblical portrait of Paul, while these new incarnational models of God emphasize the interdependence and interrelatedness of all life. The liberating and loving initiative of God is manifest in John's portrait of "the Word made flesh." The parental metaphor for God accents creative "agape" love that evokes the justice ethic. It stresses God as the giver of life, loving the weak and vulnerable as well as the strong and beautiful. Creation is not viewed as an artistic expression, but uses the "imagery of gestation, giving birth, and lactation that creates an imaginative picture of creation as profoundly dependent on and cared for by divine life." Our resistance to speaking of God as mother seems ironic since "all of us, female and male, have the womb as our first home, all of us are born from the bodies of our mothers, all of us are fed by our mothers. What better imagery could there be for expressing the most basic reality of existence; that we live and move and have our being in God?"[15]

God imaged as artist or sculptor becomes angry when the beauty or balance of creation is spoiled, or when humans rebel because of the design. When God is pictured as mother, "God is angry because what comes from her being and belongs to her lacks the food and other necessities to grow and flourish."[16] McFague argues for a caretaking image of God, contending "We should become mothers and fathers to our world."[17]

Mission as caretaking suggests a much more comprehensive calling than mission as simply converting. Stewardship or trusteeship of the creation God has entrusted to us calls us to a "universal parenthood" that seeks to preserve, not destroy, life. Instead of focusing only on saving individuals, we are called to save the total structure of life as created by a loving God, who seeks both justice and care.

All Christians will affirm that God is love, but paradoxically almost all will resist the idea that God is a lover! The latter evokes our fear of eroticism and sexuality and seems inappropriate when speaking of the divine. We would rather retreat to talking about God, the Almighty, than to think of God, the Lover. Yet the Song of Songs is part of the Bible; God is imaged as a faithful husband in Hosea; the church is called "the bride of Christ"; and in John Jesus prays "that they may be one even as we are one: I in them and thou in me" (John 17:22b-23a, KJV). God is not just love, but lover, since Christians are affirming one who actively loves. Norman Pittenger called God the "cosmic lover" who expressed divinity "decisively in the human loving which was and is Jesus."[18]

If the mission of God is to love the world, then apostolic ministers are called to be co-lovers of creation. Such passion for God's body, i.e., the world, means feeling deep emotions and experiencing pain. Lovers are not dispassionate! God as lover, says McFague, seeks to save and make whole.

The entire beloved cosmos has become estranged and fragmented, sickened by unhealthy practices, and threatened by death and extinction. God as lover finds all species of flora and fauna valuable and attractive, she finds the entire, intricate evolutionary complex infinitely precious and wondrous; God as lover finds himself needing the help of those very ones among the beloved—of us human beings—who have been largely responsible for much of the estrangement that has occurred.[19]

Lovett H. Weems, Jr. advocates that clergy and laity recover a sense of passion for ministry, for without it the church grows sterile, lifeless, and missionless.[20] The passion of Jesus was not passive, indifferent endurance, but an agony for those who suffered. Contemporary disciples of Jesus will be wounded healers and enslaved liberators, for we have endured scars from living and are enslaved by the very oppressive systems that need to be overthrown. Yet, by God's grace, we can transcend our sin and become passionate lovers of the world and healers of its wounds.

Christian mystics frequently have spoken of God as friend. The intimacy sought and experienced in meditation has enabled them to experience the close friendship of God. This bonding relationship enables political mystics to take great risks for justice and peace, because they sense tremendous divine power that supports and sustains them as they encounter the powers of injustice and evil.

C. S. Lewis once characterized sweethearts as being "normally face to face, absorbed in each other," while "friends, side by side" are absorbed in some common interest.[21] Viewed in this way, God as friend is not a self-absorbed, exclusive individualistic image, but one that suggests humans can join the Divine in common efforts of loving and liberating creation. The Quakers, known as the Society of Friends, epitomize this metaphor as they have shared and labored for a common vision of justice, peace, and the integrity of creation.

The friendship of Jesus with the nonpersons of his society, even sharing table fellowship with outcasts, models an appropriate pattern of behavior for those Christians who seek to be missional and Christlike. Such hospitality prompted critics to call Jesus "a glutton and a drunkard, a friend of tax collectors and sinners!" (Matthew 11:19). His behavior paved the path to the Cross. Likewise today reaching out to those whom the church or society label as pariahs is likely to lead to great controversy and personal costs for ministers in mission.

The church as a "fellowship of the friends of Jesus" must also be a friend of the world, daring to cross gender, racial, religious, and national barricades for the sake of love and justice. Apostolic ministry, said Jesus, means loving one another to the extent of laying down one's life for one's friend (John 15:12-17).

Whether one speaks of God as parent, lover, and friend or whether one opts for more traditional trinitarian language, the crucial question is whether one experiences the Divine in dynamic, personal terms as seeking in partnership the loving liberation of all nature and humanity. The missionary God beckons us to participate.

Being Reluctant Missionaries

However, we are unlikely to welcome this call to a new type of mission and ministry because it forces us to re-examine not only our theological convictions, but also our personal life-styles and institutional stances. Of course, no one wishes for the extinction of the earth and all of its creatures, but what this means in terms of our cherished traditions, customary thoughts, and comfortable trends may be more than we are willing to contemplate or change. Many who want compassionately to combat AIDS (Acquired Immune Deficiency Syndrome) may be afraid of promoting the use of condoms, celebrating chastity while disease runs rampant and death triumphs! We want to join the "missio Dei" in this dangerous nuclear, ecological age, but we are afraid this may require us to violate previous taboos as we build bridges of understanding and cooperation among peoples of diverse religions. Even those who accept this challenge may find themselves less than certain and more than a bit uncomfortable about revisioning mission and ministry for the twenty-first century.

Thus the Hebrew story of Jonah, the reluctant missionary, becomes a model for our time. Holy satire characterizes the Book of Jonah. Contrary to the typical missionary adventure tale, this one lacks a genuinely heroic character. Jonah is not portrayed in the same way as great missionary giants of the past two centuries—persons who willingly went to distant lands, gladly risked life and limb for a glorious cause, and gradually succeeded against all odds to develop a young church or social institution.

No, Jonah resisted the call to missionary service at every point. He traveled in the opposite way from which God instructed him; he met hazardous perils with cowardice; and he expressed anger because the people of Nineveh repented when he hoped they would be destroyed! Sent to proclaim a message of grace to the Gentiles, Jonah did all in his power to resist Yahweh, for he had no desire to see his rapacious enemies of the Northern Kingdom saved.

Ecological touches add to the drama. God appoints a missionary whale ("large fish") to rescue the reluctant Jonah! In Nineveh even the animals repent, wear sackcloth with the king, and neither eat nor drink. When Jonah pouts over his evangelistic success, God produces a miraculous plant to give him shade. But when a worm destroys it, Jonah is peeved. To which God responds: "You are sorry about the gourd, though you did not have the trouble of growing it, . . . should not I be sorry about the great city of Nineveh, with its hundred and twenty thousand people . . . as well as cattle without number?" (Jonah 4:10, 11, REB). God has compassion for all creatures, including the cows!

Jonah's story demonstrates the persistence of efforts to thwart the loving and liberating initiatives of God. Yahweh has constantly wrestled with the ethnocentrism that tempted Israel to claim Yahweh for its own and the ecclesiocentrism of the church to avoid the world.

The writer of Jonah sought to expand our understanding of the boundaries of God's compassion. The message is not really the conversion of the Ninevites but the call for us to be converted to a compassion comparable to Yahweh's. "The story's missionary significance," says David J. Bosch, "does not lie in the physical journey of a prophet of Yahweh to a pagan country but in Yahweh's being a God of compassion—a compassion which knows no boundaries."[22]

Like contemporary Jonahs, many Christians today refuse to accept God's call for mission and ministry in a nuclear, ecologically global age. We are uncertain whether we truly want God's love to cross religious, national, ideological, and sexual boundaries. Deep down, we suspect what Jonah feared. Our doctrinal barriers cannot encompass the compassion of God. With Jonah we want to flee to Tarshish because we know " 'that you are a gracious and compassionate God, long-suffering, ever constant, always ready to relent and not inflict punishment' " (Jonah 4:2, REB). How fitting is Thomas Carlisle's poem "You! Jonah!" that closes with these lines:

> And Jonah stalked
> to his shaded seat
> and waited for God
> to come around to his way of thinking.

> And God is still waiting for a host of Jonahs
> in their comfortable houses
> to come around
> to his way of loving.[23]

Coming of a Compassionate Christ

Both the Gospels of Matthew and Luke speak of "the sign of Jonah" in reference to Jesus Christ. They portray the risen Christ as "greater than Jonah" (Luke 11:32) and the time between Christ's death and resurrection is compared to Jonah's "three days and three nights in the belly of the whale" (Matthew 12:40, RSV). Far from being a reluctant missionary, Jesus accepted the call of God to cross barriers that divide people and to preach a gospel of grace for all persons. Even Jesus, however, faced temptations and prayed that the cup of danger and death might pass him by, "nevertheless, not as I will, but as thou wilt" (Matthew 26:39, KJV).

Jesus the Christ incarnated compassion in what he taught, how he lived, and in the way he died. Not to be confused with pity, compassion is empathetic love in action, identifying with the suffering of others and entering into the brokenness of all life. Unlike Jonah, Jesus gladly went to the most despised and rejected of his society, sharing a message and manner of mercy. Unlike Jonah who despised Nineveh, Jesus taught the love of enemies. Jesus did not approach people with sympathy flowing from superiority but with empathy pouring from sensitivity. Repeatedly he identified with people on the periphery of his religious and cultural society—women, lepers, Samaritans, prostitutes and other persons of questionable reputation—those called "sinners" and "the rabble who know nothing of the Law." This compassionate ministry forms the foundation for a missional understanding of Christian ministry.

Christians are called not only to be individuals of compassion, but also a community of the compassionate. What must distinguish Christian mission is its authentic quality of compassion—the unearned and unmerited free grace of God.[24] Compassionate service represents an end-in-itself, not a means for "softening-up" persons for conversion. Medical and educational mission projects exemplify expressions of God's loving and liberating initiatives, not bait for the "real" mission of conversion or church growth.[25] If persons feel drawn to Christ because of consistently compassionate actions, then Christians rejoice. However, food for the hungry, medicine for the sick, and education for the needy are not nets to entrap, but responses to God's grace toward us.

Illustrative is Mother Teresa's mission to the poor in Calcutta, India. Extreme malnutrition, untreated illnesses, and devastating poverty mutilate the small orphans served by the Missionaries of Charity. The mission accepts all sick and needy children, trying to restore their health and to give them hope. By routinely checking the city rubbish heaps, they save children left for dead. Louise L. Reiver reports that:

Sometimes the children come in to us so far gone from lack of nutrition that they are frail little wisps with stick-like arms and legs, bloated bellies and the thin orangey hair and yellowed skin symptomatic of Kwashiorkor. Despite the loving and attentive care given to these children of poverty . . . sometimes the struggle to live is too much. Whenever one of these anonymous little souls is called to God we all grieve, although we know that, at the last, they were loved and treasured and held in warm and gentle arms.[26]

Compassion for "the least of these," not conversion, is the cornerstone of Christian motivation for mission and ministry.

The compassionate Christ, though, is not limited to individual acts of mercy. Compassion seeks to relieve the pain of this world by justice making and political action that prevents catastrophe. By systematically addressing social injustices, Christians battle against the "powers and principalities" that promote and profit from wars, environmental destruction, genetic engineering, and human poverty and oppression.

Before the Vatican "silenced" him, the Dominican priest Matthew Fox wrote two provocative books entitled *A Spirituality Named Compassion and the Healing of the Global Village, Humpty Dumpty and Us* and *The Coming of the Cosmic Christ: the Healing of Mother Earth and the Birth of a Global Renaissance.* In medieval days ecclesiastical censorship triumphed, but today "banned books" only add to their popularity. What quaint irony that the Vatican rehabilitated Galileo and repressed Fox in the same year! Persons can be crushed, but the truth of their ideas cannot be suppressed. As Fox's book titles illustrate, his theological notions press the church to a more compassionate global stance appropriate to healing the broken body of God.

Compassion is the missional language of God and the Cosmic Christ belongs to all people. Fox envisions a "deep ecumenism" that will unleash the wisdom of all world religions in the quest for freedom, justice, peace, and the integrity of creation. In his view:

This unleashing of wisdom holds the last hope for the survival of the planet we call home. For there is no such thing as a Lutheran sun and a Taoist moon and Jewish ocean and a Roman Catholic forest. When humanity learns this we will have learned a way out of our anthropocentric dilemma that is boring our young, killing our souls, trivializing our worship, and exterminating the planet. Universalism is a common characteristic to all the traditions of the Cosmic Christ in the Scriptures and in Western history.[27]

The traditional wording of the Apostles' Creed asserts that after the crucifixion "Jesus descended into hell." Years ago when I asked one of my seminary professors at Boston University what that meant, I received the response: "Where would you expect Jesus to be on his three days off?" The same teacher predicted the growth of Zen Buddhism in America. Asked to explain, he cited this Buddhist scriptural passage for illumination: "If I were on my way to heaven, and saw a person suffering, I would turn back to help." Both the images of Jesus in hell and the Buddhist refusing heaven symbolize a healing core of compassion that is the spiritual dynamic of the universe.

The question posed in the second chapter was whether the earth is moving toward a world house or world havoc. By imagining the universe as God's body and affirming the "missio Dei" of love and liberation, Christians can revision mission as compassionate caretakers of God's creation. By embracing all of life, empathetically identifying with all suffering, and energetically offering ourselves in missionary service, new sacramental meaning emerges when the bread is broken and we hear Jesus saying: "Take, eat; this is my body which is given for you. Do this in remembrance of me."

Appropriating New Metaphors for Mission

Some metaphors of mission (especially the triumphalist, monarchical, and patriarchal ones) probably will not inspire or motivate a new generation of leaders, lay and clergy, to address the compelling concerns of a new century. We need a revisioning of mission to overcome past dichotomies that unnecessarily separated evangelism and social justice, personal and social, conversion and compassion, spiritual and ethical, church planting and community building. One evangelical writer, Ron Sider, declares that "The time has come for all biblical Christians to refuse to use the sentence: 'The primary task of the Church is . . .' I do not care if you complete the sentence with evangelism or social action. Either way it is unbiblical and misleading."[28]

Revisioning mission requires appropriating new metaphors for understanding the church and its ministry in the twenty-first century, images faithful to biblical perspectives and models that can motivate Christians toward greater faithfulness and action. Metaphors for mission, such as being bridge builders, global gardeners, star throwers, and fence movers illustrate how mission can be rooted in the historical, yet free theologically to shape the future.

This book uses the terms "metaphor," "image," and "model" in a synonymous fashion. In a previous book, *Contemporary Images of Christian Ministry*, I discussed in more detail the art of imaging.[29] Remember, however, that metaphors at their best can only be suggestive; pushed to an extreme they can become distorted, ridiculous, and useless. Images, however, can move us beyond sterile concepts, inflaming our imaginations and helping us to perceive realities that cannot be measured or objectified easily. By painting a mental portrait, metaphors can enable us to see beyond our customary angle of vision. All of us perceive only partial views of the world, conditioned by our own biases and pet theories. Language itself proves elusive, with the truth-obscuring power of words and dogmatic systems tempting us to confuse concepts for real things.[30] Words have meanings, but let us walk lightly, knowing that divine mysteries surpass our ordinary levels of communication. Let us probe beyond what we hear or read to discover the deeper spiritual meanings intended.

CHAPTER FOUR

A Covenant of Global Gardeners

Every part of the earth is sacred, every shining pine needle, every sandy shore, every mist in the dark woods, every clearing, and humming insect, is holy. . . . We did not weave the web of life; we are merely a strand in it. Whatever we do to the web, we do it to ourselves. Our God is the same God whose compassion is equal for all.

CHIEF SEATTLE, 1854

Francisco "Chico" Mendes Filho, the Amazonian Gandhi, had a net worth of only two dollars when he was murdered a few days before Christmas, December 22, 1988. A rubber tapper by trade, he lived and labored in the small, obscure river town of Zapuri in Acre, Brazil. In this rugged Amazonian frontier, Mendes mobilized three hundred thousand rubber tappers and a million farmers and hunters, all victims of two decades of government-supported cattle ranching and hydroelectric projects that had stolen their lands. Once a vast, undisturbed stretch of bio-mass, international banks and Brazil's ruling generals had exploited the region for its wealth since the 1970s.

Twenty million acres of virgin rain forest were burned each year, thanks to cattle ranchers profiting from government subsidies and benefiting from beef-hungry fast-food markets in the United States. The ecological costs have been global, since the fires released huge quantities of carbon dioxide into the earth's atmosphere, enhancing the greenhouse effect with potentially drastic climatic changes. Fragile jungle soils have been irrevocably harmed and the precious habitat of thousands of animal and plant species permanently eliminated.

Battling these "principalities and powers," Mendes lived simply and fearlessly, standing in front of bulldozers illegally clearing trees, persuading multinational banks to suspend financing for roads that ripped through the forests, convincing his government to designate five million acres of rain forest as reserves, and alerting the world community to the drastic environmental damage in process. Amnesty International reports that more than one thousand people died in the Amazonian land disputes in the 1980s. Five times Mendes Filho survived attempts on his life.

Influenced by Catholic liberation teachings, Mendes served as the monitor of a base community "group of evangelization." Theologian Clodovis Boff spent time with Mendes and the other tappers. To them Boff preached:

> Happy are those who fight for justice.
> Happy are those who unite with the people.
> Happy are those who go to the side of the
>   oppressed.
> Happy are those who struggle to change the
>   world.
> Happy are those who die without seeing the
>   results of their efforts.[1]

In 1987 the United Nations awarded Mendes the Global 500 prize. After also receiving honors from the Better World Society, Mendes immediately returned home to tap rubber and harvest Brazil nuts to feed his family. Worldly honors did not deter him from his lifelong struggle to stop the devastation of his people and region.

Tending God's Gardens

The incorruptible Mendes was assassinated because he served as a global gardener who gave voice to the poor and vision to the world. His life and death incarnated the risk of tending God's garden earth in the face of those who would exploit and destroy it for their own greed and gain.

Mendes prophetically illustrated emerging theological perspectives being shaped with special force by Two-Thirds World Christian feminists. Adapting the metaphor of gardening, these women have claimed an invaluable personal heritage from their mothers in particular, yet transforming this image into the cultivation of a global garden. As Marta Benavides, a Salvadoran Baptist pastor, writes: "We must understand that each of us is able to have our own garden only when we cultivate it in the context of global interdependence and mutual respect, regardless of color, sex, religion, or national size. Gardening has to do with *companerismo:* standing beside one another; being of the same company and commitment."[2]

Wesley Granberg-Michaelson suggests that "the scope of Christ's redemption beckons mission work not only to soul saving, but also to earthkeeping."[3] Stewardship of the creation God has entrusted to us calls us to a ministry that seeks to preserve, not destroy life. Instead of simply focusing on saving individuals, we are called to save the total structure of life as created by a loving God who seeks both justice and care.

The implication of belonging to a covenant of global gardeners is that each of us in our own place, wherever we may be, can embody environmental witness. This may take the form of refusing plastic foam cups, recycling paper, reducing energy waste, and so forth. Or, it could be in the way we lead worship, deepening Christian awareness of our trusteeship of God's creation. If we conceive of ourselves as global gardeners, our vision and practice of church mission and ministry will be dramatically altered.

Gardening for Christians focuses on envisioning, dreaming, and working for a new earth here and now. The authority and motivation is drawn not from the latest environmental commissions or transnational development plans but from the promises of God. Concerns for ecology, the end of exploitation and militarism, the care of children, the conservation of the soil and plants, and the fulfillment of human hopes is rooted in the Scripture. As described by Isaiah 65:19-22 (GNB):

There will be no weeping there, no calling for help. Babies will no longer die in infancy, and all people will live out their life span. . . . People will build houses and get to live in them—they will not be used by someone else. They will plant vineyards and enjoy the wine—it will not be drunk by others. . . . They will fully enjoy the things that they have worked for.

Articulating this vision of global gardening, Marta Benavides reports that:

The garden I inherited from my mother has become for me the whole of creation. We all need to join together to live as *companeras* and tend the global garden. Time is of the essence. . . . I am one with my nation just like the plants and flowers are one with the soil. But the soil of El Salvador has been plundered, and there is almost nothing for us to inherit. The land, the indigenous ways of El Salvador, our language and traditions—everything is being gradually destroyed. All that we have left is ourselves and the future we forge. Our inheritance, above everything else, is our will to survive as a self-determining people. That is also the only legacy we have for our children. What a wonderful flower! No pesticide can kill the will to survive.[4]

North American feminist theologians also have embraced this metaphor. Sallie McFague calls Christians to become the gardeners "of our Eden, our beautiful, bountiful garden, not taming and ruling it, let alone despoiling and desecrating it."[5] Linking this image to her model of God as parent, lover, and friend, she presses for a profound caring that wills the life of others (both human and nonhuman), nurtures the weak and vulnerable, and seeks the fulfillment of all. Instead of envisioning ourselves as namers and rulers over nature, we need to imagine new relationships between ourselves and the earth that are mutually sustaining and caring. In befriending the world we are its companion, advocate, and partner.

This vision of global gardening seems especially remote and utopian as we contemplate the human and environmental catastrophe in the Middle East due to the 1991 Gulf War. The United Nations conducted an unprecedented study of the war's environmental effects while it raged. The fear was that as combat engulfed the oil fields, the smoke from burning oil platforms and spills could block as much as one-fifth of the sunlight that normally warms the Northern Hemisphere, cooling average temperatures by as much as two degrees. During the 1980–88 Iran-Iraq War, attacks on ships and oil installations dumped millions of barrels of crude oil into the waters and onto the shores of the Gulf. No one knows how many millions of barrels of crude oil now have despoiled the region.

Most environmental concern focused on the possibilities of spilled or burned oil. As Kuwaiti oil wells were deliberately set on fire by Iraq, the conflagration spread to 650 oil wells and burned an estimated three million barrels of oil per day. The cooling caused by the barrier of smoke from smoldering Kuwaiti oil wells could have had global repercussions. Had the war persisted longer, not only could the price of energy have skyrocketed worldwide, with particularly damaging consequences to Two-Thirds World nations lacking their own sources, but it could have disrupted the onset, duration, and character of the monsoons, which affect hundreds of millions of people in south Asia who depend on the seasonal rains for agricultural production.[6]

The Gulf War underscored the imperative of integrating God's concerns of justice, peace, and the integrity of creation into the mission of ministry of our churches and the theological curriculum of our seminaries. Too often in the past, these commitments have been peripheral to, rather than priorities of, our churches and seminaries.

Christians need to understand their faith in the context of a more global and inclusive perspective. In a nuclear and ecological age, pastors and laity must be leaders who not only evangelize, nurture, and manage our churches, but also incorporate concern and action for justice, peace, and the integrity of creation in their ministries. Embracing the Wesleyan understanding of the world as our parish, the United Methodist bishops declared in a pastoral letter entitled *In Defense of Creation: The Nuclear Crisis and a Just Peace* that "Those who serve in church vocations are the primary gatekeepers who can either open or close the opportunities of corporate witness to the things that make for peace. Pastors must know that every aspect of their ministry—preaching, worship, education, counseling, visitation, administration, community leadership—can be an opening for peacemaking."

As anyone who has ever gardened or farmed knows, gardens and fields are not all rich with harvests or overflowing with bouquets of flowers. All metaphors have their limits. Stubborn weeds, pesky insects, and inclement weather always make agriculture problematic. Global gardeners know these limitations and must struggle against the sins of racism, sexism, and classism.

Solidarity in the struggle for life is a noble goal, but we often subvert it by our insensitivity to the suffering of others, our prejudices, and our own enslavement to high and wasteful standards of living. For example, our love of fast food results in fast food restaurants producing 1.7 billion cubic feet of plastic foam trash each year, which aids in damaging the ozone layer. Japan's use of twelve billion pairs of throwaway chopsticks each year has been largely responsible for the destruction of half of the hardwood forests of the Philippines and about a third of the forests of Indonesia.[7] The garbage "imperialism" of European and United States industries prompts the dumping of millions of tons of toxic waste in Two-Thirds World countries and in poor ethnic communities.[8] Instead of tending God's gardens, we have tended to despoil Eden not only for the next generation but for the next millennium.

The Church as Covenant

The covenantal nature of Christian community and ministry is rooted in our relationship with Christ. Persons are not bound together by contracts demanding certain legal or ethical responses. The bond comes as a grateful response to God's free grace. We love, because God first loved us.

To imagine the church and its ministers as a covenant of global gardeners means to envision that in every place where Christians live and gather they would be conscious of the totality of God's creation. By each doing what good they could to preserve and to enhance creation, a new ethos might emerge that would inspire and support politicians and other public leaders to take action to rectify past wrongs and to enhance future environmental possibilities for unborn generations.

Though ecological consciousness has increased significantly in recent years, it is not a foregone conclusion that church members will become global gardeners. Past history is not necessarily reassuring since the church is a "latecomer" to the environmental movement. Critics contend that Christians have encouraged architects of ecological desecration because of our emphasis on having dominion over all creation and our record of offering little resistance to environmental destruction. Since the Reformation, salvation theology has almost eliminated thoughtful attention to creation theology. Thus the famous evangelist John R. Mott was disappointed in 1938 when he visited Mahatma Gandhi in India. Mott asked Gandhi, "What do you want to achieve in this world?" Gandhi replied simply, "To identify myself with all creation."[9] This was not the language or imagery of Protestant North American Christians. Little wonder Mott was not satisfied with the response.

More disturbing is the possibility that contemporary churchgoers may be less environmentally oriented than nonchurch attenders. One survey of human attitudes toward nature and wildlife discovered that persons who frequently attended church services were more dominating or negative toward animals, while those who seldom, if ever, attended religious services expressed a more ecological or naturalistic perspective toward animals.[10] Teaching the stewardship and respect for all of God's creation needs a higher profile in the life of most congregations. Preaching should underscore that "the central vision of world history in the Bible is that all creation is one, every creature in community with every other, living in harmony and security toward the joy and well-being of every other creature."[11]

Mary Evelyn Jagen proposes that Christians need to enter a covenant relationship with others on the ecological journey. Drawing on the New Abolitionist Covenant developed for those committed to the abolition of nuclear weapons, she notes the six areas of practice specified in that covenant: prayer, education, spiritual examination, peace evangelism, public witness, and nuclear disarmament.[12] A similar covenant could be used by global gardeners engaged in ecological evangelism and promoting the integrity of creation.

If the church chooses to have a role in healing, then it must share the earth's wounds. The church cannot pretend to be an objective observer, simply offering remedies or prophetically denouncing others. The way of healing for Jesus the Christ required that he take upon himself the wounds and weaknesses of humanity. "By his wounds you have been healed," says I Peter 2:24-25, even though "you were going astray like sheep." The church as a covenant of global gardeners must repent of its complicity with those who have abused creation. Christians must covenant to seek liberation from enslavement to excessive energy use, wasteful consumption, misuse of animals, and so forth.

Earth-keeping responsibilities must be personalized. If we truly want clean air and water, then we have to change many of our personal habits. Practicing what we preach is never easy and ecological hypocrisy plagues many of us. "Earth Day" celebrations on university campuses evoke great attention and commitment, but frequently at even the most ecologically conscious colleges one discovers that after 350 faculty, students, and a few loyal townspeople leave a football game it takes five or six maintenance people to pick up all the accumulated litter. At a recent peace demonstration, I joined students holding a sign. Later I realized the sign urged something that I fail to do myself, namely it encouraged motorists to car pool, thereby cutting the United States oil dependency. Repentance begins with me, as I discover myself oil-addicted and enslaved to a way of life that abuses the earth. Had the Exxon *Valdez* not spilled its 240,000 barrels of oil in Alaska's Prince William Sound, its cargo would have supplied the United States with only twenty minutes of energy.[13] We depend upon the equivalent of seventy-two tankers a day—no wonder ecological accidents happen inevitably.

An experience in the life of Mahatma Gandhi provides a story that global gardeners should remember. A woman came to his place in Sevegram, India, and asked him to tell her son to stop eating sugar because it harmed him. Gandhi's cryptic reply was: "Please come back next week." Disappointed in his response, she, however, did what he directed. When she returned the next time, the Mahatma told her son, "Please don't eat sugar. It is not good for you." After joking with him for a while, Gandhi hugged him and sent him on his way. Curiously the mother asked, "Bapu, why didn't you say this last week when we came? Why did you make us come back again?" Gandhi smiled, and said to her, "Last week, I too was eating sugar."[14] Global gardeners must live what they teach and practice what they preach.

Gandhi did what most refuse to do. He changed his ways before he sought to be a teacher or preacher.

Facts Alone Will Not Save

Global gardeners know that Christ's "at-one-ment" on earth has not yet been realized. The opening words of a United Nations document released by the World Commission on Environment and Development on *Our Common Future* declares:

The Earth is one but the world is not. We all depend on one biosphere for sustaining our lives. Yet each community, each country, strives for survival and prosperity with little regard for its impact on others. Some consume the Earth's resources at a rate that would leave little for future generations. Others, many more in number, consume far too little and live with the prospect of hunger, squalor, disease, and early death.[15]

Behind that bleak portrait lie some sordid statistics. More hungry people suffer in the world today than ever before in human history. One-fifth of the persons in Two-Thirds World nations are undernourished; one-fifth in major industrial nations are overweight or obese. An hour's worth of the military expenditures of all nations would immunize 3.5 million children who are destined to die from preventable infectious diseases. Only 25 percent of the world's population use some 79 percent of the available drugs and vaccines. By the mid-1980s, twentieth-century wars had killed ninety-nine million people, twelve times as many as in the nineteenth century, and twenty-two times the count in the eighteenth century. The nuclear weapons stockpile (over sixty thousand) is large enough to kill everyone on earth at least twelve times.[16]

In the United States each year 220 million trees are cut down just to print newspapers, most destined for the trash. The entire U.S. commercial airline fleet could be rebuilt four times over with the aluminum cans American citizens discard each year. A typical American discards thirteen hundred pounds of garbage per year, and uses (or wastes) thirty-seven thousand gallons of water. With only 5 percent of the world's population, the U.S. consumes 26 percent of the oil, releases 26 percent of the world's nitrogen oxides, produces 22 percent of the carbon dioxide emissions, and creates 290 million tons of toxic waste.[17] And the litany of statistics could continue almost *ad infinitum* and *ad nauseam*.[18]

Facts alone, however, will not save us or the earth. As Archibald MacLeish once noted, "We are deluged with facts but we have or are losing our human ability to feel them."[19] The endless accumulation of facts yields no panacea; in fact, we may feel even more impotent in the face of the magnitude of the global crisis. Worse yet, it can prompt "compassion fatigue" even among the most unselfish and altruistic. How can we remember to care in a world so busy that most of us cannot recall what we had for breakfast? "Ecology needs religion," claims Fred Krueger. "A linkage of the two can serve as an antidote to rampant consumerism and hedonistic disregard for Planet Earth. Ecology by itself doesn't have the ability to bring about personal change in habits and thinking like religion does."[20]

From the perspective of Native Americans and other indigenous peoples, until one respects creation, neither justice nor peace can be realized. As my Native American faculty colleague at Iliff, George E. Tinker, says, "Every animal, every insect, every tree, every stream has its part to play in preserving the balance and harmony" of creation. Tinker contends that when Native Americans "kill a deer, they recognize that the deer itself has a spiritual consciousness and an awareness of giving itself for them. And so they return thanks also to the deer at that moment in the hunt."[21] Unless and until Christians embrace a new creation spirituality, the potentiality for justice and peace remains limited.

Knowing the facts does not guarantee salvation. "At-one-ment" in the world remains a distant dream. God's atonement in Jesus Christ may be, as some theologians say, "once and for all," but for most of the earth it is still a story to be heard and to be lived by Christian disciples in the world.

God's First Love

When I was ordained, my small home church of fifty members in Kimball, South Dakota, celebrated with a party and asked to print my favorite verse on the cake. Since John 3:16 was too lengthy for the decorators, my rural friends printed: "For God so loved the world. . . ." There, described in frosting, the people had identified a distinctive missional motif of the Christian faith: God's first love is not the church but the globe. All God's inhabited earth—from the jungle rain forests of Brazil to the prairie farmlands of South Dakota—lies within the framework of God's creative and redemptive activity.

On that ordination day I also received a gift of a carved wooden monk. The note attached read: "Always remember that your calling is not to be cloistered, but to serve in the world." The gift givers did not intend to devalue monks and monasteries, for St. Francis of Assisi and Thomas Merton must be among Christianity's greatest ecologians, but to affirm my ordination not merely to ministry within a specific local congregation, but to a mission that views the world as my parish.

Evangelical Christians rightfully criticize some ecumenical Christians for quoting only the beginning of John 3:16 "for God so loved the world" and ignoring the rest of the verse "that He gave his only Son, that whoever believes in him should not perish but have eternal life." Focusing only on God's love for the world can distort the full meaning of the gospel by not emphasizing the Christian conviction that Jesus Christ is the Savior of the world. The church as the covenant of global gardeners is not only ecologically conscious, but evangelically committed to the proclamation of God's saving grace in Jesus Christ.

However, we must realize that until God's first love becomes the church's first love, the possibilities of evangelism are restricted. Illustrative is what happened at the evangelical sponsored Lausanne II Conference in the Philippines in 1989. Outside of Manila stands Smokey Mountain, a giant garbage heap where poor Filipino families live, struggling to survive on what they can salvage from the leftovers of others. A worker from Smokey Mountain spoke at the conference, dramatically declaring that until the church and world overcome the economic disparity of the rich and the poor, "be not surprised that the people of the garbage dumps of the world will think our Gospel is just another piece of trash."

The price God willingly paid in loving the world underscores the imperative role of Christians as global gardeners. The mission of ministry is to be "earth-keepers" rather than being "earth-eaters," to use the imagery of scientist Loren Eiseley.[22]

This earth-keeping must manifest itself in reflective theological practice. G. K. Chesterton outlined the dilemma when he remarked: "One must somehow find a way of loving the world without trusting it; somehow one must love the world without being worldly."[23] The missionary activity of the church must focus not only on all six continents and in every country possible, but also on the earth's well-being.

Tending God's gardens, missionaries have made substantial contributions around the world through agricultural efforts, development projects, and famine relief work. Long before the Peace Corps and government efforts, Christian global gardeners have been teaching agricultural improvements, building latrines, helping people get water for their communities, and so forth. A former lack of ecological awareness among missionaries is not surprising since such sensitivity was rarely evident among those who sponsored them. Today the church should consider it intolerable to "send out" persons who reveal ecological illiteracy and insensitivity. In fact, indigenous peoples can teach missionaries. Ghillean Prance, an expert on the Amazon rain forest, writes:

With the Paraguay Indians, and in similar cases I have seen first-hand in Brazil, the greatest misunderstanding is failure to recognize the paramount importance to the Indian peoples of their land, and of their communal ownership of it. To change the Indians by insisting on the importance of private property, or to turn them into cotton pickers who earn a daily wage against their wills, is a serious infringement of both their basic human rights and of the thousands of years of experience such people have had in working out an ecology appropriate for their forest region.[24]

Christian Responses to the Ecological Crisis

Many Christians resemble the frog in a cruel old science experiment. The frog continued to sit in a pan of water as it slowly heated to the boiling point. However, the same frog immediately leaped out of a pan that already contained boiling water. The ecological crisis is at the boiling point, but many Christians still do not know it is time to jump!

Fortunately others are taking leadership positions. The World Council of Churches through its program on "justice, peace, and the integrity of creation" has enjoined the environmental movement to the life of the global church. Pope John Paul II issued the first ever papal encyclical addressing ecology, "Centesimus Annus" in 1991. Evangelical Christian organizations are showing new sensitivity and concern for the welfare of the planet as well.

The greatest global gardening, however, can be experienced at the local level. In the United States, four in ten Americans worship every weekend in one of the nation's 350,000 congregations. The opportunities for motivating and mobilizing ecologically minded individuals and local churches is as infinite as one's imagination and will. What is needed are leaders who understand that the missional nature of their ministry includes a commitment to caring and preserving the world as God's own body.

Possibilities include preaching on interrelationships of ecology and theology, drawing on the rich resources of the Bible. Initiating study classes that focus on global and local environmental issues can touch people's life-styles directly. Instituting energy-saving measures and monitoring a church building's heating and plumbing are practical expressions of a congregation's commitment. By investigating alternatives to plastic foam cups and plates, nonrecyclable stationery, nonorganic fertilizers and pesticides, significant learning experiences can be attained for all involved. By engaging the whole church, including the children and youth, an educational process can have consequences throughout the society.

In Montville, New Jersey, the Reformed Church and The United Methodist Church entered into a friendly competition to recycle cans and raised $5,000 for a soup kitchen, a food pantry, and a program to feed infants. St. John's Episcopal Cathedral in Jacksonville, Florida, spent six weeks studying environmental issues. As a result, church members decided to join Sierra Club members in opposing the construction of a city incinerator they believed would add to the air pollution. In Niagara Falls, New York, an ecumenical task force of Protestant, Catholic, and Jewish congregations first dealt with the Love Canal toxic waste crisis and then began to focus on five other toxic waste sites in the region. These examples illustrate how congregations in mission across the nation are launching recycling projects, protecting migrant workers, monitoring nuclear reactors, questioning toxic waste dumps, fighting soil and coastal erosion, and encouraging investments in environmentally responsible industries.[25]

Additionally, individual Christians are creatively, and often sacrificially, responding to the ecological crisis by becoming global gardeners in their own homes and communities. Many live out their discipleship as involved citizens in the politics of their region. Others illustrate the mission of the laity by becoming involved in voluntary associations concerned about the environment ranging from the National Audubon

Society and the Environmental Defense Fund to the Union of Concerned Scientists and Greenpeace.

Christians need to know that when they become ecologically conscious and involved, they are joining God's mission of ministry to the world. They are the "Chico" Mendeses of their community.

Work Our Souls Must Have

African American novelist Alice Walker penned a fitting description of what is envisioned by the metaphor of global gardening. She describes her mother in a book called *In Search of Our Mothers' Gardens*. Though living in poverty and struggling against life's hardest odds, her mother always adorned every home in which she lived with flowers. Her ambitious gardens bloomed profusely with over fifty different plants, so that Walker says even her "memories of poverty are seen through a screen of blooms."[26] She literally covered the holes in the walls with sunflowers. In doing so, she left a legacy to her daughter: "I notice that it is only when my mother is working in her flowers that she is radiant, ... She is involved in work her soul must have. Ordering the universe in the image of her personal conception of Beauty."[27]

Global gardening is truly work our souls must have. The garden provides a metaphor to open our spirits and hearts to the needs of our common garden, Earth. It offers a vivid reminder that "the earth is the Lord's, and the fulness thereof" (Psalm 24:1a, KJV).

CHAPTER FIVE

A Collegiality of Bridge Builders

The people of God cannot be changed until the outcasts are restored to its body.
UMBERTO ECO, *The Name of the Rose*

Disaster struck suddenly as a European ferry boat recently capsized in a raging storm and passengers were plummeted into the ferocious waters. Andrew Parker, his family and others were separated from the safety of a small island of metal by a six-foot-wide cascade of water. The chasm proved too wide for people to jump over, so Parker stretched his six-foot, three-inch frame into a human bridge. As one passenger later recalled: "I was the first to climb across and I was petrified when I stepped on his back." Thanks to Parker's bodily bridge, twenty people escaped safely.[1]

This contemporary embodied parable highlights the historic bridge-building dimension of the mission of ministry. The word for priest in Latin is *pontifex*, literally meaning "bridge builder." At its best the church has been a collegiality of both lay and clergy seeking to build bridges between peoples and between God and humanity. Missionaries have symbolized this bridge-building ministry between peoples and nations.

Quite often, someone loses their life when bridges are being constructed. Reflecting on the dangers of bridge building, Halford Luccock once noted how this image pictures "the truth that throwing bridges across the tragic chasms which separate group from group, race from race, and nation from nation, is a costly undertaking into which life must be put . . . for without the shedding of blood there is no great and lasting accomplishment" for humanity.[2]

In today's world the urgency of this missional ministry is dramatized especially by the global crisis prompted by the worldwide plague associated with Acquired Immune Deficiency Syndrome (AIDS). Embodied Christian bridge builders are called to stretch beyond past prejudices and paralyzing fears, creating bridges that will overcome stereotypes and stigmas, bringing Christ's love to all.

> Michael Bennett
> Dick Hanson
> Jerry Smith
> Chris Barnaskij
> Alfred Gonzales, Jr.
> Laura Shaeffer

Director of *A Chorus Line*, a farm activist, a professional football player, a nine-year-old child, a graphic artist, and a physical therapist, respectively.[3]

While attending college, I served as youth minister in a large church. On the staff at the time was the pastor emeritus, a distinguished church leader of his generation. Once he told me that when he received the clergy journal of his denomination, he always turned first to the obituary column. He wanted to see what was happening to his friends. You can imagine my dismay. But now wherever in the world I travel, I turn and read the obituary pages.

> Richard Bray
> Donald Howard
> Sunnye Sherman
> Ricardo Palomares
> Fritz Holt
> Terry Dolan

A cowboy, a Stanford scholar, a legal secretary, an Episcopal priest, the producer of *La Cage aux Folles*, and a New Right political activist, respectively.

Albert Schweitzer, noted for his reverence of life, once wrote Norman Cousins about his hospital in an isolated spot in Africa. Schweitzer said, "As you know there are only two automobiles within 75 miles of the hospital. Today the inevitable happened. The cars collided. We have treated the drivers for their superficial injuries. Anyone with a reverence for machines may treat the cars."[4]

> John Gaffney
> Susan Greenleaf
> Stewart McKinney
> Margaret Nadawula
> "N"
> Finis Crutchfield

A thirteen-month-old baby, an opera singer, a Republican congressman, an African orphan, an anonymous Soviet citizen, and a United Methodist bishop, respectively.

And the roll call could continue almost indefinitely. More than 126,000 people can be identified by name as having died from Acquired Immune Deficiency Syndrome (AIDS) in the United States. Every fourteen and a half minutes someone reports a new AIDS case. Approximately one AIDS death occurs every twelve minutes. One out of every sixty infants born in New York City, most of them incredibly poor, is infected with AIDS.

The World Health Organization estimates that by the year 2000 some thirty million adults and ten million children will be infected. North American federal health officials estimate that one million Americans are already infected with HIV, the virus that causes AIDS. In North America one out of seventy-five adult males is estimated to be infected and one out of every seven hundred women. By 1993 officials project at least 450,000 United States citizens will have been diagnosed with AIDS.

Many of these individuals will be treated by their families, friends, churches, and communities as nonpersons, i.e., persons who do not exist or never should have existed, phantoms to be dreaded and abhorred. No one can predict how many more thousands, perhaps millions, will die from AIDS. Already one out of every ten American families knows someone personally who has died. Probably each of us has a friend or loved one for whom we fear. Basketball star "Magic" Johnson's HIV diagnosis has heightened public awareness.

Within the United States, gay or bisexual men and intravenous drug abusers of both sexes account for more than 86 percent of the first one hundred thousand deaths from AIDS. In Africa, the pattern differs, with heterosexual transmission the most common. Since the church has long treated gay and lesbian persons as nonpersons (despite statistical findings that suggest that possibly up to one in ten persons may be homosexual), the stigmatizing of persons with AIDS has been compounded.

Shamefully slow and reluctant, the Christian community is beginning to respond to the AIDS crisis with compassion and care. Most parishioners hesitate to tell their pastor and fellow church members that they, or their loved ones, suffer from AIDS, because they fear rejection and expect hostility. In every congregation and community there are persons yearning for the church to be involved in Christ's healing mission. Michael J. Christensen describes in *The Samaritan's Imperative* how his Church of the Nazarene congregation overcame apathy and antipathy to create a mission outreach called "Bridge: Living With Aids." This evangelical perspective offers a nonjudgmental bridge-building approach, based on biblical perspectives and personal experience, that seeks to overcome the nonperson status and treatment too often manifested by the church to persons with AIDS.[5]

This new class of nonpersons joins many others globally who have been marginalized and dehumanized. During the Irangate hearings, Lt. Col. Oliver North sought to justify selling arms to Iran in order to fund the war in Nicaragua, by passionately describing the death of eleven-year-old Natasha Simpson at the hands of terrorists in Rome. In the midst of the Ollie North mania, columnist Ellen Goodman pointed out that "more than a few 11-year-olds, 'not perhaps a whole lot different than Natasha Simpson' . . . , surely have been killed by our weapons in the Middle East. More than a thousand civilians, 'living, breathing young men and women'—including 210 under 12—have been killed by the war we created in Nicaragua. North helped make these things happen. So did his lies to Congress." These civilians, including the children of the Middle East and Central America, are nonpersons in the minds of the utilitarian policy makers in the White House and beyond.[6]

Children, among the least able to protect themselves, have been systematically treated as nonpersons. In Romania during the oppressive regime of Nicolae Ceausescu children born with deformities, neurological problems, developmental disabilities, or crippling diseases were labeled "irrecuperable." The regime discarded more than one hundred thousand children as worthless nonpersons and placed them in institutions where they were barely fed, given no names, and never touched by another human being, except once a day when their diapers were changed. In Guatemala City five to ten thousand poverty-stricken street children are subjected to violent abuse. Eight children were recently kidnapped, tortured and killed: their ears sliced off, their eyes burned away, and their tongues carved out. "Hopefully they were killed first," commented the regional director of Covenant House, "but that's not the way it's usually done here." A tombstone erected for a thirteen-year-old street urchin, Nahaman Carmona Lopez, simply reads: "I only wanted to be a child and they wouldn't let me."[7]

Around the globe, the powerful crush the weak, torture the imprisoned, and impoverish the masses. Persons of color worldwide know the ugly pain of being treated as nonpersons. In culture after culture, women have been negatively defined by their subservient relationship to men. They are virtually nonpersons in terms of their societal and legal status. In Woody W. Guthrie's folk song "Deportee (Plane Wreck at Los Gatos)," he laments the death of Mexican migrants being deported from the United States after working the harvest. In this poignant ballad, he notes that the newspaper accounts named the pilots and attendants, but the twenty-eight Mexicans remained nameless nonpersons, simply listed as deportees. In every community there are persons who have been marginalized and oppressed to the point of being viewed as nonpersons.

Nien Cheng published an incredible account of her six and one-half years in prison during the Cultural Revolution of China. Her book, *Life and Death in Shanghai,* witnesses to her stubborn struggle to retain her personhood and dignity, even in the most degrading circumstances of prison and of public humiliation. To avoid becoming a nonperson, she would speak when ordered to be silent, argue rather than succumb to intimidation, and endure physical torture rather than yield to psychological depression. Hers is a triumphant story of the human spirit, strengthened by a confident faith in a gracious deity who knows nothing about nonpersons in the family of God.[8]

God's Eye Is on the Sparrow

The conviction that all human life is sacred remains fundamental to Christian theology. The Hebrew psalmist said "even the sparrow finds a home, and the swallow a nest for herself, where she may lay her young, at thy altars, O Lord of hosts, my king and my God" (Psalm 84:3, RSV). The individual worth and value of every human being is basic to the gospel story. Jesus asked "Are not two sparrows sold for a penny? And not one of them will fall to the ground without your Father's will. But even the hairs of your head are all numbered. Fear not, therefore; you are of more value than many sparrows" (Matthew 10:29-31, RSV).

Artists have often been inspired by the imagery of this passage. The great African American spiritual, "His Eye Is on the Sparrow," has brought hope to millions. An ecological God cares about creation; none lie beyond the pale of God's grace.

> I sing because I'm happy,
> I sing because I'm free,
> For His eye is on the sparrow,
> And I know He watches me.

In the words of Thornton Wilder in *The Bridge of San Luis Rey:*

Either we live by accident and die by accident, or we live by plan and die by plan. Some say that . . . to the gods we are like the flies that boys kill on a summer day. And some say, on the contrary, that the very sparrows do not lose a feather that has not been brushed away by the finger of God.[9]

Some critics of my book on *Christian Ethics and Political Action* questioned my assertion about the sacredness of human life.[10] "Sacred" might seem an inappropriate term to ascribe to human beings, mixing the infinite and the finite. Certainly political leaders in many cultures prefer not to think in such terms. The violations of human sacredness are too many to number, as governments all over the globe deny people basic rights. The concept of human sacredness stands as a stumbling block to those who would reduce individual worth as a means to an end. Those who believe morality consists in "the greatest good for the greatest number" willingly sacrifice certain human beings to the diseases of coal mines, accept a certain percentage of unemployment, permit medical experimentation on persons without informed consent, destroy the homes or livelihoods of large groups of persons for national development, and so forth. Yet a stubborn Christian insistence that every life is sacred and inviolable exists. God creates all persons and cares for each and every one.

This Christian persistence appears to be wavering in the United States today. The tragic human plight of the homeless across the land challenges this Christian conviction. Jonathan Kozol describes in his book, *Rachel and Her Children,* the poignancy of homeless families and their children. Rachel lived with her children for five years in a one-room basement apartment with no bathroom. Now, she leaves her children to fend for themselves in the streets of New York while she goes either to work or to beg for money. Hear her speak:

"All that I want is somethin' that's my own. I got four kids. I need four plates, four glasses, and four spoons. Is that a lot? I know I'm poor. Don't have no bank account, no money, or no job. Don't have no nothin'. No foundation. Then and yet my children have a shot in life. They're innocent. They're pure. They have a chance." The Bible by her side is opened to the Twenty-third Psalm.

"I do believe. God forgive me I believe He's there. But when He sees us like this, I am wonderin' where is He? I am askin' Where the hell He gone?"[11]

Mission opportunities appear at every doorstep. The missional call to ministry echoes unmistakably. Are our churches tombstones of the past? Or are they sanctuaries where sparrows can find rest and the homeless can find nests where they may lay their young? Families number 40 percent of the homeless and government shelters cannot meet the increasing needs for shelter and care. In Denver, the Roman Catholic archdiocese built a major complex to meet the needs of the homeless. In Portland, Oregon, congregations have identified unused rooms in their buildings and have created transitional housing units. Pastor Frank Shields of Sunnyside Centenary United Methodist Church has initiated a shelter program on a budget of only $2,000 to $3,000 per year. It offers refuge to families while parents work to earn sufficient funds for deposits on housing and utilities. The church provides an address for children so they can enroll in school. Over 350 Portland families (one thousand-plus people) have received help through a network of churches—truly experiencing a collegiality of bridge builders—in mission to the homeless in their own neighborhoods.

The Hermeneutical Privilege of Nonpersons

Nonpersons are the starting point for a Christian theology of mission. The experience and voice of nonpersons—those who have been marginalized, impoverished, and oppressed—must be accorded a certain "hermeneutical privilege."[12] The missiological accent today, says Christopher Duraisingh, should be on "bringing the peripheral people within the city gate. God brings the marginalized to centre stage, through the work of Jesus Christ, who died outside the gates."[13]

In the battle against the nuclear, ecological, and genetic threats to all life, we must express special concern for and take action with those who are persistently placed on the periphery of power, lest the "solutions" selected further disadvantage the nonpersons of the globe. Jon Sobrino of El Salvador argues that

we must adopt the viewpoint of those who lack life, power, dignity, and not pretend there can be another and better viewpoint than theirs . . . . The poor, sinners, and the despised are the necessary, though not absolutely sufficient, starting point for an understanding of what is meant by the good news of the kingdom.[14]

This does not mean that only the poor or the nonperson has a claim on God's truth. However, by first hearing these voices, which historically have been so slighted in mission theology, the possibility persists that we can escape our own cultural cocoons and discern God's liberating and loving initiatives in ways that previously eluded us. Gustavo Gutierrez reminds us: "Christ is not only come, he is the one who is to come. He is the future of our history. . . . Jesus Christ is precisely God become poor."[15]

Historically church dogmatics overlooked nonpersons. Frederick Herzog emphasizes that:

Nicea and Chalcedon did not let Jesus the refugee, the homeless one, the "nonperson," through their lofty christological grid. In the dogmatic tradition, Jesus hardly appears as a particular human being, but rather as an impersonal being (as in the old doctrinal notion of enhypostasia). Nicea and Chalcedon dealt with the divinity of Jesus, but not with the "humanity of God" in the streets—God in solidarity with the poor, wretched human being.[16]

Christians need to hear anew Herzog's assertion that "we are not allowed to reject even the most ragged shred of the human, for we do not so much hear the Word of God through 'nonpersons' as we meet the 'very God' in the 'nonperson' who struggles for justice."[17] This style of spirituality, which affirms the sacredness of all persons, should shape our mission of ministry. "No longer can conservative, confessional and liberation groups treat each other as 'nonpersons.' We need to listen to and learn from each other and we need to hear the pain of the Third World,"[18] as well as that of the nonpersons living and dying in our own communities.

Refugees around the globe epitomize nonpersons; even their numbers remain unknown with estimates ranging from ten to eighteen million. Oppressed, hungry, unrepresented, and unwelcomed anywhere, they constitute a Fourth World. Often they are imprisoned for indefinite periods of time, and threatened with return to the lands where they were persecuted and/or impoverished.

Tragically, in November, 1989, six Jesuit priests were tortured and murdered in El Salvador. Front page headlines screamed: "Salvador Wants Bishops Out: Clerics Who Side with Poor Must Go, Pope Told." Blaming the victims for the atrocity, the Attorney General wrote Pope John Paul II asserting that the Catholic bishops had "persisted in keeping alive the questionable ideology of the 'church of the poor' " and therefore deserve responsibility for "much of the violence that has devastated El Salvador for many years."[19] The priests captured the headlines because they represent the vast population of nonpersons crushed in a civil war that has claimed more than sixty thousand lives, displaced one million people, and destroyed an impoverished economy. Ironically, a library book was knocked to the floor while the priests were being killed. Its title? *The Crucified God* by Jürgen Moltmann. Need anything more be said?

Evangelization of Nonpersons

Most mainline denominations and local congregations feel isolated from people who have been marginalized by society. Churches sidelined from the center of action and marginalized by the culture, William McKinney suggests, need to realize the mission potential in their own communities. This means accepting the reality of their "own new off-centeredness" in order to have "a chance of partnership with peoples whose current experience is also not of the center but of the margins."[20]

When it comes to evangelization, it is quite apparent that the gospel has not been offered to nonpersons as often and as eagerly as to those in visible places of power and prestige. For instance, the church often overlooks or ignores persons with handicapping or retarded conditions and those imprisoned, impoverished, or otherwise marginalized.

The world has 1.6 billion persons with handicapping conditions, 80 percent of whom live in the Third World. One-third of these are children. If all the deaf and blind of the world lived in the same country, it would be the seventh most populated nation of the world. Yet in most communities we can search in vain for a mission or ministry to persons with handicapping conditions. Marilyn J. Stoddard has taught a Sunday school class for retarded persons in Denver for more than thirty years, in part because no one else will accept the assignment. Families of such persons often feel alienated from the church. Recently when Stoddard surveyed the city's churches, she discovered that it made no difference whether the church professed a liberal or conservative theology. Almost none reached out to persons with handicapping conditions with anything more than a curb ramp!

In Colorado, special summer church camps operate for persons with handicapping conditions. In the winter, imaginative programs enable persons who are blind or who have had limbs amputated or who suffer other serious disabilities to ski the Rocky Mountains. Those who experience the mission of ministry to persons with handicapping conditions report powerful spiritual experiences. Stanley Hauerwas, for example, reminds us that:

Quite simply, the challenge of learning to know, to be with and care for the retarded is nothing less than learning to know, be with, and love God. God's face is the face of the retarded; God's body is the body of the retarded. For the God we Christians must learn to worship is not a god of self-sufficient power, a god who in self-possession needs no one; rather ours is a God who needs a people, who needs a son.[21]

Ministries to prisoners and their families also have a low priority. Worldwide, Amnesty International has spotlighted the brutal torture and the inhuman conditions of the imprisoned. Prison populations are escalating in the United States. More than one million persons were imprisoned by the beginning of the 1990s, and unless rates abate, two million will be incarcerated by the year 2000. The insatiable public demand for more imprisonment and the low priority on rehabilitation provides opportunities for mission in nearly every community. Some years ago when I chaired the Governor's Commission on Corrections, I learned the bitter truth that no political constituency cares about prisoners. Others have their advocates and lobbyists, but the youth and adults languishing behind bars remain powerless nonpersons.

More than ten thousand people "disappeared" in Argentina—lost in the prisons and torture chambers of the military generals. Entire families were wiped out, covered with cement, and tossed into the river. Working closely with the Mothers of the Plaza de Mayo, Rabbi Marshall Meyer regularly visited the netherworld of Argentine prisons. On Friday, when the Jewish sabbath began, he often received threats on his own life, but he persisted in visiting those whom authorities had deemed as nonpersons. Frequently, after belabored efforts with a mother, trying to identify ways the Rabbi might find her child or relative, she would say, "Rabbi, I think I should tell you I am not Jewish." To which he always replied, "Madam, I didn't ask if you were Jewish." Nor did he ever ask the prisoners, because he believes suffering is the common religion of humanity. Remembering this prison mission to nonpersons, Jacobo Timerman dedicated his award-winning book, *Prisoner Without a Name, Cell Without a Number*, to Rabbi Meyer.[22]

The prison mission of John and Charles Wesley distinguished their movement. Their championship of prisoners was not always considered strategically wise. Oxford was astounded with the scandal of John Wesley's lack of discretion after he emphatically denounced the injustice of imprisoning a young man by the name of Blair for homosexual practices.[23] Perhaps Wesley's thinking paralleled that of Jesse Jackson's when the latter explained his support of gay and lesbian people: "You must really love people the most when they need it the most. People don't need much love when they've got a tail wind blowing. They need love when they are facing head winds and cross winds."[24] Wesley's prison mission prompted him to proclaim in his famous sermon "Salvation By Faith":

Here is comfort, high as heaven, stronger than death! What! Mercy for all? For Zacchaeus, a public robber? For Mary Magdalene, a common harlot? Methinks I hear one say, "Then I, even I, may hope for mercy!" And so thou mayest, thou afflicted one, whom none hath comforted! . . . Whatsoever your sins be, "though red like crimson," though more than the hairs of your head, "return ye unto the Lord, and He will have mercy upon you; and to our God, for He will abundantly pardon."[25]

The homeless, drug addicts, and the mentally ill are not welcome in most congregations. Lacking affluence, these nonpersons seldom add significantly to church income. Around the globe, many persons live isolated or sealed off from conventional Christian view. Evangelicals speak of these "hidden peoples" and urge further research so they can be identified and reached.[26] Actually, many are far from "hidden"—we just do not want to become entangled in the complexity of mission and ministry to them.

Noreen Towers in Sydney, Australia, does not shrink from God's call to serve the nonpersons in her community. Assigned to pastor a large, nearly empty, fading metropolitan church, she boldly crossed the street to the park and invited the homeless to join her congregation. She recounts the beginning of that mission:

I happened to see across the street two men sitting in the gutter. They were dirty; they were unshaven; they had bottles in their pockets, and they were trying to warm themselves in the sun. I said to one of my friends, "I don't suppose they would like to come to church here. After all, nobody else wants to." The idea seemed crazy to me, but I went across the street and invited them to church. They looked at me, and they said, "Well, lady, as a matter of fact, we were on our way there." And I said, "That's great." A few minutes later they got up out of the gutter and they came to church.[27]

And that began a great mission and ministry, resulting in an enlarged congregation, soup kitchens, homeless shelters, and alcohol treatment facilities. By building bridges, she not only proclaimed Jesus Christ to them as the "bread of life" (John 6:35) but gave them the manna necessary for living. Her apostolic ministry has been a missional ministry after God's own heart.

South Korea has demonstrated spectacular church growth in recent years. Megachurches of fifty thousand to even five hundred thousand members exist. Evangelism is a high priority. Korean Methodists, for example, have sent fifty-one missionary couples to twenty-one different countries around the world. Korean churches are growing rapidly in the United States. However, generally overlooked in South Korea are the minjung people, the oppressed masses who suffer from injustice and poverty. Minjung theology seeks social transformation and criticizes the other-worldliness and individualistic piety of conservative evangelicals who neglect social justice and social service. Korean women theologians, themselves often oppressed, especially are seeking to bridge the gaps between the Korean rich and poor, the established and the disenfranchised. Since they themselves experienced the pain of dehumanization, they are crying out for justice and human dignity for the minjung.[28]

The genius of the early church in the "wild West" of Montana, Colorado, Wyoming, North and South Dakota was a willingness to reach out to all persons, excluding no one from the family of God. Ministers preached in the streets and in the saloons. They reached out to Native Americans and white settlers, to gamblers and prostitutes, to miners and cowboys, to the newly rich and the impoverished. When everyone else refused to give Calamity Jane a decent burial, the Methodists of Deadwood did not hesitate. Sermons on the prairies and in the mountains were not literary documents, but addresses punctuated by human need and discourses with the practical appeal of the heart-cry of humanity. In his 1927 journal entitled *The Last of the Old West*, George Mecklenburg wrote that "humanity is open, bare and raw in a pioneer country. The need for religion is immediate and terrific. Sin is open and blatant. Salvation becomes a real need and religion a reality, rather than a mere philosophy."[29] As one man, shot in a fight, said to the preacher bending over him, "If your God can do anything fer a feller like me, tell him to do it quick."

There were no nonpersons in Christ's Kingdom of the "Old West." The ground at the foot of the cross was level. All stood—and knelt—as sinners in need of God's grace. They welcomed broken humanity into the family of God. When they sang hymns in a dirty saloon or around a lonesome campfire, they meant it when they cried:

> Amazing grace! how sweet the sound
> That saved a wretch like me!
> I once was lost, but now am found,
> Was blind, but now I see.
> Through many dangers, toils, and snares,
> I have already come;
> 'Tis grace hath brought me safe thus far,
> And grace will lead me home.

A mission theology of evangelism that begins with the shunned neighbors instead of ourselves or our favorite neighbors stands in sharp contrast to previous theologies that focused primarily on individual salvation. Jesus serves as the model for this spirituality and movement of mission. As Emilio Castro has articulated: "The dynamic of mission in Christ's way must always start from the marginalized sectors of society and move upwards towards the domes of power. It is from the starting point of the poor that the fabric of God's kingdom will be woven."[30] An evangelism open and seeking nonpersons—the homeless, the prisoners, the poor, the disabled, and the oppressed is a gospel closer to the Christ of compassion. As one Cuban Christian testified:

I am a Christian because I came to know the Christ of the gospel, not the one of magnificent cathedrals, or the one of great theological constructions, but rather the simple and unassuming Christ who was followed by fishermen, called upon by lepers, and loved by repentant prostitutes and rehabilitated politicians.[31]

The Church as Collegiality

Traditionally, churches have been organized according to hierarchical, patriarchal, racist, and heterosexist principles. Power and authority have flowed from the top down to the masses. Popes and bishops, or their equivalents, have been at the pinnacle of power. The clergy has been ranked next, with the laity at the bottom. Men at all levels have dominated women. White persons have acted superior to persons of color. Heterosexuals have been valued over homosexual persons. If one drew a power and authority chart, it would appear that almost every level has sought to make nonpersons out of some other classification of people.

Vatican I anticipated the argument for the hierarchical conception of authority, rejecting democratic or representative forms, but has parallels in the Protestant tradition:

But the Church of Christ is not a community of equals in which all the faithful have the same rights. It is a society of unequals, not only because among the faithful some are clerics and some are laymen, but particularly because there is in the Church the power from God whereby to some it is given to sanctify, teach, and govern and to others not.[32]

This institutional model of the church treasures the grace God has given and reserves it for its own members. Not indifferent to those outside its membership, it historically advocated a strong missional effort. But, as Avery Dulles, notes:

it seeks to save their souls precisely by bringing them into the institution. For the proverbial old-style missionary—who is not a totally mythical figure—success is statistically measurable: How many baptisms have been performed, how many persons have entered the Church, how many continue to come regularly to church and receive the sacraments?[33]

The idea of collegiality—that all are equal in authority, power, and value in God's eyes—has rarely been fully institutionalized or realized within the church. Collegiality sometimes refers to the association in which the Pope and bishops of the Roman Catholic Church share collectively the ruling power over the church. Churches endorsing a theory of church government called collegialism maintain that the highest ecclesiastical authority is vested in the whole community, and not in a clerical order or ruling class. United Methodists function with a College of Bishops, but insist that only the General Conference (composed of equal lay and clergy) can speak for the denomination.

Emil Brunner in *The Misunderstanding of the Church* claimed that from a biblical perspective the church was not an institution but a brotherhood and sisterhood, "a pure communion of persons *(personengemeinschaft)*." Yves Congar in his *Lay People in the Church* argues that the church in its ultimate reality represents a fellowship of persons.[34] Explicit in the understanding of the mission and ministry of the laity is the image of the church as collegiality. Laity represent not mere appendages of the apostolate of the clergy hierarchy. The vision of the church as "the people of God" and "the body of Christ" both embody metaphors of collegiality, suggesting a relationship of associates. First Peter 2:9-10 declares: "You are . . . God's own people, in order that you may proclaim the mighty acts of him who called you out of darkness into his marvelous light." Romans 12:5 says that "so we, who are many, are one body in Christ, and individually we are members one of another." In contrast to Vatican I's institutionalism, Vatican II documents reflect this vision of the church and Irenaeus: "Where the Spirit of God is, there is the church and every grace."[35]

The dilemma with the collegiality model of the church is that the stress on interpersonal relationships and *koinonia* sometimes results in an ecclesiology that fails to provide a clear sense of mission for ministry. If, as Avery Dulles notes, "we cannot take it for granted that evangelization, baptism, or church membership coincides with the bestowal of the Holy Spirit, the motivation for Christian mission is left obscure."[36] If, however, Christians understand their mission as an extension of the spirit of collegiality of bridge building to and for others, including the so-called nonperson, we can imagine and implement powerful possibilities for missional ministry. Combined with the powerful biblical metaphor and mandate of hosting strangers, collegiality takes on new meaning.

Hospitality to Strangers

Hospitality is a distinctive and essential mark of the people of God. "Welcome one another, therefore, just as Christ has welcomed you, for the glory of God" (Romans 15:7). Christian community envisioned as the collegiality of hosting strangers is stated most dramatically in Matthew 25:31-46 when at the Last Judgment Jesus speaks of the poor, hungry, naked, diseased, and imprisoned as God incognito in nonpersons: "And when did we see thee hungry and feed thee, or thirsty and give thee drink . . . a stranger and welcome thee, or naked and clothe thee . . . sick or in prison and visit thee? . . . as you did it to one of the least of these . . . you did it to me" (RSV).

Hospitality to strangers is a pivotal mission metaphor for Christians. In Exodus 23:9 we hear: "You shall not oppress a stranger; you know the heart of a stranger, for you were strangers in the land of Egypt" (RSV). In Hebrews comes this advice: "Do not neglect to show hospitality to strangers, for thereby some have entertained angels unawares" (Hebrews 13:2, RSV). The Bible emphasizes not only compassion for the person in need but also the idea of the stranger as a bearer of truth. God often appears in the face and the voice of the stranger. The stranger the dejected apostles met turned out to be the risen Christ. "In every encounter with every stranger," says Parker J. Palmer, "we are given the chance to meet the living Christ."[37] Jack Nelson-Pallmeyer suggests that the purpose of missional ministry is ". . . not to bring Jesus to the poor but rather to discover Jesus among the poor and oppressed, and enter into concrete struggles for liberation with them."[38]

The ultimate test is not the orthodoxy of our words—do we have the doctrinally correct theology?—but the orthopraxy of our actions—do our deeds reflect the spirit of Christ? The test of our faithfulness to God depends not on where we stand on the conservative to liberal spectrum, but in how we treat the "nonpersons" we encounter—the orphans, the widows, the hungry, the thirsty, the oppressed, the poor. The church is unlikely to save the poor, but perhaps our encounter with "nonpersons" will save us. God is unexpectedly present in the ordinary experiences of life.

Hospitality to the stranger, writes Thomas W. Ogletree, is a metaphor for the moral life. On the one hand, caring for another can mean providing sustenance and shelter, protecting against vulnerabilities, and promoting the well-being of a neighbor. On the other hand, it offers a rich opportunity for meeting someone new, being challenged by differing perspectives, and possibly being transformed. Just as the stranger may need us, so we may need the stranger, for often they bear spiritual gifts. The experience of John Koenig when he was serving as a hospital chaplain intern in Atlanta illustrates the gift of hospitality. One night he came into the duty chaplain's office and discovered an older African American man stretched out between two chairs. The gentleman explained he was waiting to perform a wedding in the chapel next door, and neither the bride nor the groom had yet arrived.

Maybe, I thought. But how could I know if he was telling the truth? Lots of strange folks wandered about here, especially on the week-ends. Just two weeks before, in this same office, I had found myself trying to humor an armed man spaced out on drugs. But this person was clearly different, more at ease with himself and with me. We talked, easily from the start, about summer weather and the imponderables of wedding ceremonies. Gradually I dropped my guard. "By the way," I said, "I'm John Koenig. I don't think I caught your name." "Nice to meet you, John," he responded. "I'm Martin King." There was silence for a moment while part of me turned inside out. I had thought this man was invading my territory. Now I felt more like a guest than a host.[39]

Meeting the father of the famous civil rights leader truly was like entertaining "angels unawares."

Hospitality to the stranger cannot be viewed as a superior/inferior relationship but as a meeting of equals. In the history of mission, "sending" churches too often acted as if they had nothing to learn from "receiving" churches. Christian colonialism of the spirit dominated. Now as all churches are envisioned as being both "sending" and "receiving," a reciprocity of hospitality may prevail. Nearly 90 percent of all the world's missionaries for the past two hundred years have come from Europe and North America (80 percent from the English speaking world). Today Two-Thirds World churches are sending over twenty thousand missionaries to other peoples, including the United States and Europe.

By the year 2025, some estimate that 50 percent of the global missionary community will be sent by churches of the southern hemisphere.[40] Mission agencies must move from paternalism to partnership, sharing and surrendering decision-making power, listening to the truth as it emerges from other peoples and cultures. Local congregations and pastors likewise need to reject paternalism and to embrace partnership in order to experience a new collegiality in the Holy Spirit.

As persons with differing historic faiths meet, Christians will discover ways God has witnessed in other cultures and times. Hospitality is neither a passive form of interaction, nor simply a matter of being nice or gracious but an active way of engaging other persons. Hospitality builds bridges between strangers. Certainly with the earth an endangered species, the imperative of finding ways to span the gaps between peoples is urgent. Historically Christian-Muslim relations have been conflictual. Throughout the globe the possibility for a revival of this conflict seems immanent, unless bold religious leaders attempt to break out of past patterns, rein in fanaticism of all faiths, reduce the estrangement of minorities, and enhance tolerance in every place. In an era of nuclear proliferation and of world problems crying for global solutions, Christians and Muslims need to search for ways together to affirm commitments to justice, peace, and other human values. By developing a theology of Christian hospitality, Christians can contribute significantly to a global reduction of tensions and to the resolution of difficulties.

Amid social oppression, hospitality is an insufficient moral response, particularly if the host benefits from unjust political and economic structures that capitalize on nonpersons. It does not suffice to fund soup kitchens or shelters for the homeless or to support medical missions, if the very societal structures are designed to perpetuate inequality and injustice. Christians in mission must repent of such moral bankruptcy and seek to participate in God's initiatives for "a new heaven and a new earth" (Revelation 21:1).

The daring Christians and congregations that have provided illegal sanctuary to sojourners and strangers who have fled the bloodshed and terror of Central America exemplify such participation via hospitality. Just as persons took enormous risks during the days of the Underground Railroad in order to liberate African Americans from slavery and death, so many Christians engage in a collegiality of building bridges to strangers by defying government policies in order to aid persons from El Salvador, Honduras, and other war-ravaged countries. Ethicist Dana W. Wilbanks of The Iliff School of Theology contends that:

As we respond to the urgent needs of Central American refugees in our midst, sanctuary is an expression of compassion, a symbol of resistance against injustice and a sign of hope that the American community will see the refugees' plight and extend national hospitality and protection. In these ways, sanctuary is a faithful response to the liberating God who calls us into solidarity with the oppressed.[41]

Thomas Ogletree does not urge everyone to drop out of the social contexts in which they live in order to become victims of social oppression themselves. Rather he encourages us to live within those contexts with sufficiently transformed attitudes and commitments that we may live in the new age. In solidarity with others, may we discover what it means to be a stranger, living by God's grace. Ogletree envisions a pilgrim people, drawn diversely from every race, nation, and class. With none enjoying special privilege, pilgrim people celebrate diversity, mutually respect one another and labor together with patience. Ogletree claims that "since all are strangers, no one is a stranger any more. Through their shared commitments, they are becoming sisters and brothers, the new family of God by faith."[42] The idea of a religious journey or quest may very well be universal. The vision of pilgrim people seeking a new future radiates a special symbolism.

If Christians take seriously the idea of hospitality, then perhaps we should reappropriate the act of washing feet. Louis J. Luzbetak claims most Christians find washing another's feet "as much out of place as brushing someone else's teeth."[43] Most denominations have dropped the practice or ritualized it in this pantyhose generation. Yet what greater gentleness or humbler hospitality could one offer? A Buddhist monk in Sri Lanka was creating a wall sculpture of Jesus washing the disciples' feet. One day the monk remarked, "If you Christians had looked like this (and he pointed to the kneeling Jesus) we Buddhists would not have turned to Marxism." For, as Kenneth Cracknell, points out "The panoply of wealth and power of Western Christendom, and its individual representatives, some of whom have the temerity to call themselves 'born-again' Christians, impress the monks and nuns of the east very little."[44]

Extreme xenophobia—the fear of strangers, foreigners, and outsiders—is a deadly disease in a nuclear age. Xenophobes exhibit hostility, not hospitality to strangers. Frightened people are rarely peacemakers. They hoard nuclear weapons, stockpile poison gas, and threaten genetic warfare. Neither do they dare cooperate in finding global ecological solutions. Suicidal xenophobia could lead to the extinction of all life. As President Dwight D. Eisenhower once lamented: "Every gun that is made, every warship launched, every rocket fired, signifies, in the final sense, a theft from those who hunger and are not fed, those who are cold and are not clothed."[45] Encouraging Christian hospitality therefore is more than good personal etiquette, but rather a corporate way to connect with God's loving and liberating initiatives for freedom, justice, and peace.

No Nonpersons in God's Family

When William R. Persons formally retired from the pastoral ministry, his wife spoke on his behalf since he had suffered for the previous seven years from Alzheimer's disease and had moved beyond the realm of ordinary discourse. Mildred Persons traced the joys of their earlier ministry and spoke of the grandeur of climbing some of their career summits. But then she recounted the ugly pain of slowly discovering Alzheimer's and what it felt like to become nonpersons, losing stature and status in the church and community. Instead of being involved and influential in matters, they were marginalized and on the periphery of power.

At that point, however, she paused and in a very poignant moment said:

But, The Iliff School of Theology was the one exception. The Board of Trustees kept Bill as a member. He was sent all the materials. Another Trustee picked him up and took him to every meeting, as long as he could physically attend. After one Trustee session, I asked him what happened. He replied, "I don't know, but Iliff still thinks I'm a people."

The collegiality of building bridges to strangers is a metaphor for missional ministry that opens endless opportunities for caring evangelism and service. Whether it is Alzheimer's or AIDS, whether First World or Third World, whether male or female, whether lay or clergy, whether liberal or conservative, whether urban or rural, whether straight or gay, whether white or Native American, whether bishop or bartender, no nonpersons populate the inclusive family of God. God's eye *is* on the sparrow!

CHAPTER SIX

A Company of Star Throwers

Until the lions have their historians, tales of hunting will always glorify the hunter.
AFRICAN PROVERB

In *The Star Thrower*, the poet scientist, Loren Eiseley, paints a word portrait of life and death along an unidentified beach called Costabel. Personally suffering a dry emptiness, a massive sense of futility, and a foretaste of annihilation, he often arose early due to insomnia and walked along the surf. Just before dawn, especially after a storm, flashlights bob up and down along the beach like fireflies on the sand as shell hunters scavenge for treasures.

A greedy kind of madness often overcomes these collectors. With vulturine activity, they scoop up living specimens, favoring starfish. Gathering huge bags, they hurry to outdoor kettles, where they boil alive "the beautiful voiceless things." One early morning Eiseley discerns an even odder spectacle—a person he called the star thrower. Moving toward him and away from the shell collectors, Eiseley felt the full blast of the wind as the sun began to rise above the horizon. Just then he saw a "gigantic rainbow of incredible perfection" with "a human figure standing, as it seemed to me, within the rainbow."[1]

The man reached into the sand, picked up an object, and threw it into the breaking surf. As Eiseley walked the half mile across the wet sand toward him, he again noticed the man kneel, pick up something, and toss it into the ocean. When Eiseley finally reached him, the man was looking at a starfish raised stiffly on its legs. Eiseley said, "It's still alive." "Yes," replied the man, as he gently threw that starfish into the surf. "It may live," he said, "if the offshore pull is strong enough." The man stopped again, picked up another starfish and skipped it gently across the waves. "The stars," he said, "throw well. One can help them." Eiseley wrote:

109

I nodded and walked away, leaving him there upon the dune with that great rainbow ranging up the sky behind him.

I turned as I neared a bend in the coast and saw him toss another star. . . . For a moment, in the changing light, the sower appeared magnified, as though casting larger stars upon some greater sea. He had . . . the posture of a god.[2]

Eiseley noted that this star thrower contradicted everything that he had learned about evolution and the survival of the fittest. "Death is the only successful collector." Here on the beach in Costabel, the strong reached down to save, not crush, the weak. The star thrower stands in opposition to the entire inclination of the universe. Starfish cookers know their victims have lost; they do not worry about the losers of life. But Eiseley comes to realize that he cannot accept the evolutionary verdict. " 'But I *do* love the world,' I whispered to a waiting presence in the empty room. 'I love its small ones, the things beaten in the strangling surf, the bird, singing, which flies and falls and is not seen again.' I choked and said, . . . 'I love the lost ones; the failures of the world.' "[3]

His affirmation of love included not only the lost ones of nature but the lost ones of humanity, in particular his deaf, mentally ill mother from whom he had been long estranged. Daisy Corey Eiseley epitomized all "the lost ones" and embracing her meant renunciating a cold scientism that could not comprehend how one freely chooses not only to be merciful to nonpersons, but to identify with them.[4] Parker J. Palmer speculates: "Is there a star thrower at work in the universe, a God who contradicts death, a God whose nature (in the words of Thomas Merton) is 'mercy within mercy within mercy?' "[5]

This existential essay concludes with Eiseley joining the star thrower on the beach, spinning living starfish beyond the danger points, beyond "the insatiable waters of death."[6] He joins the company of the star thrower, not as a scientist but as a fellow sufferer. By loving life, even the lost ones, Eiseley points to a God who not only creates unfathomable worlds of nature but who is also the God of the lost ones. Scientific language attains religious symbolism as the images of a rainbow and the star thrower become emblems of divinity. The rainbow metaphor represents for Eiseley a sign of compassion, perfection, and the ecologic unity of nature. The star thrower is an image of Christ. As Eiseley hurls starfish, he recalls there have always been those who have cherished "the memory of the perfect circle of compassion from life to death and back again to life—the completion of the rainbow of existence."[7] As Eiseley's biographers note:

To choose the way of love requires a risk, the pains of which no science can ease. But if taken, the risk leads to the discovery of a deity also freely embarked on a vast project of reconciliation. Humans are invited to be star throwers, cooperators in a stupendous and perhaps impossible venture. At the same time, they themselves are doomed starfish, rescued by a hurler of stars who walks, "because he chooses, always in desolation, but not in defeat."[8]

The Church as Company

To speak of the church as a company can prompt negative corporate institutional images: First Church, Inc. or Denominational Ltd. Sometimes our language reinforces this perception when we talk about the congregational buildings as part of the "church plant" or when we speak of ministry as management. The language of business emerges in conversations when our bishops and other leaders become CEO's (chief executive officers) and "bottom line" mentality begins to dictate our mission and ministry. While by necessity the church needs an institutional shape for enacting God's mission of ministry, the fundamental focus of imaging the church as company accents its character as a fellowship in faith, heralding or proclaiming the liberating, saving love and mercy of God in the world.

In contrast to the conglomerate church model, the vision of the church as company resembles instead the idea of a small band of apostles such as "Paul and his company" setting sail on their mission (Acts 13:13). The Bible affiliates the term *company* with a fellowship of persons with a mission or purpose. Sometimes this suggests negative meanings, for instance when the psalmist declares "a company of evildoers encircle me" (Psalm 22:16) or "I hate the company of evildoers" (Psalm 26:5). The psalmist who sings "I will give thanks to the Lord with my whole heart, in the company of the upright" (Psalm 111:1) expresses a more positive connotation.

Imaging the church as a company recalls the basic Latin meaning of the word *company*, literally to "share bread together." The early church is envisioned in Acts 4:32 as being a communitarian, if not a socialist, company: "Now the company of those who believed were of one heart and soul, and no one said that any of the things which he possessed was his own, but they had everything in common." They laid resources "at the apostles' feet" and "distribution was made to each as any had need" (Acts 4:35). Thus, the early church was a company of Christians who shared their bread together. In a world where forty thousand persons die daily from starvation, what does such apostolic practice mean for us who seek to be contemporary disciples of Jesus Christ in mission and ministry?

In response to evangelical efforts, Scripture reports that "a large company was added to the Lord," when Barnabas preached in Antioch (Acts 11:24). In Iconium the apostles preached and "a great company believed" (Acts 14:1). Remembering D. T. Niles' classic definition of evangelism "being one beggar telling another beggar where to get food,"[9] the idea of the church as company takes on new meaning. As the company of apostles shared Jesus Christ, "the bread of life" (John 6:35) lives changed and Christ's church grew.

Saving life is central to the company of star throwers. Whether a popular activity or not, Christians seek to say "no" to death and "yes" to life. They express salvific mission in a variety of ways. It may be the environmentalist who struggles to save endangered species of birds and animals. It may be the lonely vigil and vision of the pacifist who works for peace even when others are persuaded that war is a necessary evil. It may be the dedicated social worker who strives to rescue families ripped apart by economic forces. It may be the volunteer business leader who reaches out to help the homeless, the chemically dependent, or the abused. Or it may be the Christian who simply tells another beggar where to get the spiritual food necessary for new and abundant life in Christ. Proclamation by word and/or deed of the *kerygma* (the good news of God's saving and liberating love in the life, death, and resurrection of Jesus) is fundamental to the missional ministry of the company of star throwers.

James Forbes calls the trilogy of parables in Luke 15 the "Magna Charta of evangelism": the stories of the lost sheep, the lost coin, and the lost son. The context for Jesus' parables is that he faces criticism for associating with the marginal and unworthy people of his society. Worse yet, he partakes of table fellowship with them—sharing bread together. Keeping company with such nonpersons prompts critics to murmur: "This man receives sinners and eats with them" (Luke 15:1).

In response, Jesus asks what persons caring for one hundred sheep would be satisfied to find only ninety-nine and not go looking for the missing one. And when that lost lamb was found, would there not be great joy? The imagery, rich with ecological implications, portrays a clear message: God seeks to save everyone and to exclude no one. Lest the point be unclear to his critics, Jesus repeats the theme in a second parable about the lost coin. When a woman loses even one coin she seeks diligently to find it. Once she discovers it, she rejoices in celebration with her friends and neighbors. Mingling with "sinners" is to embrace all of God's people and to reaffirm God's searching love for everyone.

The third parable of this trilogy—traditionally called the story of the prodigal son, but more appropriately labeled the story of the loving father—must rank among the top ten favorite stories in the Bible. (When I preached in a prison, however, the chaplain urged me to select another passage because the inmates get a bit tired of this text!) In this context, Jesus again stresses the joy in God's heart when the lost are found, relationships are restored, and grace flows freely. Jesus declared: "It was fitting to make merry and be glad, for this your brother was dead, and is alive; he was lost, and is found" (Luke 15:32). The company of star throwers are both bread-givers and grace-donors. Evangelism is an experience of joy; God offers his company not bread and water, but bread and wine.

Struggling with Temptations

The temptation to escape from mission responsibilities always imperils the Christian movement. Being in the company of star throwers appears less attractive than being identified with more successful and prestigious organizations. But as Emil Brunner insisted, "The Church exists by mission just as fire exists by burning. Where there is no mission, there is no Church, and where there is neither Church nor mission, there is no faith."[10]

The temptation experiences of Jesus prove instructive for they recall both the ways the world says "no" to life and the way Jesus said "yes." In the forty days in the wilderness Jesus was tempted to be an impostor: to forsake his intended mission as God's servant in order to become a wonder-worker, an economic messiah, or a political revolutionary. He wrestled against interpreting his messiahship in terms of power, strength, and conquest, rather than as God's servant leader. He struggled for authenticity, for purpose, and for the foundations of his faith and existence. Lay and clergy responding to God's call for the mission of ministry face similar temptations.

Jesus' first temptation is always ours—the inclination toward materialism. He knew the pain of not having enough to eat and understood the popular appeal of transforming stones into food. Politicians who have promised prosperity and higher standards of living have always won applause.

British economist E. F. Schumacher has challenged the massive materialism and industrialization of our age. He has called for new technologies for the developing Two-Thirds World and new life-styles in other nations. For the survival of humanity, we must challenge the materialism of modern economics with religious and spiritual values.

Just as a modern European economist would not consider it a great economic achievement if all European art treasures were sold to America at attractive prices, so the Buddhist economist would insist that a population basing its economic life on non-renewable fuels is living parasitically, on capital instead of income. Such a way of life could have no permanence and could therefore be justified only as a purely temporary expedient. As the world's resources of non-renewable fuels—coal, oil, and natural gas—are exceedingly unevenly distributed over the globe and undoubtedly limited in quantity, it is clear that their exploitation at an ever-increasing rate is an act of violence against nature which must almost inevitably lead to violence between men.[11]

Jesus rejected the demonic impulse to minister to human economic needs to the exclusion of his spiritual mission. Drawing upon his Hebrew religious heritage, he reaffirmed the words of Deuteronomy by saying: "It is written, 'One does not live by bread alone, but by every word that comes from the mouth of God' " (Matthew 4:4). It is not a choice between prayers and prosperity, for either alone is insufficient; both the spiritual and the material play an indispensable role in giving meaning and worth to life. What hinders authentic evangelism, however, is the great gap between the rich and the poor in this world. The income differential between One-Third World and Two-Thirds World persons is reminiscent of the rich man clothed in purple and Lazarus full of sores (Luke 16:19ff.).

On a global scale, we need new attitudes that go beyond materialistic goals, for in and of themselves they prove self-defeating. Missionaries through the ages have embodied a personal generosity that has demonstrated that one can live more frugally and be other-centered. Their lives have often been symbolic judgments on those of us who have chosen to exercise our ministries in more materialistic settings.

Increased human prosperity provides no panacea for world justice and peace, since the pursuit of material ends alone may be built on greed and envy. Internationally we need new spiritual attitudes of sharing and cooperation. There are limits to economic growth and natural resources. Mahatma Gandhi's insight that "earth provides enough to satisfy everyone's need, but not everyone's greed" remains prescient.

The second experience of Jesus in the wilderness was the temptation of power. Scripture says "the devil led him up and showed him in an instant all the kingdoms of the world" (Luke 4:5). Satan offered him all the power any political messiah could ever desire. What always amazes and depresses me is how often the most caring, loving Christian turns "power-hungry" when it comes to nationalism. Christians worldwide would not consider kneeling before the devil, but they will prostrate themselves before the flag of their particular nation regardless of how evil its policies may be.

The Sermon on the Mount incites subversion, for Jesus speaks the unspeakable—he thinks the unthinkable—he calls us to love our enemies—to respond to violence with nonviolence—to be peacemakers, not apostles of the arms race. How true it is that "We have grasped the mystery of the atom and rejected the Sermon on the Mount. . . . Ours is a world of nuclear giants and ethical infants. We know more about war than we know about peace, more about killing than we know about living."[12] The evolution of war has reached such monstrous proportions that now the United States (and other super nuclear powers) not only has the power to obliterate its enemies but all future generations as well, reducing itself, in Jonathan Schell's graphic description, to nothing but "a republic of insects and grass."[13]

Christians must become a company of star throwers, affirming life, questioning our knee-jerk loyalty to every patriotic appeal, and asking about the possibility of severe spending reductions on military expenditures. Jesus rejected the path to earthly power, using his influence to question those in power. As a result, he suffered a political execution—death on a cross. Likewise, Christians who challenge the powerful in terms of human rights, basic justice, and possibilities for peace can anticipate resistance and martyrdom.

The third temptation Jesus faced was arrogance—pressing God to the limits—confusing the created with the Creator. Satan exhibited a most ingenious seductive spirit. Whisked away to the highest point of the temple, Jesus was baited: "If you are God's Son, throw yourself down from here. Let the angels protect you!" (Luke 4:9, paraphrase).

The temptation always is to believe that God will provide special protection if we are good, moral, and law-abiding. One-Third World Christians imagine that we as a people can consume 40 percent of the world's resources while composing only 6 percent of the earth's population—and yet escape God's judgment. Such arrogance—to believe we can be exempt from the laws of creation because we have experienced the grace of God in Christ! We are part and parcel of the universe. Who do we think we are—putting God to the test—as we race forward threatening the future of life by our nuclear arms race, destruction of the biosphere, capricious genetic engineering, and environmental pollution?

Jesus successfully resisted the temptation of arrogance—of pushing God to the limits—of asking the impossible. By God's grace the company of star throwers can also resist, stooping down to save, not to crush. Star throwers become co-creators with God in an effort to preserve, not destroy life.

Star Throwers as Peacemakers

Preserving, not destroying, life calls the star thrower to be a peacemaker. Though Jesus taught "Blessed are the peacemakers: for they shall be called the children of God" (Matthew 5:9, KJV), the powerbrokers of the world persistently view peacemaking as a subversive activity. Those who resist violence often are viewed as unpatriotic because they stand in opposition to those who would wage war. At the height of the Vietnam War, Bishop James Armstrong asked "Is Peace a Dirty Word?"

In his sermon to the United Methodist General Conference, he answered his own question, declaring:

For us peace is not a plank on a political platform or the fervent hope of the administration of our choice. It is a tenet of the faith; an imperative of the Gospel. . . . If peace is a dirty word, then Christ was a dirty liar and history is a dirty joke; life is a cruel wasteland, and violence and hate have license to prevail. No! This we do *not* believe. We are Christians, and we have been raised up for such a time as this.[14]

Far from being subversive, Christian commitment to a just world order, a revitalized United Nations, and a peacemaking mission and ministry may ultimately represent the most patriotic and loyal stance citizens can give their nations. If war industries could be converted to productive civilian enterprises, a nuclear Armageddon could be avoided and the health and welfare of the world enhanced. If we eliminated the $100 billion spent on Trident II submarines and F-18 jet fighters, ten thousand of the worst toxic waste dumps in the United States could be cleaned. If the United States did not spend $4 billion manufacturing nuclear warheads every six months, child-care legislation could be funded twice over. The $68 billion spent on stealth bombers could subsidize national health insurance, thus covering forty million Americans now without protection. The United States may have "won" the Gulf War against Iraq, but ultimately we may be the "losers" if the "peace dividend" of approximately $150 billion promised by the end of the Cold War never materializes.[15] If Christians as a company of star throwers can contribute to decreasing the dangers of war, our "subversiveness" will support that biblical ideal envisioned when "nation shall not lift up sword against nation, neither shall they learn war any more" (Micah 4:3b, RSV).

Perhaps a story from Kurt Vonnegut's novel, *Slaughterhouse Five*, best captures what it means to be a Christian star thrower.[16] The hero of the book, Billy Pilgrim, a man caught in a middle-age crisis, a Rotarian/Chamber of Commerce type, has literally gone crazy as he sought to cope with the ambiguities and anguish—the complications and contradictions—of life.

In his youth Billy Pilgrim was a patriotic American, who as a German prisoner of war, lived through the dreadful fire-bombings of Dresden. Filled with patriotic idealism, he had believed in the justness of the Allied cause, until the night the American planes fire-bombed that beautiful, fragile city, and left its lovely cathedrals, its men, women, and children, in a burning rubble.

With that truth "buttoned-up" inside him for years, Billy became quite crazy. He lived "unstuck in time" traveling from the present back into Dresden, then ahead to the day of his death, then back to the war, then briefly into the present again, then off to his imaginary planet of Tralfamador. Then one night Billy saw a World War II movie backwards.

Seen in reverse, the harmful blows of war were transformed into healing acts. Damaged American airplanes, with wounded men and corpses, took off from British airfields. They met German fighter planes flying backwards over France, who miraculously sucked out bullets and shell fragments from the planes and soldiers. The same occurred for wrecked American bombers on the ground and they flew backwards up to join the formation.

Over a German city in flames, the backward flying American bombers withdrew the bombs from the ground and the flames were extinguished by a "miraculous magnetism." The bombs were gathered in cylindrical steel containers and neatly stored in racks. Back in England, the bombs were unloaded and shipped back to the United States of America, where women took them apart and turned them back into minerals, and shipped them to remote areas. Then, specialists replaced the minerals cleverly in the ground, where they could never injure anyone ever again.

By all our academic, therapeutic and even "common sense" definitions, Billy Pilgrim was crazy. But perhaps—yes, just perhaps—he was the only sane person in an insane world—a star thrower on another coast of Costabel. Peacemaking star throwers are not just fictional characters for life often imitates art. For example, who can forget the horror of watching the bombings of Beirut in the 1980s and seeing the mounting casualties of civilians? Amid the urban Lebanese battlefield, no safe place to hide existed; even hospitals and orphanages were destroyed. And then a "crazy" star-throwing woman broke through the battlelines and went to the shell-shattered mental hospital in West Beirut where she began embracing starving, hurting retarded children—those whom Eiseley might have labeled "lost ones" and Jesus would have called "the least of these." And the bombs stopped and the guns ceased—for a seventy-year-old Mother Teresa walked the streets where even the brave feared to tread.

Peacemaking must be a priority for all Christians. Sometimes this seems easier to affirm on a global scene than in our more intimate relationships with family, friends, and professional colleagues. We nurse grudges, harbor hostilities, and rub raw the sores of distrust. Instead of reaching out to heal, our inclination to slash back and to hurt prevails.

Christians personally are not immune from such sin, not even star throwers. If only we would run the films of our lives backwards—sucking out the words that wounded others, withdrawing the fine sabers that cut so needlessly, burying the disputes that divided us—then perhaps we could become a company of star throwers, overcoming temptations of materialism, power, and arrogance, in order to exercise a peacemaking ministry of healing in Christ's name.

Aficionados of Hope and Life

Christians have always been in a company of star throwers. They have never shared a vision of defeat and death, but instead have been aficionados of hope and life. Had they limited themselves by the defined boundaries of what others deemed "reality," they would not have pushed back the borders of Gentile Christianity, evangelized Europe, or taken the gospel to the six continents. Had missionaries been "realists," they probably never would have left home, much less dreamed of conquering hunger, defeating illiteracy, stopping epidemics, translating the Bible, improving the status of women and children, planting churches, and so forth.

Any sane analysis of statistics would demonstrate that at any given moment in history the problems are too great and the resources of the church too small. But star throwers see beyond the ordinary, hope beyond the usual, and act beyond the expected. They possess faith in a God who not only created the universe, but loves the lost ones—the sparrows, the starfish, the suffering. Since they seek neither fame nor fortune, they identify with the nonpersons of the earth and claim God's liberating love for all. The star thrower suggests, says Parker J. Palmer:

an image of a God who threw the stars and throws them still. It speaks of how ordinary men and women can participate in God's enveloping mercy. And it suggests a vocation that each of us could undertake on our inward way of the cross: to recognize, to identify and lift up those moments, those acts, those people, those stories which contradict the ways in which the world says no to life.[17]

The story is told of a holy man who, during his morning meditation, noticed that the river was rising and threatening to drown a scorpion caught in the tree's roots. Slowly the meditator crawled near the water's edge and tried to free the scorpion. At every attempt, the scorpion struck at him. A passerby warned the holy man, saying: "Don't you know that's a scorpion, and it is in the nature of the scorpion to want to sting?" To which he replied, "That may well be, but it is my nature to save, and must I change my nature because the scorpion does not change its nature?"[18]

As aficionados of hope and life Christians are willing to take risks for a missional ministry. Albert Schweitzer forsook a brilliant career in music to become a missionary. Martin Luther King, Jr. sacrificed his life for the civil rights of all Americans. Archbishop Oscar Romero was assassinated in El Salvador when he spoke on behalf of the poor in his country. The

Anglican Bishop of Kenya, Alexander Muge, was murdered because he argued for justice and against oppression in his own country. Political despots always fear aficionados of hope and life. Whether singing hymns or folk songs, star throwers articulate the dreams of the masses. When General Pinochet seized power, his junta severed the hands of Victor Jara whose songs on guitar had catalyzed the oppressed nonpersons of Chile.

Many local pastors and laity have endured slander and suffered persecution because they have prophetically stood with so-called nonpersons in their communities. Brazilian Bishop Don Helder Camara noted that "I brought food to the hungry, and people called me a saint; I asked why people were hungry, and people called me a communist."[19]

The outside public rarely comprehends or appreciates the enthusiasm and energy Christian star throwers invest in lives of sacrificial service. Star throwers live and die in local parishes and communities. A few win Nobel Peace prizes or get honorary doctorates, but most spend their existence in humble obscurity and obedience. They stake their lives against seemingly insurmountable injustices. The victories seem few and far between, but the company of star throwers senses that they are participating in God's liberating and loving initiatives both now and for the next millennium.

Donald J. Shelby spotlights Sister Emmanuelee as illustrative of a person who represents Christ in the garbage pits of Cairo, Egypt. Those who struggle there for a livelihood live in perpetual serfdom, salvaging what they can for resale, subsisting on what food they find in the refuse, and feeding the rest to pigs that coexist with them. Infant mortality reaches an appalling 40 percent. As the only missionary among ten thousand garbage pickers, she teaches literacy to some forty children in her tiny hut with its dirt floor. With the Coptic Christians she shares Bible stories. When this Belgian-born nun was asked why she chose to live and serve there, she replied: "My task is to prove that God is love, to bring courage to these people."[20] An aficionado of hope and love, Sister Emmanuelee, like the lonely star thrower, beckons others to join in God's life-saving operation.

Uniting Two So Long Divided: Evangelism and Social Justice

What distinguishes a company of star throwers is their vision of missional ministry as the unity of evangelism and social justice.[21] Unwilling to accept the inevitable demise of the weak and the survival of the strong, star throwers identify with the Good Shepherd who looks for the lost sheep, with the Good Father who rejoices when a prodigal son comes home, and with the Good Samaritan who cares for the outcast. However, star throwers are never content with only personal actions of amelioration; they are committed to systemic change. Personal compassion and sharing remain imperative, but these must be accompanied by a systems approach to global problems. Issues of global debt, inequality, substance abuse, or apartheid relate to personal evangelism, but they defy individualistic solutions alone. Offering Christ to the imprisoned or enslaved offers the possibility of new personal life, but it is shallow and deceptive without efforts to restructure and redeem the social situation. Nonpersons around the world need both personal conversion and social change.

Typically Christian "evangelicals" and "ecumenists" have severely disagreed on this issue. At times even our language acts to divide. Terms like "evangelicals" and "ecumenists" seem arbitrary and lack precision, but they serve for the moment as a handy typology for analysis. Understand, of course, that such "ideal types" in the Troeltschian sense are always abstractions; flesh-and-blood persons differ in varying degrees. Peter Beyerhaus, for example, has distinguished no fewer than six evangelical groupings, and Arthur F. Glasser classifies five types of evangelicals. Both scholars identify Christians who claim to be both evangelical and ecumenical.[22]

Usually evangelism is identified with phrases like "winning souls for Christ," "spreading the Good News of the gospel," and "being born again." The spotlight focuses on one-to-one conversion experiences, most dramatically personified in the public mind with Billy Graham's altar calls at the close of his mass stadium rallies, when he appeals for repentance and warns about the moral degradation of the nation and the imminent Second Coming of Christ. Theologically, there has been much escatology talk—being saved for heaven's sake! Evangelical Christians place great emphasis on church extension and membership growth. Ethically, the evangelical command has emphasized a new way of life—often accompanied by a somewhat lengthy list of specific sins to avoid. Overcoming sin is not so easy, however, as evidenced by a recent Roper pool which reported that "born-agains" admitted to somewhat higher rates of drunken driving, illegal drug usage, and adultery after their conversion experience![23]

Ecumenically-oriented Christians, especially in North America, have tended to accent the motif of "changing society" at the expense of "saving souls." Since they believe that only by transforming social structures can persons be liberated from oppressive situations that degrade human dignity and destroy the human spirit, they stress the theological theme of the kingdom or reign of God. Their favorite prayer has been "Thy kingdom come, thy will be done, on earth as it is in heaven." Social ethics often receives a higher priority than personal ethics; eradicating racism and eliminating sexism predominate over personal moral codes. Sin persists, however, since institutional racism and sexism often pervade ecumenical bodies and actions.

David J. Hesselgrave analyzed the missionary strategy patterns presented in 444 books published in the 1970s and 1980s, as well as the major themes in articles appearing in the *International Review of Missions* and the *Evangelical Missions Quarterly* over a twenty-one year period. He concluded that ecumenical materials devoted over four times as much attention to sociopolitical action than did evangelical books and articles. Surprisingly, he found that the concerns of evangelism and church growth received approximately equal attention by both groups, though he says "witness is not always understood in the more traditional terms of preaching the gospel and aiming for conversion."[24]

Over the years the World Council of Churches has been vehemently attacked by its opponents because of its social justice stances. However in 1989, the Lausanne II International Congress on World Evangelization, meeting in the Philippines, muted somewhat its criticism of the ecumenical movement, and even made dramatic calls for global social justice. By way of illustration, one declaration said: "World evangelization will make little headway unless Christians face the challenge of reaching the poor, which make up nearly half the world's population. [Those at Manila] who mainly represent the church of the well-to-do must squarely face the dilemma."[25]

Increasingly, evangelicals recognize a biblical imperative to relate the gospel to the social problems of our time. The historic evangelical position has demonstrated less involvement in social and political activism. Notable exceptions, of course, are evident. The evangelical emphasis clearly played a central role in the crusade to abolish slavery and in the effort to impose prohibition. Evangelicals are now recovering this aspect of their tradition. Waldron Scott, General Secretary of the World Evangelical Fellowship and an active participant in the Navigators, argues that the making of disciples must be related to a commitment to social justice. He openly admits the past failure of evangelicals to be involved in social action and insists evangelicals "must be foremost in the pursuit of the justice of God."[26]

The Evangelical Newsletter surveyed fifty-seven evangelical leaders about ways in which their minds had changed in the last decade. Some 70 percent said they now believe in social responsibility more than previously; 44 percent said they evince less interest in questions of eschatology. Billy Graham speaks of his "born again" conversion to the necessity of speaking out about the madness of the nuclear arms race. Richard Mouw calls lay persons to "holy worldliness," seeking to demonstrate to more conservative Christians the biblical basis for a broader understanding of discipleship and the implications for questions of poverty, racism, ecology, and world hunger.[27]

One should note that "doing justice" as a basis of mission involves far more complexity and controversy than the "saving souls" approach. Reaching consensus about what justice means in a given context, particularly at the congregational level, presents problems. Opposing apartheid may have a high consensus but the steps Christians should take regarding the global debt may be less clear. Supra-congregational-level boards and committees often favor actions that they deem in accord with God's justice, but people in the local congregation often oppose these actions. Whether "evangelicals" deal with this dilemma any more effectively than "ecumenists" is yet to be tested.

Ecumenically-oriented Christians are becoming more committed to the evangelical mandate of the gospel. While evangelicals are expressing more social gospel concern, ecumenists have been reappropriating their own evangelical heritage. The founder of the social gospel movement, Walter Raschenbusch, would have called himself an "evangelical" because he did not see himself departing from the personal dimensions of the gospel. Sometimes liberals have departed from the evangelical vision to such an extent that occasionally they have interpreted declining church membership as a divine sign of approval of the "remnant" community's controversial struggle for social justice.

Evangelical and ecumenical scholars have credited Mortimer Arias with calling the World Council of Churches back to the "essential priority" of evangelization with his speech, "That the World May Believe," at the WCC 1975 conference in Nairobi, Kenya. "Evangelism," says David J. Bosch, again assumed a "place of honour in the ecumenical movement, especially because of the stimulating contribution of Mortimer Arias and the ensuing discussions."[28] How ironic that in 1989 the United Methodist-related Foundation for Evangelism withdrew $125,000 intended for Arias' three-year contract as professor of evangelism at The Iliff School of Theology, claiming that Arias did not believe in personal conversion. Arias, who suffered imprisonment in Bolivia in 1980 for his courageous opposition to oppression, reminds Christians that:

Authentic evangelism will not be achieved without paying a *high price* for it. Cheap evangelism cannot be a very evangelical evangelism. What price did Jesus pay for evangelizing? What price did the Apostles pay? Do we believe that we shall pay today a cheaper price thanks to a cheap and comfortable circulation of the gospel? An evangelical evangelism will force us to pay in serious renunciation, painful changes and radical options, particularly an option in favor of the oppressed, rejecting the temptation of false neutrality or an open alliance with the oppressive powers. There is no evangelism without a cross.[29]

Evangelicals and ecumenists, however, do not necessarily agree, and may seem more like boats passing in the night than ships setting sail on similar life-saving missions. In certain instances, Christians find themselves in passionate opposition with one another on social issues, discovering more in common with persons of other faiths and/or no religious persuasion. Questions such as abortion, prayer in public schools, gay and lesbian rights, and the Equal Rights Amendment deeply divide Christians in the United States. Yet the company of star throwers must seek to bridge differences and identify ways of linking Christians together in order to face the major perils facing the earth. Evangelical theologian Carl F. H. Henry reminds us that:

Our task remains that of lighting and salting an otherwise dark and putrefying world. In a generation for which SALT has become an acronym for Soviet-American adjustments in a vicious arms race, and LIGHT is a phenomenon that scientists computerize in inter-planetary correlations, even Christians easily forget that lighting and salting is their mission to the world.[30]

Likewise perspectives on evangelism sometimes diverge. Not everyone agrees about what distinguishes a "saved soul"! Virginia Ramey Mollenkott rejects a style of evangelism that fails to transcend racism, sexism, heterosexism, classism, ageism and economic imperialism. An evangelism that accepts certain destructive assumptions of traditional Western culture proves objectionable,

that bigger is better, so that evangelism's purpose is to enlarge Christian institutions; that competition is necessary and desirable even in the life of the church; that human fulfillment stems chiefly from measurable achievements; that Christians should strive to transcend the condition of ordinary humanity; that at the same time Christians must properly remain in a state of small-child dependency upon a God-Out-There; that salvation is personal and perhaps justice-oriented, but is certainly not intended to challenge the current structures of society; and that some people (such as evangelists and other clergy) are in a special position of authority that gives them the inside track of God's intentions, so that others must assume a position secondary to themselves.[31]

While the wording is Mollenkott's own formulation, many share her expression of a new evangelism. Grace, not perfection, provides the major motif of this new emphasis on evangelism. She rejects the politics of exclusion, used to keep women and persons of color from leadership positions in the church. Accenting a witness to human unity in Christ, this new evangelism listens to and empowers the oppressed, practicing a politics of inclusion.

As the company of Christian star throwers reformulates evangelism for the twenty-first century, a fuller understanding of the whole gospel, both personal and social, may prevail. Perhaps both "evangelicals" and "ecumenists" will begin to join company and share bread together and demonstrate that evangelism is indeed one beggar telling another beggar where to get food. This represents an invitation to acknowledge the malnutrition of all our souls and to feast together on the life-giving nourishment of the gospel of Jesus Christ.

The company of star throwers must seek to transcend the differences of "evangelicals" and "ecumenists." Times together in prayer must accompany intentionally structured opportunities for disciplined dialogue and study, focusing on the biblical, theological, and political ramifications of differing concepts of evangelism and social responsibility. If we simply continue to go our own ways, we not only suffer personally from not growing by the witness and insight of Christians who disagree with us, in addition we send out mixed and confused messages to a world hungry and hurting for the Good News we are committed to sharing.

Conversion as Essential

The movement from a maintenance mentality to a mission mind-set in the church requires conversion. A renewal of personal commitment and faith is essential. Radical changes of the heart *(metanoia)* become imperative for individual persons and the church, if the world and all God's creation are to have continued life. New ways of thinking, believing, and acting must be mandatory. A renunciation of sin and evil, both personal and social, are needed if we are to be peacemakers in a violent world or ecologians on a polluted globe. The call of mission, declares theologian John B. Cobb, Jr., must be both personal and social. Cobb claims:

We can make no lasting and significant contributions to world peace or to feeding the hungry and bringing liberation to the oppressed that does not involve personal conversion to Jesus Christ. And there can be no authentic personal conversion to Jesus Christ apart from involvement in the working of Christ for peace, feeding the hungry and freeing the captive. To offer the gospel to hungry people while refusing them food is an utter travesty.[32]

We must transform our world views and intellectual paradigms. For the Christian, a reawakened love of God in Christ prompts a rededicated love of neighbor. A decisive encounter with the love of God on a personal basis opens one to a greater love of God's creation. John testified "We love, because he first loved us" (I John 4:19), and Jesus declared of the prostitute, "Her sins, which are many, are forgiven, for she loved much" (Luke 7:47, RSV).

The Presbyterian Church of New Zealand reportedly discovered new life only when it opened itself to the Holy Spirit and each person began to pray individually: "Lord, revive your church, beginning with me." Graeme Murray contends that God calls the church "to make a heart commitment to intentional growth by gentle evangelism." "Growth" is understood as people coming to faith in Jesus Christ, due ultimately to the work of the Holy Spirit, but accompanied by the witness of Christians by word and life-style. Christians are called both to plant churches and serve humanity. "Gentle" evangelism describes a style of reaching out to others in daily experiences of life that creates "a mood and attitude in their activities that motivates them to reach out to others and encourages them to discover the truth of the gospel."[33] More than just practicing Christian presence, it includes inviting others to know the saving joy and hope and love of our faith. If we are to remain faithful to the spirit of Christ, it dare not appear manipulative or threatening, but rather be kindly and caring.

"Gentle" evangelism requires passion, not passivity, but it does not condone demeaning or distorting other religions or making excessive claims for the Christian faith. Open dialogue without deception must replace arrogant attempts at proselytizing people of other faiths. People should feel free to convert if an honest search for truth leads them to such a conviction, but conversion should never be imposed arbitrarily. "Gentle" evangelism requires a unity of testimony and living of word and deed, in order that others may not only hear, but also see, the transforming power of Christ in the star thrower's life.

Conversion is essential if the church as a company of star throwers intends to affirm social justice and action as well as "gentle evangelism" and church growth. Extending and forming new communities and congregations of Christian faith rest at the heart of missional ministry. Star throwers are not shy about sharing the Good News and grace of Jesus Christ. They agree with the Hong Kong theologian and evangelist, Raymond Fung, when he notes that "frequently the world's poor are also those who have not yet heard the good news of the Gospel; to withhold from them justice as well as the good news of life in Christ is to commit a 'double injustice.' "[34] People need both social justice and new spiritual life in Jesus Christ. "We should be doing a disservice to the poor," asserts Emilio Castro, "if we were to deprive them of the knowledge of him who for love of them and of us . . . became poor even to the point of death on the cross. . . ."[35] A missional ministry neither apologizes about the possibilities and power of personal conversion nor becomes defensive about the imperative and immediacy of global caretaking.

An incident from the civil rights struggle in Selma, Alabama shows the essentiality of conversion for the star thrower. A large crowd of black and white activists outside Ebenezer Baptist Church became quite angry when they heard reports of serious injuries to demonstrators in Montgomery. Across the street stood Sheriff Jim Clark, who symbolized the oppressive police forces of the state and city. Sensing what might happen if the crowd became more restive, a young African American preacher grabbed a microphone, shouting out that "It's time we sang a song."

Lifting his voice, he sang, "Do you love Jesus?" to which the crowd responded "Certainly, certainly, certainly, Lord." Then, the pastor recited a litany of the leaders of the nonviolent movement, calling Martin Luther King, Jr., and the others by name. Each time the demonstrators, warming to the song, sang loudly, "Certainly, certainly, certainly, Lord." Then suddenly, the preacher sang out, "Do you love Jim Clark—the sheriff?" "Cer . . . certainly, Lord," came the stunned reply. "Do you love Jim Clark?" the preacher sang again. "Certainly, Lord," came the reply, only this time a bit stronger. "Do you love Jim Clark?" the preacher asked again. By this time, he had made the point and the protestors' voices rang out: "Certainly, certainly, certainly, Lord." Taking the microphone, Reverend James Bevel reminded everyone that "We are not just fighting for our rights, but for the good of the whole society. It's not enough to defeat Jim Clark—do you hear me, Jim?—we want you converted!"[36]

The company of star throwers are committed to joining in God's loving and liberating initiatives because they want the world converted. Thus in a nuclear, ecological, and global age, they go and stand on every coast of Costabel and seek to save the lost, the lonely ones, and "the least of these."

CHAPTER SEVEN

A Community of Fence Movers

What life have you if you have not life together?
There is no life that is not in community,
And no community not lived in praise of God.
T. S. ELIOT, "The Rock," *Collected Poems*

Immediately after the devastation of the First World War, Quakers distributed food and clothing to the impoverished people of Poland. One relief worker, who had served a variety of villages, suddenly contracted typhus and died within twenty-four hours. Only Roman Catholic cemeteries existed and canonical law forbade burying anyone not of that confession in consecrated ground. Therefore, they buried their cherished missionary friend in a grave just outside the cemetery. The next morning, however, it was discovered that the villagers had moved the fence during the night so that the cemetery now included the grave.[1]

This community of Polish fence movers embodies an enacted parable for our time. Defying outdated dogmas that denied the true reality of their faith and friendship, these Roman Catholic laity redrew the boundaries defining whom to include or exclude. Their story illuminates and illustrates the challenge facing the mission of ministry as we seek globally to move fences and destroy walls that divide and alienate the human community in its spiritual quest for God and for justice, peace, and the integrity of creation.

The metaphor of moving fences portrays the heart of the church's mission and ministry as we approach the twenty-first century. Fence movers are persons who see broader visions beyond given boundaries. They are not hemmed in by historical accidents or cultural conditioning, but respond freely to God's continuing revelation in the world. Embracing ecumenism, ensuring inclusiveness, and engaging other faiths are urgent priorities for a church faithful to Jesus Christ and fruitful in human service. In a nuclear, ecological, and global era, the church must move beyond trivialities and tribalism and become a community of fence movers.

The Church as Community

Presumably, the framers of the clerical canon law, who decreed who could be buried in the church's cemeteries, had developed a systematic, rationalistic theology to justify their legalism. But the community of lay fence movers felt that such abstractions betrayed their experience of the love of Christ and neighbor, so they evolved their own theological practices. Similarly, contemporary Christians, lay and clergy, are challenging other anachronistic church teachings and practices, calling into question their value and authority in a world threatened by extinction. Not only Catholics, but also Protestant and Orthodox Christians are being forced to rethink what the faith means and what God calls the church to be in the next millennium. The threat this poses to patriarchal, hierarchical, and institutional leaders often creates political tension and a backlash of criticism and controversy.

Affirming the church as community contrasts sharply with the image of "the church as institution," which has dominated much of Christian history.[2] Rejecting the idea of the church as a democratic or representative society, the ruling classes of the church have argued traditionally that all the faithful do not possess the same rights, and that propounding theology must be reserved for the powerful elite. The image of the church as a communion or community of persons through the grace of God suggests a drastically different way of doing Christian theology and ethics. The visions and voices of all the people of God, lay and clergy, need to be shared and considered. No one in God's global family is excluded.

Noting that Jesus lived and died primarily among his enemies, the theologian Dietrich Bonhoeffer declared that "the Christian, too, belongs not in the seclusion of a cloistered life but in the thick of foes."[3] Operating an "illegal," clandestine seminary in Germany, he experienced "life together" in Christ with twenty-five vicars while struggling against totalitarian evil. Imprisoned in 1943 and executed by hanging in 1945 for his courageous witness against the Nazis, Bonhoeffer knew the cost of Christian discipleship and the gift of grace in Christian community. While incarcerated he ministered to the prisoners, saved some from certain death, and even inspired his guards sufficiently that a few smuggled out his papers and poems. Living in and loving the world, he called other Christians to engage in suffering service and to experience a "costly grace" that goes beyond just following Jesus by preaching, teaching, and evangelizing. He affirmed Christian community, not as a way of retreating from responsibility in the world, but as a base for transforming evil and doing good.[4]

The fellowship of fence movers is a community created, sustained, and motivated by God the parent, lover, and friend. In St. Paul's language, community is rooted in "the grace of the Lord Jesus Christ, the love of God, and the communion of the Holy Spirit" (II Corinthians 13:13). *Koinonia*, the Greek word in the New Testament usually translated as communion or fellowship, is centered in Jesus Christ and manifested in the activity of the Holy Spirit: "But we have this treasure in earthen vessels, to show that the transcendent power belongs to God and not to us" (II Corinthians 4:7).[5] One receives authority within this community not as automatic privilege, but rather one earns it by caring service. Servant leadership in a world cherished as God's body determines greatness in ministry.

In the early church, one of the first "fences" to be moved was the barrier of circumcision. This obligatory male practice symbolized community membership for both the Jewish synagogue and the Christian congregation. Today, the intensity of the controversy over whether male Christians had to be circumcised in order to be saved seems hard to imagine, but Scripture repeatedly stresses the dispute and the differences of opinion. At a conference in Jerusalem about A.D. 50, however, the apostles moved this fence so that circumcision became optional for Christians, since one achieves salvation by grace, not by actions (Acts 15:1-11 and Galatians 1 and 2). From the perspective of the first great missionary, St. Paul, "neither circumcision counts for anything nor uncircumcision, but keeping the commandments of God" (I Corinthians 7:19). Paul and Barnabas and the other early Christian fence movers prevailed, when it was decided that persons could be circumcised or uncircumcised and still be Christian. Ultimately inclusion triumphed over exclusion, grace over works. In the community of fence movers, "there is neither Jew nor Greek, there is neither slave nor free, there is neither male nor female; for you are all one in Christ Jesus" (Galatians 3:28).

Experiences of the church as community can occur anywhere two or three persons, or even two or three thousand people, experience the grace and power of the Holy Spirit. Amid the civil rights struggle, Clarence Jordan's Koinonia Farm in Americus, Georgia witnessed to a new kind of community of fence movers. The "base communities" of Latin American liberation theology seek to cross previously uncharted territory in opposition to oppression and poverty. Korean Christians, meeting together in homes as *sokhewes*, or class meetings, know the sustaining power of community during years of personal crisis and revolutionary change. We may experience this sense of the church as a *koinonia* of fence movers at a march on Washington, a lonely prayer vigil, an exhibition of the quilt memorializing persons who have died from AIDS, a congregational administrative meeting, or whenever Christians decide to move beyond fear to hope, from phobia to faith.

The power of *koinonia* is illustrated dramatically in the life of Linda and Millard Fuller. A millionaire at the age of twenty-nine, Millard had money but no meaning in his life. He and his wife separated, but reconciled at Clarence Jordan's Koinonia Farm. They sold their possessions and gave their wealth to churches and charities. At Koinonia Farm they discovered a mission replacing the dilapidated shacks and shanties of poverty-stricken persons around Americus. Their mission later became known as Habitat for Humanity, which now has replaced, with volunteer help, thousands of homes for poor people in hundreds of U.S. cities and more than twenty-five nations around the world. The church as *koinonia* or community can change lives, creating a fellowship of fence movers and house builders.

Embracing Ecumenism

A community of fence movers commits itself to shifting the fences of denominationalism and to embracing ecumenism. Though they may joyfully and gratefully identify themselves with a particular denomination or tradition, they underscore the catholicity or universality of Christianity. Fence movers concur with H. Richard Niebuhr's assertions regarding the "scandal of denominationalism" and the "ethical failure of the divided church."[6] The vision is of a uniting church in a divided world that acknowledges "one body and one Spirit . . . one Lord, one faith, one baptism, one God . . . of us all" (Ephesians 4:4, 5).

Fence movers endorse the vision of a world house, believing with Martin Luther King, Jr., that unless persons learn to live together as brothers and sisters, we will perish together as fools. Fearful of world havoc if we do not transcend the divisions of the past, the community of fence movers understands its mission and ministry as reaching across barriers and finding unity in the human household, including the church of Jesus Christ.

A biblical way of imaging the world is *oikos*, or house. *Oikos* serves as the root word for three key terms: ecumenics, ecology, and economics. Ecumenics refers to viewing the whole inhabited world as a single family, human and nonhuman, and to encouraging unity and cooperation in that family. Ecology speaks of the intricate interdependence of organisms and environments upon which the whole household depends. Economics means providing sufficient resources for managing the global household. Larry L. Rasmussen notes that "one of the classic theological expressions for bringing creation to full health is the unfolding drama of 'the divine economy' (*oikonomia tou Theou*).'"[7] As a banner reads outside the World

Council of Churches headquarters in Geneva: "The Oikoumene is the whole inhabited earth, not just the Christian part of it."

A community of fence movers identifies with the missional ministry of Paul and Silas, both described as persons who "have turned the *oikoumene* upside down" (Acts 17:6). Turning the world upside down meant challenging the status quo, threatening the imperial powers, and "acting against the decrees of Caesar, saying that there is another king, Jesus" (Acts 17:7). Embracing ecumenism entails adopting a style of mission and ministry that not only seeks unity and cooperation among Christians but assertively proclaims a higher authority than the nation-state. By crossing customary borders of denominationalism and nationality, the church emerges as greater than any particular institutionalized expression and subject to only one ruler, Jesus Christ.

The ecumenical vision and movement is rooted deeply in centuries of Christian thought, but the persistence of denominational separatism cannot be denied. Great ecumenical conferences occur virtually unnoticed in the United States today. Pronouncements by the National Council of Churches and the World Council of Churches exercise little impact on the thinking of either the churches or society or church members. In many ways, ecumenism seems unfashionable. Efforts to bring organic unity to denominations find little support. Documents of the Consultation on Christian Unity (COCU) tend to go unread, with only hesitant or nonexistent official church endorsement. Instead of diminishing, the scandal of denominationalism and religious tribalism and triumphalism may be increasing.

Even those who embrace ecumenism often quarrel among themselves, unwilling to recognize the validity of each other's clergy, traditions, and practices. When the World Council of Churches gathers, they cannot celebrate Holy Communion together. How can Christians expect the world to listen to their witness for justice, peace, and the integrity of creation and against hunger, war, and environmental degradation, when we cannot agree to share the Lord's Supper among ourselves? Reportedly, a Muslim had to control the key to the Church of the Holy Sepulchre in Jerusalem for many decades because the Christian bodies that shared the sanctuary believed their fellow Christians would lock them out. Everywhere we need fence movers who will imitate the spirit of Pope John XXIII, who said, "Whenever I see a wall between Christians, I try to pull out a brick."[8]

Ensuring Inclusiveness

Fence movers dare to dream of more inclusive communities in terms of gender, ethnicity, race, nationality, and sexual orientation. These boundary crossers claim as their mission of ministry to ensure inclusiveness by overcoming the division, fears, and hatreds that separate and alienate God's family. The world thinks "Good fences make good neighbors," but to use the words of Robert Frost: "Something there is that doesn't love a wall" in the heart of God.[9] God's free grace means unconditional love for all.

Being open to such diversity has parallels to the circumcision debate of biblical days. The biblical debates focused on whether a Gentile had to convert to Judaism before becoming a Christian and whether certain cultural and ritual practices had to be observed or not. Contemporary ways of posing this question include asking whether persons have to be middle class to be Christian, or male to be pastors, or white to have influence in the church, or Western in one's theology, or heterosexual in one's life-style. Fence movers tend to view these distinctions as artificial barriers to faith and life. Believing and proclaiming a gospel of grace, they embrace all of God's creation as good, and they emphasize that no nonpersons exist in the family of God.

The mission of ministry meets resistance and enmity at many points. Christian fence movers, led by Martin Luther King, Jr., moved many legal barriers of discrimination, but Sunday morning at 11:00 A.M. endures as the most segregated hour in the United States. Cross-racial pastoral appointments remain the exception, not the general practice. Overcoming racism in the church and its structures proves to be as difficult as eliminating it in society.

While attending college in India in the early 1960s, I purchased a Bible on a narrow, dirt village street of Tambaram from a man named M. Joseph. Born the son of an "untouchable" beggar, M. Joseph learned about Christ through a missionary from the United States. His life had been transformed and he had devoted his life to spreading the "Good News." Many an evening I saw him stand beside his table of Bibles and proclaim their value to passers-by. Once he told me that many people refused to buy Bibles because they had heard of racial prejudice, segregation, and violence in the United States. If that is what it means to be Christian, they said, they did not want to know about Christ. "If you believe in God's revelation in Christ," pleaded M. Joseph, "then do something when you get home to change the situation. And please tell your good American Christian friends to do something too." Racism has been and continues to be a major stumbling stone discouraging Christian evangelism.

Racism manifests itself in expressions of fear about the Japanese buying too many properties in the United States. Two purchases in 1989 by "foreigners" are illustrative. When Mitsubishi Estate Company bought controlling interest in Rockefeller Center, it was front page news and prominently mentioned on all three network evening news programs. However, when a British firm, Bass PLC, bought fourteen hundred

Holiday Inns across America, paying twice the amount of the Rockefeller Center deal ($2.3 billion), the story was buried in the financial pages and never mentioned on television network news programs. Britain far exceeds Japan as a property holder in the United States, but great fear and prejudice is expressed toward the Japanese.

Worldwide, the ugly head of racism appears in almost every culture, with the majority imposing its will and prejudices on the minority. In 1990, when the World Council of Churches convened a consultation in Seoul, Korea, on justice, peace, and the integrity of creation, the participants cited the need for combating racism as one of its four highest priorities. Far from being a world house, the globe is divided by racial and ethnic fences.

Women are excluded systematically from positions of influence and authority in many churches and cultures, their dignity denied and their calls from God for the ministry rejected by a patriarchal dominated church. Compared to the ordained ministry, missionary service has offered more of an equal opportunity vocation. Gender discrimination and suffering, however, have inflicted women in missionary service as well. Church women established their own missionary organizations due to discrimination. Without constant vigilance, mission agencies often overlook the needs of women and children. Isabella Thoburn almost failed to establish her famous school for women in India, because her brother Bishop James Thoburn, refused to recognize her missionary calling to education work as valid and, thus, kept her busy doing secretarial work. Rosalind and Jonathan Goforth lost five of their eleven children in infancy or early childhood. When she resisted travel to remote Chinese villages for fear of the health of their children, Jonathan threatened that she would be punished by God if she did not obey.[10] In 1989 the Southern Baptists would not return a divorced woman to her mission post, even though they acknowledged that she was the victim of adultery![11]

An estimated 58 percent of all Christians will live in Two-Thirds World countries by the year 2000, compared to the beginning of the twentieth century when 85 percent of all Christians lived in the West. David J. Hesselgrave reports that the percentage of evangelicals in the West (including Eastern Europe) has been declining while rapidly rising elsewhere. Since 1980 the Two-Thirds World evangelicals have outnumbered those in Europe and North America.[12] Yet it has been very difficult until recently for these Christians to be included in world assemblies or for their theological ideas to be heard.

As Christianity's center of gravity shifts from the economically rich One-Third World to the poorer Two-Thirds World, we can anticipate changes. On certain matters, Two-Thirds World Christianity supports more conservative (e.g., sexual mores) standards, but on others, more radical (e.g., social justice) positions. As the editor of *The Economist* notes:

The new majority sees itself as dispossessed. Their savior is not the triumphalist Christ the king of old Christendom. New Christendom's savior is Jesus the liberator, the crusader against injustice. He will comfort the afflicted and afflict the comfortable.[13]

The development of liberation theologies by Christians all over the world indicates these changes. The theology and history of mission and ministry is no longer written solely by white Westerners.

When the first great world mission conference convened in Edinburgh, Scotland, in 1910, Caucasian men dominated. No women served among the twelve hundred delegates, despite the existence of powerful women's missionary organizations. Very few "natives" of the areas then designated as "mission fields" participated. In contrast, in 1989, the ninth ecumenical mission enclave in San Antonio, Texas, overwhelmingly represented the Two-Thirds World, and women members composed 41 percent.[14] The conference program and its resolutions integrated themes of social justice and evangelism. The entrails of Europeanism were evident at the 1989 evangelical world mission conference called "Lausanne II" though held in Manila, Philippines. Although it bore the name of a Swiss city, the large number of Two-Thirds World participants and the social justice resolutions adopted signaled a seismic shift in the evangelical center of gravity. The sessions manifested a minimum of hostility toward the World Council of Churches. A joint ecumenical/ evangelical world mission conference appears as a distinct and hopeful possibility in the immediate years ahead.

Fence movers confront great opposition and hostility to including gays and lesbians in the Christian community. Despite social science findings suggesting that possibly as many as one in every ten persons may have a homosexual orientation, ecumenical and evangelical Christians often share an emotional and ethical antipathy toward homosexuality. Though Jesus apparently opposed divorce in three of the four Gospels, and theologians opposed divorce for the first seventeen hundred years of Christian history, fortunately both evangelical and ecumenical churches now have adopted a more humane and understanding position on this issue. Yet when faced with homosexuality, a subject on which Jesus said nothing, most Christians suddenly become biblical literalists when they interpret five scattered biblical passages regarding certain homosexual practices. Despite propensities for championing social justice and civil rights issues, ecumenical conferences and leaders generally avoid prophetic statements or actions on this question. Homosexual persons and their families experience treatment as nonpersons, like the "lepers" of biblical times and the "untouchables" of India. Like the mandatory circumcisers of old, churches condition acceptance and grace on heterosexuality or, at least, chastity, before they welcome persons into the church and its leadership.

Efforts by the predominantly gay and lesbian denomination, the Metropolitan Community Church, to join the National Council of Churches have met only delaying tactics and outright opposition. Likewise, because of prejudice and homophobia, churches have responded exceedingly slowly to the health needs of persons with Acquired Immune Deficiency Syndrome (AIDS). Amid a global threat of immense proportions, the church has not distinguished itself either in promoting programs to help in preventing the disease or caring for persons living with the virus.

The true story of a young man dying from AIDS in an Atlanta, Georgia hospital illustrates the difference between fence makers and fence movers. Abandoned by his family, the patient lay alone during these crucial hours. Concerned nurses asked a visiting clergyman to speak to him. To their horror, the pastor stopped at the doorway and simply shouted a prayer, asking God's forgiveness for this prodigal son. After hearing of this incident, a seminarian in training at the hospital hurried immediately to the patient's room. Entering, she spoke gently and held the man in her arms until he died. Later friends inquired: "Sally, whatever did you do during that long wait?" "Oh," she replied, "I prayed; I quoted Scripture; I sang hymns; and I kept telling him how very much God loved him."[15]

Engaging Other Faiths

The fences Christians face as they consider "crossing the theological Rubicon" in relating to persons of other faiths present even more controversial and perplexing problems. In a global village, we require a theology of religions—ways to articulate our faith amid global religious plurality—in order to avoid world havoc and to advance a world house. The Gulf War in the Middle East dramatically spotlighted the appalling ignorance of most Christians about Islam and Judaism and the incredible danger war poses to both human life and the environment. The alternatives to the future seem clear: death or dialogue. Unless monologue yields to dialogue, fear, hate, and misunderstanding will multiply and will threaten all of creation with annihilation.[16] Dialogue must forever replace diatribe.

My own exposure to persons of other world faiths began at age twenty when I left Dakota Wesleyan University to study at Madras Christian College in southern India. My year-long journey abroad helped me begin to overcome my parochial perspectives and to discover for the first time the variety of religious expressions in the world. One cannot live in the homes of Muslim and Hindu friends and not realize that God, in different ways and in distinct expressions, touches with love all peoples of all religions in all cultures. I am persuaded that humanity yearns for God's *shalom* and that the religions of the world provide the spiritual basis for justice, peace, and the integrity of creation.

Engaging and understanding other faiths dare not remain simply the esoteric prerogative of the scholar, but must become an essential prerequisite for ministry. Religious diversity and pluralism characterize contemporary cultures and nations. In the United States, Islam may pass Judaism as the second largest religion. Muslims outnumber Episcopalians and Buddhists may total more than Presbyterians. Yet generally, churches and seminaries live in isolation from these vital foci of spiritual life and thought. Thus when The Iliff School of Theology appointed a Buddhist to the faculty, we watched in amazement how this action threatened some church members. However, if interfaith relationships fail to be expressed and embodied in the theological schools that prepare persons for ministry, then the probability diminishes that these pastors and other religious leaders will be able to engage, understand, and work with other religious communities.

In relating to other world religions, Christians may manifest extreme anxiety due to a fear of syncretism, absorption, loss of missionary vocation, compromising the faith, or simply because faith and practices differ. This fear surfaced when South Korean theologian, Chung Hyun Kyung identified a Korean Buddhist bhodisattva with the third person of the Trinity during a dramatic address at the 1991 Canberra Assembly of the World Council of Churches in Australia.[18]

Psychologically, phobias are exaggerated and often disabling fears that create high anxiety and prompt persons to experience an intense desire to avoid feared situations, people, or ideas.[17] People may be described as suffering from agoraphobia (fear of contact with other people), hydrophobia (fear of water), claustrophobia (fear of enclosed spaces), or acrophobia (fear of heights).

When looking for a word to describe the genuine and obsessive fear many Christians have of engaging persons of other faiths, I have explored terms like *heathenaphobia* (fear of anything but Christianity), *allophobia* (fear of the other) and *theophobia* (fear of other gods).[19] None quite fit, but I am inclined toward the latter, if one understands *theophobia* as fear of other religions. Theophobia is foreign to the community of fence movers. They do not fear other religions, but openly seek ways to engage in dialogue and cooperation with differing faith perspectives.

In the decades ahead, no missional issue may divide evangelical and ecumenical Christians more than the question of interfaith dialogue and relationships. The limits of this book do not permit an extensive analysis of the vast literature and debate on this subject; however, three basic positions can be identified. The *exclusivist* perspective with regard to world religions argues that Christianity is utterly unique or absolute. Salvation comes through Christ only. Other traditions may be avenues of God's saving love, but in themselves they remain inadequate. In missional theology, Karl Barth and Henrik Kraemer have articulated this viewpoint.

The *inclusivist* position contends that Christ's normative saving love exists incognito in all the world's religions. God in Christ is manifest or latent in all religions. Jesus remains universal and decisive, but not absolute and exclusive. For example, Catholic theologian Karl Rahner speaks of anonymous Christians among other religions. The *pluralist* posture views Christianity as one religion among many, an expression of God's reaching out to humanity and, in return, persons responding to God's grace. Wilfred Cantwell Smith and John Hick insist that Christians move away from claiming the superiority or finality of Christ and Christianity. Rosemary Ruether and Marjorie Suchocki suggest that to declare Christ or Christianity the "norm" for all religions is just as exploitive as attempting to make male experience the normative criterion for all of humanity. The crossing of this theological Rubicon stimulates major controversy within the community of fence movers.[20]

Former President Jimmy Carter exemplifies what it means to be a Christian fence mover, who evolved from exclusivism to inclusiveness, if not pluralism, without rejecting his Christian commitments. Well-known for his "born-again" Baptist convictions, Sunday school teaching, and church involvement, Carter volunteers each year to build and restore houses with Habitat for Humanity. As President, he presided over the extraordinary Camp David agreements that brought a framework for peace between Egypt and Israel. Since leaving office, he has worked for justice and peace by seeking to negotiate diplomatic differences around the globe.

Carter portrays himself as emerging from "a parochial experience, where you are sure you are right, you know that your particular religious interpretation is certain, and those who disagree with you are somehow inferior in the eyes of God." Early in his life, he believed that missionaries from Plains Baptist Church should be sent to Latin America to convert Catholics to be Baptists. Carter reports that:

Since then, as I've developed a broader perspective, I have begun to see two or three things, and without being overly glib about it, one is that there is a lot of commonality among religions. Almost all of them call for justice, peace, service, equality, some humility. And the finer aspects of our faith are expressed in those terms. But at the same time I have become aware that many of the horrendous wars of history, and today, are caused by conflicts in religious beliefs. And an additional factor is that the "true believers" have very little inclination to accept contrary opinion.

Reflecting on his Camp David experiences with Egypt's President Anwar Sadat and Israel's Prime Minister Menachem Begin, Carter describes how interreligious dialogue influenced international diplomacy. He believes their common faith in the God of Islam, Judaism, and Christianity made a major difference. Sadat was the first Muslim believer, Carter says, with whom he ever engaged in extensive conversation. In fact, Carter claims that Sadat first "pointed out to me that his was a faith of peace, of reconciliation, of brotherhood, the same principles found in the faith of other people of the Book, Jews and Christians."

While many Christians will continue to suffer from "theophobia" and missiologists and theologians will dispute distinctions and differences, three devout laymen (a Muslim, a Jew, and a Christian) have provided a lasting witness of practical theology. They demonstrated what can happen when persons transcend their religious parochialism and prejudices to engage in dialogue. And did President Carter fall into heresy, syncretism, or compromising the faith? James M. Wall of *The Christian Century*, who interviewed Carter, concludes:

And each Sunday, if he is in Plains, Jimmy Carter teaches the Baptist Church's adult Sunday school class. The former president's appreciation for, and openness to, Jews and Muslims with whom he has dealt around the world has not changed his basic orientation. Discussing his weekly lessons, he says they cover "the plan of salvation." No compromise there, just plain, direct proclamation.[21]

Dialogians of the Faith

Christians as a community of fence movers realize that monologue cannot be the language of God's loving and liberating mission of ministry. Our God is a God of dialogue, seeking to hear and heal the world's wounded and to share the grace of life and love. The dialogic teaching style of Jesus that responded to a person's greatest fears and confronted people at their deepest levels of spiritual and human need instructs us. Christian fence movers do not pretend to know all the answers to the world's problems, but they express an openness to seek and to find solutions with others.

Dialogians of the faith reflect the spirit of John Wesley's famous sermon on "The Catholic Spirit" (Sermon XXXIV). Wesley recalled a kind of interfaith conversation recorded in II Kings between Jehu and Jehonadab, a fanatical Yahwist and the founder of an extremist sect opposed to the sedentary culture of the Canaanites.[22] Though the two men represent opposing perspectives, Jehu asks: "Is thine heart right, as my heart is with thy heart?" And Jehonadab answers: "It is." "If it be, then give me thine hand" (II Kings 10:15, KJV).

Commenting on this text, Wesley asserted that persons will reflect different minds in religion as well as in everyday life—"So it has been from the beginning of the world and so it will be 'till the restitution of all things.' " Wesley recognized the fallibility of all human thinking, including the differing ways persons worship. Instead of being dogmatic, Wesley was dialogical, saying: "We must both act as each is fully persuaded in his own mind. Hold you fast that which you believe is most acceptable to God and I will do the same." A high point of the universal love theology for interfaith relations comes when Wesley adds:

Love me not in word only but in deed and in truth so far as in conscience thou canst (retaining thine own opinions, thine own manner of worshipping God) join with me in the work of God and let us go on hand in hand, . . . Speak honourably wherever thou are, of the work of God by whomsoever he works and kindly of his messengers.

A Christian community of fence movers, entrusted with the challenge of creating Martin Luther King's "world house" of "black and white, Easterner and Westerner, Gentile and Jew, Catholic and Protestant, Moslem and Hindu" in justice and peace can build upon the heritage and theology of Christianity. Wesley's eighteenth-century words fit the contemporary context of dialogue:

While he is steadily fixed in his religious principles, on what he believes to be the truth as it is in Jesus; while he firmly adheres to that worship of God which he judges to be the most acceptable in His sight, and while he is united in the tenderest and closest ties to one particular congregation—his heart is enlarged towards all mankind, those he knows and those he does not; he embraces with strong and cordial affection neighbours and strangers, friends and enemies. This is catholic or universal love. And he that has this is of a catholic spirit. For love alone gives the title to this character: catholic love is a catholic spirit.

With hearts enlarged with love, communities of fence movers do not fear dialogue with those who differ from themselves. As Christians, our affection for Christ often results in the use of love language. The Bible flows with wonderful metaphorical expressions of the ways in which God's people speak of the divine. With hearts overflowing with appreciation, early Christians ascribed their highest honors and titles to Jesus. Much of the New Testament might be described as love letters. This confessional language differs from propositional or philosophical language. As Paul F. Knitter suggests, "the titles and images given to Jesus by the early church are better understood as literary-symbolic rather than literal-definitive attempts to say who Jesus was for them."[23]

When I tell my wife that she is "the most wonderful woman in the world," or my children that they "are the best on the whole earth," I am speaking love language, not necessarily offering empirical descriptions verifiable by others. I am speaking from my heart of what I feel and know to be true. Likewise when I share my Christian convictions and express my deepest feelings for Christ, the hyperboles of my language may exceed what I can rationally justify or demonstrate. Presumably other devotees, whether Muslim, Buddhist, Hindu or of other faiths, will utter the language of love as they communicate their deepest spirituality and beliefs. A problem only arises, says Wesley Ariarajah, "when we take these confessions in the language of faith and love and turn them into absolute truths. . . . begin to measure the truth or otherwise of other faith-claims."[24] For me to speak about my wife and family in extravagant terms of love seems appropriate, but I should not then begin to judge others in the neighborhood by that norm! If hearts are enlarged by love, then dialogue focuses not on diminishing another's faith, but rather on engaging that spirituality for deeper understanding, mutual enrichment, and the search for truth.

We engage in dialogue with others not with a tourist's mentality or simply as a recreational adventure or a game of religious one-upmanship, but instead as an effort to enhance our understanding and to find new ways of cooperation. Conversion of any person may occur in the process because honest dialogians of the faith remain open for change as truth leads. The potentiality for new life and vision always exists as people seek to discover God's liberating love in their lives and universe.

Indeed we live in a new world, fraught with perils and possibilities. We must remove dividing fences. Toxic theologies poisoning human relationships must be overcome. Never before has humanity contemplated both the end of the earth and the end of nature. As we prepare for the twenty-first century, we must have a new generation of apostles, ordained clergy and committed laity, who are not only theologians, but dialogians of the faith. Inclusiveness does not respond to a passing phenomenon. Neither does ecumenism reflect an esoteric enterprise, nor interreligious concerns represent an idiosyncratic intellectualism, but both reflect the quest for global unity and understanding on the frontiers of the church's mission and ministry. In the spirit of John Wesley, a community of fence movers declares: "If your heart is as my heart, give me your hand."

As a guide, dialogians of the faith can utilize four principles of dialogue drafted by the British Council of Churches and developed by Kenneth Cracknell.[25] *The first asserts that dialogue begins when people meet each other.* This means people meeting and talking with people, not abstract systems or theoretical religions in conversation. No single person ever represents the totality of any faith, but simply speaks from their own perspective and experience. We engage people, not stereotypes or categories. Labels identify cans, not people.

This approach contrasts sharply with how the Christian theological "giants" functioned in previous generations. Their textbook knowledge of other religions actually proved to be a type of ignorance. Sri Lankan theologian, D. T. Niles, reports that at his first meeting with Karl Barth in 1935, Barth declared, "other religions are just unbelief." Niles asked: "How many Hindus, Dr. Barth, have you met?" Barth replied: "No one." Niles next queried: "How then do you know that Hinduism is unbelief?" Barth said: "A priori." Niles simply shook his head and smiled.[26]

Second, dialogue depends upon mutual understanding and mutual trust. Dialogue seeks to overcome misunderstanding and to develop friendship. The language one uses is meant to heal, not inflame. People should define themselves in their own terms with care taken to ensure that people describe their own faith. False interpretations of what people say or think or feel undermines mutual understanding and trust. Dismissing with a cavalier attitude the ideas or religious beliefs of another only undercuts the process.

Regrettably, persons entering dialogue sometimes appear eager to find fault with others, questioning motives or integrity. Rhetorical questions are raised not in order to learn but to embarrass, confuse, or harass others. Joy apparently prevails in proving another wrong or exposing an extreme position in their argument. Intensifying polarization never leads to greater trust and understanding.

Third, dialogue makes it possible to share in service to the community. Dialogue represents an expression of love to God and neighbor, caring enough to engage in an exploration for understanding. It is not a secret weapon or propaganda tool, but a way to reduce barriers and move fences. Only through dialogue can persons of differing perspectives transcend divisions sufficiently so they can labor together for mutual purposes. Reflective action, not just intellectual contemplation, emerging from dialogue can lead to steps to stop suffering, oppression, and death.

Fourth, dialogue becomes the medium of authentic witness. Dialogue happens not just for dialogue's sake nor as ecumenical entertainment in the endless carnival of church meetings. We must speak the truth in love. People must have open commitments, not concealed ideologies. Manipulation is *verboten*; it is a time for sharing from one's heart and mind. When persons witness to each other, the possibility of conversion always exists. As Lesslie Newbigin says, "A dialogue which is safe from all possible risks is no true dialogue."[27]

Moving, Not Removing, Fences

Not every Christian finds moving fences sufficient; they favor the more radical response of removing fences. They argue that the time has come to cross the theological Rubicon and to embrace a pluralism with no barriers or distinctions. Others tire of gender, ethnic, and racial sensitivities and goals, yearning for less attention to these dimensions. Some claim denominationalism is dead, while others assert that the euphoria over ecumenism has faded. Let us remove the boundaries or at least pretend they do not exist.

However, critical differences and distinctions remain that we cannot ignore or wish away into utopia. We have not erased the obvious and latent consequences of racism and sexism. We can ensure the inclusiveness we seek only with intentional action. Desires for Christian unity and interreligious understanding do not diminish the differences that exist. Not all religious beliefs and practices are true or worthwhile or humane. We do not advance critical thinking or spiritual goodwill by degrading our own Christian beliefs or by pretending that theological differences and distinctions between Christians and among the religions of the world do not exist. We are who we are—a Christian community of fence movers. We make no apologies for our witness to Jesus Christ and our love of Christ's church.

Although certain fences may remain, we must openly explore ways to see how they may be moved toward creating greater understanding, goodwill, justice, and peace. Let our fences not be new Berlin Walls, guarded by snarling dogs of dogma and scholarly soldiers of orthodoxy. Rather keep our fences so low that good neighbors can lean across them for dialogue and on occasion even leap over them. Allow for gates aplenty to encourage us to move borders and discover what God is doing among other peoples and religions.

Impatient with the restrictive fences of cultural and national boundaries, some Christians encourage trespassing. They send missionaries from their denomination, or their ideological wing of the denomination, into the same countries or areas where their denomination is already established or has assented to ecumenical agreements with other Christians. Restrictions on types of mission, evangelism and social service do exist and need to be recognized, if not respected. Past missionary practices have created negative legacies in certain countries. Fears that proselytization undermines societal cohesion creates other fences. Politicians use concern for social stability in places like Singapore, China, and elsewhere to justify limitations on missionary activity and evangelism. Religious majorities refuse to grant full religious freedom to others in their nations. Lest Christians be too anxious to condemn and remove others' fences, may the Holocaust and Hiroshima serve as symbolic reminders that Christianity, like other world religions, has often failed to demonstrate an ethical superiority in its lived existence.

Fence moving can become imperialistic and paternalistic if we presume that we know more than we do and carelessly intervene in the cultures and churches of other peoples. Finding the appropriate balance between moving and removing fences is never simple. Missionaries now come from other countries to Europe and North America, but the vast majority of Protestant mission agencies are still based in the West. Of the eighty-one thousand Protestant missionaries around the world, North America accounts for approximately sixty-seven thousand—more than double the number serving in 1960.[28] The vast increase in numbers has not occurred in mainline denominations, but among evangelical and fundamentalist groups.

In recent years, churches and mission agencies have shifted power and authority to the local, indigenous, self-governing Christian congregations around the world as a way of attempting to struggle with issues of imperialism and paternalism. The missionary becomes a potential servant of the receiving church, not a power symbol of the sending church. The missionary becomes a gift from one community of Christians to another, expressing mutual caring and symbolizing what Christ did in another church or culture. This philosophical shift (along with other factors such as the end of colonialism, calls for a "moratorium" on sending missionaries, new government restrictions, declines in missionary support, etc.) has reduced the number of missionaries requested by many receiving churches. Mainline denominations in the United States affiliated with the National Council of Churches have witnessed a significant reduction in the number of lifetime missionaries (from 8,279 to 4,349 from 1969 to 1989).[29]

Critics of this approach stress the "terrible failure of nerve about the missionary enterprise" in many circles today. They believe ecumenical Christians have become "overly sensitive" to the complaints registered about previous mission "insensitivities" and have irresponsibly withdrawn in the face of global ambiguities. Two billion (80 percent) of the "unreached peoples" of the world are separated by significant barriers with no local Christian churches or missionaries among them. Those persuaded by an "exclusivist" theology of Christianity contend that denominations should have moved boldly ahead and not reduced their missionary personnel. Great mission opportunities now beckon the global church as the high restrictive fences surrounding the former Soviet Union and Eastern Europe are dismantled. "Unreached peoples" will never receive the gospel of Christ unless someone crosses those frontiers or fences.[30]

Evangelistic work and church growth, however, do not necessarily correspond with increases in numbers of missionaries from other countries. China experienced its greatest growth in church membership after the exclusion of missionaries. The Pentecostals, who utilize relatively few missionaries from abroad, represent the fastest growing churches on the South American continent (and worldwide).[31] Generally, evangelism and church growth prove most effective when nationals, who understand and participate in the culture and country, direct these activities. K. P. Yohanna of India notes that only 20 percent of North American missionaries engage in evangelism in his country. For the amount of remuneration one missionary receives, the churches could employ thirty Indian Christian evangelists.[32] Although perhaps too simplistic a response to financial problems, he raises questions about alternative approaches to sending missionaries and responsible steward-ship of funds. We must not dismiss the value of crossing cultural and national barriers; but the euphoria of increasing the number of missionaries must be balanced by the responsible economics of optimal investment of mission monies.

Beyond Borders

Floating above the earth in outer space, astronauts frequently observe and comment on the absence of artificial borders separating peoples and nations. The ecological unity of all of God's creation appears evident. The world truly is God's body. Fences are real, but ultimately artificial, and a community of fence movers faces the challenge of finding ways for God's loving and liberating ways to break through the barriers. It has been noted that:

We are called to the border to follow the One who crosses all boundary lines and tears down all barriers. Jesus was a Jew who dared befriend Samaritans, a carpenter who did not hesitate to challenge scholars, a male who was sensitive to women's experience, an activist who prayed continually, a Nazarene who confronted the power structure in Jerusalem. Jesus showed special concern for the poor and the marginalized, yet knew how to speak to the powerful. He stood rooted in the past while giving birth to a new heaven and a new earth.[33]

Being a fence mover means participating in the missional character of ministry with global gardeners, star throwers, and Christians building bridges. These metaphors of mission do not pretend to be exclusive or exhaustive of the possibilities, but rather reflective of the potentiality of rethinking and revisioning the church's role in the world. In light of global challenges and catastrophes, no single image suffices. Each metaphorical dimension is needed if the body of Christ is to discern and join in God's liberating and loving initiatives. Being a contemporary apostle of Jesus Christ signifies giving one's life in a divine conspiracy of goodness.

CHAPTER EIGHT

A Conspiracy of Goodness

If you save one life, you save the whole world.
TALMUD

The Baal Shem-Tov, the founder of Hasidism, once said, "In remembrance resides the secret of redemption." If one finds the secret of redemption in remembering, then one loses it in forgetting.

All of us know the horrible history of the Holocaust when six million Jews perished, along with countless other persecuted minorities such as political opponents of the Nazis, homosexual persons, gypsy people and others. Auschwitz and Dachau symbolize Hell, representative of the ultimate degradation of humanity. Most of us, however, know little about those relatively few Christians and others who defied authorities under the penalty of possible death in order to rescue Jews and other persecuted persons. In a time when the future of the world and all God's creation is endangered, it becomes imperative that we not forget the "weapons of the spirit" they used. The secret of our redemption may reside in remembering their conspiracy of goodness.

The Witness of Christian Rescuers

Philip P. Hallie in *Lest Innocent Blood Be Shed* shares the story of a French Protestant community, Le Chambon, that sheltered and saved about twenty-five hundred Jewish people during the World War II occupation. He probes the questions of why and how a small village in France, under the leadership of a pastor, became what he calls the safest place for Jews in Europe. Not a single act of betrayal occurred. Why, when so many in the world remained indifferent, did these few villagers in France rise to the necessity of doing good?

145

In a time when Nazis were breaking and rebreaking the bones of six- and seven- and eight-year-old Jewish children in cruel experiments to study the natural processes of healing in young bodies, how was it that others risked themselves, their families, and their community to rescue Jewish children with no thought whatsoever of converting them to their Christian faith? These Huguenot Protestants refashioned their community into an Old Testament "city of refuge," re-enacted the story of the Good Samaritan, and resisted the Nazis with nonviolence in accord with the Sermon on the Mount. Hallie discovered that if you asked "why did Le Chambon do these things . . . while the nearby Protestant village of Le Mazet did not?", the people always responded: "It was Pastor André Trocmé."

Hallie identifies Reverend André and Magda Trocmé of Le Chambon as signposts of faith, hope, and dignity. He tells their story of transforming a small community into a center of rescue, when they befriended strangers, shared scarce food, risked death, and persuaded others to follow their leadership in caring for the outcasts. Le Chambon was considered an obscure, unimportant, "backwater" parish when Pastor Trocmé received his assignment as pastor. Through their missional ministry André and Magda bequeathed a lasting legacy of love to the world.

Once when the authorities came with buses to arrest the refugees, Pastor Trocmé was told that they knew he was hiding Jews. They asked him to provide the officials a list of names and to help in the roundup. He was threatened with arrest and deportation. To this Trocmé replied: "These people have come here seeking aid and protection from the Protestants of this region. I am their pastor, their shepherd. It is not the role of a shepherd to betray the sheep confided to his keeping."[1] Instead he mobilized the leaders of his Bible study classes and the Boy Scouts and organized the "disappearance of the Jews" into the woods as planned in advance.

Rabbi Harold M. Schulweis and the Jewish Foundation for Christian Rescuers estimate that in World War II up to one million Jews were rescued. The Encyclopedia of the Holocaust says twenty thousand "righteous Gentiles" assisted the Jews, but Rabbi Schulweis believes there were at least fifty thousand "righteous Gentiles" and possibly up to five hundred thousand.[2] In other words, only one out of four hundred Europeans at best provided assistance, and some estimate only one out of every four thousand in these predominantly Christian nations. In recognition of this courageous remnant, a Holocaust Memorial called Yad Vashem has been erected outside Jerusalem where eight thousand are honored in the "Alley of the Righteous."

The largest and most dramatic rescue occurred in Denmark where 90 percent of the eight thousand Jews were saved. Led by King Christian X, the entire population conspired against the Nazis. When the invaders ordered Jews to wear the Star of David, the king displayed one on his clothing and urged all citizens to do likewise. Seminarians hand-delivered a letter of defiance and resistance from the Lutheran bishops, and pastors read it from their pulpits across the land

> Why Denmark? It was because of the Church;
> and clergymen who dared to speak out and to demand
> greatness from their people; and individual
> Christians who were willing to risk their own
> lives to save their brothers and sisters.

> Why Denmark? It was because of the King.
> When King Christian X was asked about the Jewish
> Question he replied: "There is no Jewish
> Question. There are only my people."

> Why Denmark? It was because of the people.
> They said "The Jews are our countrymen." They
> elevated patriotism to a noble height.[3]

Besides the Danes and the people of Le Chambon, historical evidence exists recording the heroic, caring activities of others who conspired to save Jews and others destined for death by the Nazis. The final fate of the Swedish diplomat, Raoul Wallenberg, still remains unknown. By the age of thirty-two he was manufacturing and distributing bogus Swedish passports. Called "an angel in hell," his personal mission to save Jews resulted in at least thirty thousand, and possibly one hundred thousand escaping death. Though he rescued so many, he himself perished—apparently in a Soviet prison.

The names of many Christian rescuers are lost, but we know some who conspired for goodness. A Dutch woman, Miep Gies, recently received Germany's highest medal for civilians because of her crucial role in hiding Anne Frank and her family. Bruno Reynders, a Catholic Belgian monk, engineered a huge operation that created false baptismal and identification papers that saved an estimated 350 Jewish children from death camps.

The Bulgarian Orthodox Church and the Bulgarian Parliament defied the Nazis and refused to deport the Jews. Bishop Kiril threatened to lead a campaign of civil disobedience and promised to lie down himself on the railroad tracks to stop the trains from carrying Jews to death camps.

The Nazis arrested the Catholic priest Bernard Lichtenberg of St. Heldwig's Cathedral in Berlin for subversive activities. He insisted on joining the Jews being deported and died on the way to Dachau. Father Charles Devaus headed a Catholic missionary organization in France that saved 443 Jewish children and 500 adults. Nuns in Belgium arranged private homes for Jewish children after the Gestapo learned that the sisters had concealed the youngsters in their convent.

The Citizens of Assisi, the home of St. Francis, sheltered Jews in their ancient monasteries and convents. Jewish refugees accepted fake identity papers, dressed in religious habits, received rosaries, and became temporarily transformed into monks and nuns piously saying their prayers. False documents, sent through Italy, helped protect some thirty-two thousand Italian Jews, representing 80 percent of Italian Jewry.[4]

Ordinary people acted in extraordinary ways to hide Jews in their homes, monasteries, attics, schools, barnyards, pigsties, and sewers. A Dutch rescuer used the expression, "the conspiracy of goodness," when he asked: "Do you think that I could have hidden that Jewish family without the knowledge and the cooperation of the grocer, the milkman, the policeman?" They acted under the threat of death. How many Christian rescuers the Nazis martyred we do not know. However we do know that officials killed ninety-six Polish men in the village of Bialo for hiding and feeding Jews, and in Stary Ciepielow, the Nazis forced twenty-three Polish men, women, and children into a barn and burned them alive because they had protected Jews.

The evil of the Holocaust should never be minimized, but neither should the goodness of the rescuers be forgotten. As Rabbi Schulweis notes "Goodness challenges us in a way that evil does not." If I compared myself to Adolf Eichmann, I am a saint. But if I compare myself to the Christian rescuers, how do I measure up?

Would I unlock the door? Would I take into my home a sick man, a pregnant woman, a frightened family, and keep them for days, weeks, months or years, knowing that if the Nazis discovered my act they'd imprison, torture and perhaps even kill my family?[5]

The witness of all these faithful people gives credibility to Christians when we sing:

> We've a story to tell to the nations,
> that shall turn their hearts to the right,
> a story of truth and mercy,
> a story of peace and light,
> For the darkness shall turn to dawning,
> and the dawning to noon-day bright;
> and Christ's great kingdom shall come on earth,
> the kingdom of love and light.

Mission as a Conspiracy of Goodness

We usually associate words like *conspire* and *conspiracy* with negative connotations. Literally *conspire* means "to breathe together" or work intimately together in joint action. When Christians respond to God's call to join in the divine mission of liberating love, the church engages in a conspiracy of goodness that transcends earthly political powers. The church in mission to the world runs the risk of being subversive, conspiring to bring good amid evil, compassion amid violence, and peace amid war.

We usually think a conspiracy involves secret planning to do something wrong or unlawful. The Christian rescuers committed unlawful acts by the norms of the Nazis, but not by the standards of God. Their civil disobedience conspiracy was "illegal," but not wrong. Instead they acted in the spirit of the Greek novelist Nikos Kazantzakis who wrote of signaling his companions "with a password, like conspirators," that they might unite for the sake of the earth.[6] They demonstrated what Pierre Teilhard de Chardin called a "conspiracy of love," seeking to raise the edifice of life.[7]

Conspirators of goodness emerged in Kuwait and Iraq during the Middle East War of 1991. Citizens of those countries, Muslim and Christian, sheltered Americans and other foreigners. Their stories have not yet been told and, unfortunately, many will be buried forever in history. One American hostage, however, reported in *Newsweek* that "they have fed and protected us and all other foreigners under the threat of hanging. Five members of one family were shot because the Iraqis found an American passport in their home on a search."[8]

The vision of church members as conspirators applies not only to the drastic life-and-death social and political situations confronting the globe, but also to the personal and pastoral dimensions of a missional ministry. Ironically, while I wrote this chapter, my family experienced what it means to be the focus of care by this conspiracy of goodness. My wife, Bonnie, suddenly was diagnosed as having a very large brain tumor, which required immediate surgery. As we rode a roller coaster of emotions over a period of weeks, we were sustained and strengthened by the "conspiracy of love" of which de Chardin spoke. We were overwhelmed by expressions of goodness and kindness from family, friends, students, professional colleagues, and church people from across the country. Reaching out to us, persons created an incredible chain of communication that literally encircled the earth. People we have never met wrote to say they were praying for her well-being. Her successful operation and complete recovery prompted us to sing the words of the old gospel hymn: "When nothing else could help, love lifted me."

At its best, the church responds as a conspiracy of goodness in the spirit and name of Christ to care for all persons and all of creation. Participating in deeds of kindness, justice, and mercy means identifying with God's liberating and loving initiatives in the world. We manage and maintain the structure of the church in order to express and extend its mission and ministry.

Weapons of the Spirit

In an era of unprecedented militarism and the potential of nuclear annihilation, I hesitate to use military metaphors, but clearly the Christian rescuers understood themselves as employing "the weapons of the spirit." Above all, they took seriously the words of Ephesians:

Put on the whole armor of God . . . . For we are not contending against flesh and blood, but against the principalities, against the powers, against the world rulers of this present darkness . . . . Therefore take the whole armor of God, that you may be able to withstand in the evil day . . . . Stand therefore, having girded your loins with truth, and having put on the breastplate of righteousness, and having shod your feet with the equipment of the gospel of peace; besides all these, taking the shield of faith. . . . And take the helmet of salvation, and the sword of the Spirit, which is the word of God. (Ephesians 6:11-17, RSV)

As we struggle and seek to live out our own lives with moral integrity and witness, as well as to lead communities to personal and social transformation, we need to appropriate "the weapons of the spirit" that motivated, inspired, sustained, and strengthened the Christian rescuers. Against these criteria we can measure our own understanding of the mission and ministry of the church today.

First, Christian rescuers acted on their conviction that no nonpersons exist in the family of God. All human life is sacred and inviolable. God creates all persons and cares for each and every one. The Divine demonstrates no partiality; every person is a child of God. Every war represents a civil war in a global village. Every person who dies is my sister or brother.

Christian rescuers during World War II saw persecuted Jewish people as their sisters and brothers. They resisted those who condemned to death gays, lesbians, gypsies, and others deemed unworthy. They experienced God in their encounters with those whom authorities labeled as nonpersons. They did not seek to convert Jews to Christianity, but to save Jews from death and to preserve Judaism from destruction. They opened their hearts and homes to the persecuted. Attitudes of superiority and exclusiveness contradicted their Christian faith.

Once a German-Jewish refugee approached a farm near Le Cambon to buy some eggs. A woman invited her into the kitchen. Quietly the woman who asked her to enter asked: "Are you Jewish?" Having been previously tortured for her Jewishness, she began to tremble. She became even more frightened when the woman began shouting up the stairs to her family: "Husband, children, come down, come down!" But her fear subsided as the family came down the stairs, and the woman declared: "Look, look, my family! We have in our house now *a representative of the Chosen People!*"[9]

Nonpersons exist not only in wartimes or in distant places; they dwell in all of our communities. They are the homeless, the retarded, the persons with handicapping conditions, persons with AIDS and their families and partners, prisoners and their families, the mentally ill, and drug addicts, to name but a few. Their names are legion. God offers liberating love unconditionally for all. Fence moving Christian rescuers concur with Carl Sandburg who once declared that "the ugliest word in the English language is the word *exclusive*."

Building bridges between diverse people was a second "weapon of the spirit" epitomized by Christian rescuers. When they saw a persecuted Jewish person or other oppressed minority, they remembered that Jesus said "I was a stranger, and you welcomed me" (Matthew 25:35). They believed the writer of Hebrews when he advised: "Do not neglect to show hospitality to strangers, for thereby some have entertained angels unawares" (Hebrews 13:1-2).

One reason Christian rescuers risked themselves and their relatives is because they viewed the Jews not as outsiders but as members of their own families. They epitomized the church as a collegiality of bridge builders by hosting strangers. When Philip Hallie asked the people of Le Chambon

why they helped these dangerous guests, they invariably answered, "What do you mean?, 'Why?' Where else could they go? How could they turn them away? What is so special about being ready to help . . . ? There was nothing else to do." And some of them laughed in amazement when I told them I thought they were "good people."[10]

But "they *were* nevertheless good people," declares John Koenig, "because they acted so consistently out of their own characters."[11] Two explanations account for their remarkable behavior. First, the Chambonnais were Huguenot Protestants, a marginal people in Catholic France, who empathized with the Jews because they too had been a despised and hunted-to-the-death minority. Second, their pastor, André Trocmé, never stopped reminding them that "every human being was like Jesus, had God in him or her, and was just as precious as God himself."[12]

Hospitality creates bridge building between strangers. Certainly since the earth is an endangered species, the imperative of finding ways to span the gaps between peoples becomes more urgent. Historically conflict characterizes relations between various religions. We have not yet realized the dream expressed one hundred years ago at the World Parliament of Religions in Chicago: "Henceforth, the religions of the world will make war not on each other but on the giant evils that afflict mankind!"[13] Tension and violence, reinforced by religious intolerance, permeate many cultures and nations. Visionary and courageous religious leaders must attempt to break out of past patterns, to rein in fanaticism of all faiths, to reduce the estrangement of minorities, and to enhance tolerance in every place. Persons of differing faiths need to investigate ways to affirm together shared commitments to justice, peace, and the integrity of creation. By incarnating a theology of Christian hospitality, Christians can contribute significantly to a global reduction of tensions and resolution of difficulties.

Third, the courage to care characterized Christian rescuers. Surely in Europe during World War II more than one-half of 1 percent (using the highest estimate) of the total Christian population living under Nazi occupation were good and decent folk, sympathetic and compassionate toward the Jews. But why did so few possess the courage to carry a "weapon of the spirit"?

Samuel P. and Pearl M. Oliner explored this question in their study of *The Altruistic Personality: Rescuers of Jews in Nazi Europe.* Noting that skeptics believe persons are incapable of acting out of any motive other than their own self-interest, or at best, enlightened self-interest, nevertheless they identified altruistic behavior when it involved a high risk or sacrifice, was accompanied by no external reward, and was voluntary. Heroically saving a drowning person or pulling people from burning buildings clearly represent altruistic actions. However, the altruism of Christian rescuers was distinguished by the duration of their activity, the fact that they were helping society's most condemned people, and the lack of cultural rewards for their actions.[14]

Not all rescuers were religious people, but they were all caring persons. When asked to help, they responded almost immediately, typically consulting no one else. Research indicates that helping Jews reflected deeply ingrained ethical principles that included all of humanity. These ethical principles, while incorporating concerns for equity and justice, were deeply rooted in care and inclusiveness.[15]

The Christians with the courage to care were primarily persons who had internalized the norms of their faith. The commandment to love one's neighbor had become an integral part of their being. Combined with an empathetic response to another person's pain and a sense of personal responsibility to do good, these persons responded with love in times of crisis. As Samuel P. and Pearl M. Oliner note, "the step from inclination to action is a large one," but "helping Jews was less a decision made at a critical juncture than a choice prefigured by an established character and way of life."[16]

Iris Murdoch contends that one cannot embrace ethical living during a particular crisis, but rather it takes place continuously in the small moments and habits of life. Hence, "at crucial moments of choice most of the business of choosing is already over."[17] Christian rescuers generally possessed the courage to care because they felt they "had no choice"; they just did what they had to do. They reasoned that the Jews and others had fallen "among thieves" and, as rescuers, they were called to be Good Samaritans.

Caretaking of God's body, the earth, requires similar courage and hope. A covenant of global gardeners demands altruistic actions if the earth is to avert ecological catastrophe. If apathy or indifference prevail in regard to nuclear proliferation, genetic experimentation, or global warming, then world havoc threatens to triumph over visions of a world house. The courage to care must ever distinguish Christian mission and ministry.

A fourth "weapon of the spirit" used by the Christian rescuers was nonviolent, noncooperative civil disobedience. Some Christian conspirators of goodness engaged in violent actions of resistance and sabotage, but their primary orientation focused on life, not death; love, not hatred. By dictionary definitions the Christian rescuers were indeed guilty of conspiracy in that they acted in defiance of what the governmental authorities deemed the law. But their Christian faith prompted them to obey the higher laws of God and inspired them to love, not destroy, their Jewish neighbors.

The Christian rescuers of Le Chambon put their little village in grave danger of massacre, especially in the last two years of the war as the Nazis grew increasingly desperate. Being nonviolent, they refused to join in the underground resistance armies. Faithfulness to their consciences meant jeopardizing their lives. For them:

Following their consciences meant refusing to hate or kill any human being. . . . human life was too precious to them to be taken for any reason, glorious and vast though that reason might be. Their consciences told them to save as many lives as they could, even if doing this meant endangering the lives of all the villagers; and they obeyed their consciences.[18]

In order to do good, the Christian rescuers became artists of deception and deceit. Some prided themselves on clever ways of technically not lying. One woman, for example, responding to a nosy and untrustworthy neighbor, declared: "I wouldn't have a single Jewish person in my house." In fact, she had two Jewish guests! They used coded language, such as saying "Three Old Testaments have arrived." This suspension of basic ethical patterns of life grieved faithful Christians, but they had no recourse in the situation if they hoped to save lives. They learned that the righteous often must sacrifice their own ethical purity and must experience "dirty hands" for the sake of goodness. They worried that by teaching their children to lie, the younger generation might never again know the importance of truth. Pastor Trocmé's daughter, Nelly, however, says that the children of Le Chambon never had trouble discerning between types of lying. They saw what was happening; people were being saved from death by lies. And the children were convinced this truly exemplified righteousness and goodness.[19]

The possibility of converting the "enemy" or opponent epitomizes the power of a nonviolent conspiracy. Both Mahatma Gandhi and Martin Luther King, Jr., stressed that courageous nonviolent love can change the attitudes of those on the opposite side. Some evidence suggests that both German and French leaders in the Le Chambon region knew what was happening, but did nothing to stop the conspiracy. Emboldened by the witness of these Christians, they too were converted to the conspiracy of saving Jews.

The Christian rescuers exemplified the peacemaking envisioned by a company of star throwers. At the heart of their faith, they sang a song of peace. They dedicated their lives to making peace, to encouraging reconciliation, and to establishing justice and harmony among peoples and nations. They were prepared to live amid the pain of misunderstanding and controversy. Contemporary missional leadership that seeks high Christian goals of justice, peace, and inclusiveness will find the path neither easy nor quick. Whether on the lonely shore of Costabel or the isolated village of Le Chambon, seeking to save the outcast means living without hope of immediate reward, but with a sense of the eternal.

Fifth, Christian rescuers were willing martyrs of their faith, open to conversions but opposed to proselytization. In documenting the willingness of rescuers to witness to their Christian faith, researchers have been impressed by how they internalized their values. The rescuers united love of God and love of neighbor not only in their minds and spirits, but in their words and deeds as well. Many died because they sought to save the Jews and others from annihilation.

The conservative, Bible-believing, evangelical Protestants of Le Chambon conspired against the Nazis because of their own great respect for human life, as mediated to them by the Old Testament and the teachings of Jesus. The Sermon on the Mount and the story of the Good Samaritan, both favorite biblical passages, informed their faith and inspired their actions.

The Christian rescuers did not attempt to convert those whose lives they sought to save. Hidden in monasteries and clothed as priests and nuns, complete with rosaries and prayer books, the Jews were encouraged to observe secretly their own religious holidays. The rescuers forbade the conversion of children to Christianity without the knowledge of their parents. Philip P. Hallie outlined Pastor Trocmé's basic principles regarding conversion and proselytization:

Help must never be given for the sake of propaganda; help must be given only for the benefit of the people being helped, not for the benefit of some church or other organization that was doing the helping. The life and the integrity of the person helped were more precious than any organization. And so Trocmé would never try to convert the Jewish refugees who came in need to Le Chambon.[20]

The conspiracy of goodness of the Christian rescuers serves as a contemporary model for the mission and ministry of the church. Amid great crisis, they responded in love and with justice to everyone in need. As we face the current global crises that threaten justice, peace, and the integrity of creation, they offer a model of how Christians and persons of differing faiths and perspectives might cooperate for sustaining life on this planet.

Sixth, this conspiracy of goodness by the Christian rescuers required leadership and organization. Individual efforts dare not be discounted, but combating social evil necessitated strategic planning, networks of contacts and financing, competent leadership, and high levels of trust and understanding. If ever a community of fence movers existed, who dared to move beyond established boundaries, certainly the Christian rescuers of Europe qualify.

Pastor Trocmé did not act as a solitary leader of noncooperation. He used the power of his pastoral office to organize the people of Le Chambon to resist the Nazis and to assist the Jews. His sermons stimulated the rescue efforts. He transformed Bible study groups into action agencies. After carefully choosing thirteen lay Bible group leaders, he met with them twice a week, not only to study the Scriptures, but to develop a system for sheltering and hiding refugees. Thus he engaged the whole community in weekly Bible study as well as practical planning on how to overcome evil with good. In these sessions they explored how the Good Samaritan story and the Sermon on the Mount related to their day-to-day decisions. Pastor Trocmé summarized the work of the *responsables* in his notes:

It was there, not elsewhere, that we received from God solutions to complex problems, problems we had to solve in order to shelter and to hide the Jews. . . . Nonviolence was not a theory superimposed upon reality; it was an itinerary that we explored day after day in communal prayer and in obedience to the commands of the Spirit.[21]

Creating and leading communities of faith that move from compassionate inclination to caring action presents a great challenge in our own time. In Civil War days, Christians helped operate an Underground Railroad to free the slaves. Missionaries globally challenged cultural customs that denigrated women and children. In recent years, courageous clergy and congregations have given sanctuary to refugees from Central America. Worldwide, Christians struggle with the dilemma of conscientious objection to war. We have yet to determine the courageous actions necessary to preserve the earth from toxic contamination and destruction, but pray that not only Greenpeace and other secular organizations, but also that Christians will take prophetic steps for protecting God's creation. The lessons learned from the Christian rescuers need reappropriating in the 1990s and beyond, if the church of Jesus Christ is to be true to God's mission and ministry.

How can we fathom such bravery? Yet the courage to care repeatedly manifests itself in the history of Christianity. As an example, when the Nazis ordered Christians to acknowledge Hitler's supremacy in Norway on Easter Sunday, the Bishop declared this unacceptable and closed all churches Easter morning. The Nazis were outraged at Christians for defying the Führer's command.

Easter afternoon the people of one community gathered in the town square and determined to march to the church to protest the Nazi action. As they walked, they also sang, drawing on the rich heritage of their faith. As they neared the church, they began singing Martin Luther's great hymn:

> A mighty fortress is our God,
> A bulwark never failing;
> Our helper he amid the flood
> Of mortal ills prevailing.
> For still our ancient foe
> Doth seek to work us woe;

Just as they reached the church steps, an S. S. man waved his submachine gun at them and ordered the Christians to stop. He pointed his gun directly at an impoverished pregnant women in front. "Make one more sound and she will be the first to die." Silence fell across the crowd. The pastor looked down; the church elders dropped their gaze to the dirt. Then suddenly a lone voice began to sing:

> Did we in our own strength confide,
> Our striving would be losing,
> Were not the right man on our side,
> The man of God's own choosing.

By then the whole crowd was singing and the Nazi had stepped back.

> Dost ask who that may be?
> Christ Jesus, it is he.

But who, you may ask, dared to sing and endanger the life of this woman? Why, who else but the woman herself. She possessed a faith that conquered fear and gave her the courage to care. A fence mover, she led her people in nonviolent, noncooperative civil disobedience.[22]

"Putting on the whole armor of God" and using the "weapons of the spirit" will call and challenge us as clergy and laity of Christ's church. If Christians living under the Nazi threat of death dare to engage in a conspiracy of goodness, can we in this time discover the requisite courage to care in our own churches and communities? Troubled as we are by our own complicity with militarism, genetic engineering, and environmental pollution, and recognizing our own ignorance and insensitivity to persons of other races, cultures, and religions, we need to find ways to be moral people in an immoral world. By remembering these Christian rescuers we may find the secret of our own redemption. By remembering their benevolent acts of goodness, and their unwillingness to do harm, we may catch a vision of alternative actions amid sinful structures and ambiguous historical moments.

Beyond Compassion Fatigue

The danger of compassion fatigue ever threatens. Difficulties occur because of the stubborn intransigence of the evils we deplore. We tire from the constant struggle against seemingly intractable forces. To borrow the words of St. Paul, we "grow weary from well-doing." How easy to lose one's idealistic heart and join the cynical on the sidelines of life. Thank God some people do not yield to their weariness and persistently struggle against all odds. Praise God for those who have affirmed in their own lives and work the full promise of Paul's words: "And let us not grow weary in well-doing: for in due season we shall reap, if we do not lose heart" (Galatians 6:9, RSV).

John Woolman, a young Quaker in the mid-1800s, refused to succumb to compassion fatigue even though he felt outrage at the fact that other Quakers owned slaves. He committed his life to persuading his people to free their slaves and to oppose slavery. For thirty years, mostly by foot (in protest of the treatment of post boys who cared for the horses), he visited Quaker slaveholders until 1770 when the Quakers finally renounced slavery—nearly one hundred years before the Civil War.[23] What if other Christians had also persisted in their well-doing and had not lost heart? Perhaps the inhumanity of slavery could have ended earlier without a war that resulted in six hundred thousand casualties?

William Proxmire of Wisconsin who recently retired from the United States Senate also refused to lose heart. Right after World War II, President Harry Truman asked the Senate to endorse a treaty outlawing genocide. The treaty committed the United States to work to prevent any attempt to destroy a national, ethnic, racial or religious group and to punish offenders. But for decades a handful of political conservatives kept the treaty from passing. Senator Proxmire was not dissuaded. Every legislative day from 1967 to 1988—twenty-one years!—he opened the Senate with a speech in favor of the treaty. Surely after he delivered some three thousand speeches on behalf of its passage, he must have grown "weary of well-doing," thinking his colleagues would never pass the treaty. However, he persisted and in "due season"—just before he retired, the Senate approved it and President Reagan signed it, and at long last the United States joined ninety-seven other countries in a treaty outlawing genocide.

The Romanian revolution began when secret police wanted to evict a Reformed Hungarian dissident pastor, Laszlo Tokes, from his home in Timisoara. Members of his church, along with Roman Catholic and Orthodox priests, and an Orthodox congregation, became a conspiracy of goodness and took up a vigil around his home. A twenty-four-year-old Christian brought a large number of candles and distributed them to the crowd. He lit his candle and others followed. Later the secret police opened fire on these demonstrators and shot the young man. Doctors were forced to amputate his leg. In his hospital bed, he later told his pastor: "I lost a leg, but I am happy. I lit the first light."[24]

Those engaged in God's missional ministry in the world enroll for the long term, believing that in "due season" God's kingdom will be manifest. Woolman and Proxmire and the Romanian Christians represent examples of star throwers and fence movers who persist though others despair. They light candles of hope and seek to keep the conspiracy of love burning. We could cite an infinite list of "do-gooders." It would include people like Rosa Park and Martin Luther King, Jr., who never gave up in their fight against the evils of segregation and racism. It would include the famous and the forgotten who sought to break down the walls of hostility separating the United States and the People's Republic of China and the Soviet Union. It would include those who have fought to preserve the whales of the Pacific, the elephants of Africa, the rain forests of Brazil, and so forth. What an endless line of splendor—those who have said "never again" to specific evils and then pledged their lives and their resources in the quest for justice, peace, and the integrity of creation.

Moving into Mission

The Christian rescuers did not place a high priority on their own survival. Their willingness to take up the cross and risk imprisonment and death amazes us because we seldom see communities of Christians who prize mission over maintenance, service over security. Their conspiracy of goodness sets a standard for us to emulate as we struggle with the complexities of a missional ministry in a global, nuclear, and ecological age.

Moving our local congregations and national denominations from survival mentalities to visions of mission challenges us to find new metaphors and means for expressing God's invitation to join in the divine liberation of love on earth. The images explored in this book—a company of star throwers, a covenant of global gardeners, a community of fence movers, and a collegiality of bridge builders—attempt to articulate the biblical and theological concerns and commitments of the church for serving and preserving the world as God's body.

Unless these images become embodied in particular congregations of faith, however, the probability for influencing global crises are minimized. Passing denominational resolutions and joining national and international coalitions for justice and peace are important, but pale in significance to the imperative of moving local churches into missional ministries. As congregations become revitalized, the potentiality for personal and social transformation increases and the possibilities for justice, peace, and the integrity of creation multiply.

Many local churches suffer from a malignancy mentality, a kind of congregational cancer of hopelessness. Typically they believe that the best days for their church were in the past, that no future exists in their neighborhood of strangers, and that it is only a matter of time before the doors must be closed or the programs severely reduced. No evangelistic and mission outreach occurs since maintenance and survival absorb all energies. Daniel Buttrey in *Bringing Your Church Back to Life: Beyond Survival Mentality* contends that one can identify "vision deficiency" as the root cause of this deadly disease.[25]

Sharing a renewed vision of God can overcome the stunted faith of survivalist churches. People often have lost their belief in the power of prayer and the mystery of grace. They may imagine a remote, judgmental, and uncaring God. Introducing them to visions of God as parent, lover, and friend can help them once again feel the personal dimension of the divine.

In every congregation, of course, God's faithful remnant continues to believe and to hope in Jesus Christ, but they need leadership and love. Affirmation of a God who appears present and active in the life of a congregation and the world is vital to a renewed congregation in missional ministry. The future survival of churches depends ultimately on the work of the Holy Spirit.

A dynamic worship life that connects people with the living God reminds persons of the *missio Dei*. People do not need moralistic lectures full of guilt, complaints, and despair. Instead pastoral preaching overflowing with love, care, and hope opens people to new ministries of concern. To overcome compassion fatigue and the daily stresses of parish life, pastors and laity need the spiritual stamina of a daily devotional life and regular corporate worship. The survival of the church requires our best efforts, but finally the future belongs to God.

Second, a renewed vision of the church must replace the stunted ecclesiology of survivalist churches. Buttrey suggests that unbiblical images of the church cripple Christ's body. Concepts of the church as club, massage parlor, fortress, failing business, nursing home, museum, or musty theater showing old classics hurt the institution. One pastor told me that when he assumed his current appointment he discovered that the people expected him to perform primarily as a chaplain, preaching on Sunday and burying the dead. They had not had a confirmation class for twenty-five years and only a couple of baptisms for visiting grandchildren in the past ten years.

Revitalized churches embrace visions of the institution like those reviewed in this book. If members see the church not as a fortress trying to keep neighborhood strangers out, but as a collegiality of bridge builders hosting strangers as "angels unawares," they can discover new possibilities for evangelism and fellowship. By emphasizing the inclusive nature of the church, people of diverse backgrounds, races, cultures, and life-styles are welcomed to participate in the reconciling body of Christ. Envisioning themselves as a company of star throwers, a community of global gardeners, a collegiality of bridge builders, or a community of fence movers can unveil new vistas of service for the mission and ministry of the laity.

Third, a renewed vision of mission can triumph over the stunted outreach of survivalist churches. Only when the church begins to move out in service and witness, inviting others to participate in God's mission, can the church find new life. Evangelism based on waiting for people to drop in on Sunday morning hastens doomsday.

Too many local churches function with the old foreign "mission compound" mentality. Their structure recalls a bygone era and a different group of people. They see their local neighborhoods as alien places, full of folk who think and act differently, sing unusual music, eat exotic foods, and share a hostile culture. Ironically, some of these congregations continue to support missionaries in distant countries, but they treat their neighbors as nonpersons. These congregations need to learn from the experience of missionaries and to begin to understand and translate the language and culture of their neighborhoods.

Daniel Buttrey emphasizes that revitalized churches require an "upward journey" to God through worship, an "inward journey" of nurturing members, and an "outward journey" toward the world. Every church must become a missionary church, proclaiming the Good News of Jesus Christ through evangelism, meeting human needs by acts of compassion and justice, and speaking prophetically to contemporary contexts. In Buttrey's words:

A church with a renewed vision for mission will go into the world as Christ's ambassadors to carry on his work. Instead of being the worthless, insipid salt of survivalism, the mission-minded congregation will be genuinely salty, bringing salvation, healing, and liberation to humanity and glory to God.[26]

Fourth, the revitalization of churches depends upon vision bearers who see beyond survivalism. Usually, the pastor, supported by key laypersons, bears this vision. A pastor without vision, says Buttrey, cannot "lead the people of God out of their valley of dry bones."[27] Discouraged pastors only add to the downward spiral. Lay people can and do fill leadership vacuums, but for them to lift a church out of a malignant mentality remains very difficult. Pastoral leadership burning with passion for the kingdom or reign of God can ignite new fires of faith and service. Laity will respond with additional visions and challenges for compassion and care.

Over the years I have repeatedly witnessed the rebirth of seemingly dead churches thanks to the appointment of dynamic, energetic pastors of vision. When Bill Selby received an appointment to Saint Luke's United Methodist Church in Highlands Ranch, Colorado, efforts were underway to sell the property because of the dwindling membership and high debt. But within a few years, thanks to a loving pastor, dedicated lay persons, and a supportive denominational network, the church had grasped a new inclusive vision of its mission and responded with the fastest growing membership in the region.

For the past twenty-five years I have watched the progress of congregations after my college roommate, M. Kent Millard, was appointed to serve them. In Boston, he was given a dying congregation as his student appointment. Within months, the members made headlines by protesting slum landlords. Assigned to a small rural church in South Dakota, he motivated the congregation to become involved in a school for Native Americans. In his next pastorate he helped the people envision ministry related to Native Americans at nearby Wounded Knee, as well as to gays and lesbians in the city. At a large steeple church he led the congregation to become involved in new ministries to the divorced and the widowed as well as in mission work efforts in Haiti. In each case, his pastoral preaching and care, steeped in love and compassion, motivated congregations to reach outward and become involved in God's liberating and loving initiatives in the world.

Organizing conspiracies of goodness in the world takes different forms and distinct approaches depending on the context and circumstances of ministry. No single pattern can be prescribed, but clearly vision-bearers can lift congregations to new inclusive images of God, the church, and mission. When laity and clergy share a renewed commitment to loving and serving their neighbors in a global village, they enhance the possibilities for attaining justice, peace, and the integrity of creation. The dream of a world house begins wherever we are. As we become God's star throwers, fence movers, global gardeners, and bridge builders, we experience the kingdom of God on earth.

Notes

Introduction

1. Nelson Mandela quoted in Juan Williams, "Nelson Mandela, Out of Bondage," *The Washington Post National Weekly Edition,* June 18-24, 1991, p. 10.
2. Robert Cummings Neville, "The Apostolic Character of Ordained Ministry," *Tower Notes,* Boston University School of Theology, no. 1 (Spring 1990) p. 2.
3. "Mandela Says He's No Messiah," *The Denver Post,* February 11, 1991, p. 3A. Viewing de Klerk also as an apostle may be even more controversial, since he once was Mandela's jailer and represents an apartheid government. Some evidence suggests, however, that de Klerk's self-perception is influenced by his membership in the small Dopper Church that never sanctioned official racial doctrines of the state. According to de Klerk's pastor, he believes that "dialogue is God's style." If the abolition of apartheid is achieved and a new order of justice and peace established in South Africa, this may result from the dialogical processes encouraged by Mandela, Tutu, and de Klerk. See John F. Burns, "Understanding de Klerk, Party Man with a Twist," *The New York Times,* April 1, 1990, and Roger Thurow, "F. W. de Klerk Holds, with Nelson Mandela, South Africa's Future," *The Wall Street Journal,* February 28, 1990, p. 1.
4. Donald E. Messer, *Christian Ethics and Political Action* (Valley Forge, Pa.: Judson Press, 1984), pp. 37 and 107.
5. Orlando E. Costas, "The Mission of Ministry," *Missiology: An International Review,* vol. XIV, no. 4 (October 1986): 465.
6. See Max L. Stackhouse, *Apologia: Contextualization, Globalization, and Mission in Theological Education* (Grand Rapids: William B. Eerdmans Publishing Company, 1988).
7. Keith R. Bridston, *Mission, Myth and Reality* (New York: Friendship Press, 1965), p. 33.
8. For a criticism of this approach, see Arthur F. Glasser and Donald A. McGavran, *Contemporary Theologies of Mission* (Grand Rapids: Baker Book House, 1983), pp. 29, 53-54.
9. Ron Sider, *Evangelism, Salvation and Social Justice* (Barncote, Nottingham, U.K.: Grove Books, Inc., 1977), pp. 17-18.
10. Emilio Castro, *Occasional Bulletin of Missionary Research,* vol. 2, no. 3 (July 1978): 87.
11. Emil Brunner, *The Word and the Church* (London: SCM Press, 1931), p. 108.
12. "The evangelization of the world in this generation" watchword was coined by Arthur T. Pierson, whom Dwight L. Moody had invited to preach at a student conference in Mt. Hermon, Massachusetts in 1886. One hundred of the two hundred and fifty-one students present responded to this challenge and the Student Volunteer movement for Foreign Mission was founded. The original challenge had been to evangelize the world by 1900, but when in the mid-1890s it became evident the task was not going to be achieved so quickly the emphasis changed to "this generation." The year 2000 has now been targeted by many evangelicals for world evangelization. See David Hesselgrave, "World Evangelization

by the Year 2000? " *World Evangelization,* March-April 1988, p. 13. and *Today's Choices for Tomorrow's Missions: An Evangelical Perspective on Trends and Issues in Missions* (Grand Rapids: Academie Books of Zondervan Publishing House, 1988), pp. 48-50.

13. Lynn N. Rhodes, *Co-Creating: A Feminist Vision of Ministry* (Philadelphia: Westminster Press, 1987), pp. 16-18.

14. Kennon L. Callahan, *Effective Church Leadership: Building on the Twelve Keys* (New York: Harper & Row, 1990), p. 3.

15. See Donald E. Messer, *Contemporary Images of Christian Ministry* (Nashville: Abingdon Press, 1989), p. 65.

16. Ibid., p. 73.

17. See Colin W. Williams, *Where in the World: Changing Forms of the Church's Witness* (New York: National Council of Churches, 1963), and George W. Webber, *The Congregation in Mission* (New York: Abingdon Press, 1964).

18. Samuel Moffett, *Occasional Bulletin of Missionary Research,* vol. 2, no. 3 (July 1978): 88.

19. See Clark H. Pinnock and Delwin Brown, *Theological Crossfire: An Evangelical/Liberal Dialogue* (Grand Rapids: Zondervan Publishing House, 1990), pp. 190-93.

20. See Robert K. Merton, *Social Theory and Social Structure* (New York: The Free Press, 1949), pp. 197-200.

21. Gregory Baum, "The Catholic Church's Contradictory Stances," in William K. Tabb, ed., *Churches in Struggle: Liberation Theologies and Social Change in North America* (New York: Monthly Review Press, 1986), p. 127.

1. The Mission of Ministry

1. John Hersey, *The Call: An American Missionary in China* (New York: Alfred A. Knopf, 1985), pp. 68-69.

2. Dan E. Solomon, in an unpublished manuscript, "Leadership: Needs and Expectations," as a response to the author's address at a forum on "Spiritual Leadership into the 21st Century," sponsored by the General Council on Ministries of The United Methodist Church, Atlanta, Georgia, January 17, 1991.

3. This section draws upon a previously published sermon, "God Is Calling: RSVP," by the author in *The Christian Ministry,* September 1986, pp. 28-29.

4. John W. DeGruchy, *Theology and Ministry in Context and Crisis* (Grand Rapids: William B. Eerdmans Publishing Company, 1987), p. 34.

5. Phillip Berryman, *Liberation Theology: The Essential Facts About the Revolutionary Movement in Latin America and Beyond* (New York: Meyer Stone Books, 1987), p. 195.

6. Idea from Frederick Buechner, *Whistling in the Dark* (San Francisco: Harper & Row, 1988), p. 98.

7. Charles H. Kraft, *Christianity in Culture: A Study in Dynamic Biblical Theologizing in Cross-Cultural Perspective* (Maryknoll, N.Y.: Orbis, 1979), p. 287.

8. Hans Küng, *The Council in Action* (New York: Sheed and Ward, 1963), p. 259. For a theoretical and historical discussion of various mission models, see Louis J. Luzbetak, *The Church and Cultures: New Perspectives in Missiological Anthropology* (Maryknoll, N.Y.: Orbis Books, 1988), pp. 64-105.

9. Aloysius Pieris, S. J., *An Asian Theology of Liberation* (Maryknoll, N.Y.: Orbis Books, 1988), p. 63.

10. Arthur F. Glasser, "The Whole Bible Basis of Mission," in Glasser and McGavran, *Contemporary Theologies of Mission,* pp. 30-31.

11. The first four are mentioned by J. Verkuyl, *Contemporary Missiology: An Introduction,* trans. and ed. Dale Cooper (Grand Rapids: William B. Eerdmans Publishing Company, 1978), pp. 91-100. Increasingly, Christians are speaking of the Hebrew Bible instead of the Old Testament in respect to Judaism and the possible perjorative use of the term "old."

12. See J. Verkuyl, *Break Down the Walls,* trans. and ed. Lewis B. Smedes (Grand Rapids: William B. Eerdmans Publishing Company, 1973), p. 40.

13. Don S. Browning, "Globalization and the Task of Theological Education in North America," *Theological Education,* vol. XXIII, no. 1 (Autumn 1986): 43-44.

14. Verkuyl, *Contemporary Missiology,* p. 95.

15. Statistics vary widely. These statistics are based on David B. Barrett, "Annual Statistical Table on Global Mission: 1990," *International Review of Missionary Research*, January 1990, p. 27.

16. "The Third World Reaches to the Ends of the Earth," *Christianity Today*, December 13, 1985, pp. 63-64 and *The Futurist*, March-April 1989, p. 12.

17. Austin P. Flannery, ed., "Vatican II, Ad Gentes Divinitus, 7 December, 1965" in *Documents of Vatican II* (Grand Rapids: William B. Eerdmans Publishing Company, 1975), p. 841.

18. Luzbetak, *The Church and Cultures*, pp. 3, 4, and 8.

19. Cited by Donald J. Shelby, "Being Religious Is Not Enough," sermon at First United Methodist Church, Santa Monica, Calif., May 31, 1987.

20. David J. Bosch, *Witness to the World: The Christian Mission in Theological Perspective* (Atlanta: John Knox Press, 1980), pp. 50-51.

21. Abraham J. Heschel, *The Prophets* (New York: Harper, 1962), p. 287.

22. Cf. Joachim Jeremias, *Jesus' Promise to the Nations* (London: SCM, 1959), pp. 41-46, and Walter Grundmann, *Das Evangelium des Lukas* (Berlin: Evangelische Verlagsanstalt, 1974), pp. 118-23.

23. Bosch, *Witness to the World*, p. 56.

24. See Glasser and McGavran, *Contemporary Theologies of Mission*, p. 128, Hesselgrave, *Today's Choices for Tomorrow's Missions*, pp. 51-52, and Verkuyl, *Contemporary Missiology*, pp. 106-9.

25. Gerald Anderson cited in Editorial, "Mission Evangelism: To Make Disciples," *New World Outlook*, May 1988, p. 9.

26. Billy Graham cited in Clifford Longley, "Runcie Warns of the Perils of Fundamentalism," *The Times*, July 10, 1989, p. 1.

27. Sallie McFague, *Models of God: Theology for an Ecological, Nuclear Age* (Philadelphia: Fortress Press, 1987), p. 52. See also McFague, *Metaphorical Theology* (Philadelphia: Fortress Press, 1982), Leander Keck in *A Future of the Historical Jesus* (Nashville: Abingdon Press, 1971), p. 244, and John Donahue, "Jesus as the Parable of God in the Gospel of Mark," *Interpretation* 32, 1978, p. 386.

28. Elisabeth Schüssler Fiorenza, *In Memory of Her: A Feminist Theological Reconstruction of Christian Origins* (New York: Crossroad, 1983), pp. 120-21.

29. Address by Bishop Anastasios of Androussa, "Thy Will Be Done—Mission In Christ's Way," World Conference on Mission and Evangelism, San Antonio, Texas, May 22–June 1, 1989, p. 7.

30. See Donald E. Messer, "The Revolutionary Hope of the Resurrection," *Together*, April 1973, pp. 28-29.

31. See Philip L. Wickeri, "Development Service and China's Modernization," *The Ecumenical Review*, vol. 41, no. 1 (January 1989): 84-87, and David J. Hesselgrave, *Choices for Tomorrow's Missions* (Grand Rapids: Academie Books of Zondervan Publishing House, 1989), pp. 153-54.

32. Costas, "The Mission of Ministry," 467.

33. Lesslie Newbigin, *The Household of God* (New York: Friendship Press, 1963), p. 163.

34. Robert Runcie, "The Nature of the Unity We Seek," *Ecumenism*, no. 93 (March 1989): 5.

35. Elizabeth Schüssler Fiorenza, *The Book of Revelation: Justice and Judgment* (Philadelphia: Fortress Press, 1985), p. 1. See also p. 9.

36. Mortimer Arias, *Announcing the Reign of God: Evangelization and the Subversive Memory of Jesus* (Philadelphia: Fortress Press, 1984), p. 98.

2. World Havoc or World House?

1. Martin Luther King, Jr., *Where Do We Go From Here: Chaos or Community?* (Boston: Beacon Press, 1967), p. 167.

2. Ibid., p. 171.

3. See Jonathan Schell, *The Fate of the Earth* (New York: Alfred A. Knopf, 1982), Jeremy Rifkin, *Algeny* (New York: Penguin Books, 1984), and Bill McKibben, *The End of Nature* (New York: Random House, 1989).

4. Cited in James A. Joseph "Leadership for America's Third Century: The Imperatives of a Civil Society," *National Forum* (1991):6.

5. Quoted in King, *Where Do We Go From Here*, p. 169.

6. See Donald K. Swearer, *Dialogue: The Key to Understanding Other Religions* (Philadelphia: Westminster Press, 1977), pp. 28-29. Quotation is from F. S. C. Northrop.

7. Gordon D. Kaufman, *The Theological Imagination: Constructing the Concept of God* (Philadelphia: Westminster Press, 1981), p. 181. In an era of unprecedented danger, Sallie McFague (*Models of God*, p. ix), says: "We must ask whether the Judeo-Christian tradition's triumphalist imagery for the relationship between God and world is helpful or harmful. Does it support human responsibility for the fate of the earth, or does it, by looking to either divine power or providence, shift the burden to God?"

8. "Doomsday Clock Hands Retreat," *The Denver Post*, November 27, 1991, p. 3A.

9. Matthew L. Wald, "Guarding Environment: A World of Challenges," *The New York Times*, April 22, 1990, p. 17. See also, Karen Wright, "Heating the Global Warming Debate," *The New York Times Magazine*, February 3, 1991, pp. 24-31.

10. Cited in the foreword of J. Sholto Douglas and Robert A. de J. Hart, *Forest Farming: Towards a Solution to Problems of World Hunger and Conservation*, rev. ed. (London: Walkins, 1980), p. ix.

11. See Joanne Jacobs, "On Christmas Day, 40,000 Children Died Throughout the World," *The Denver Post*, December 29, 1989, p. 6B and "U.N. Group Seeks Money for Health," *The New York Times*, May 2, 1990, p. C22.

12. Jane Perlez, "Spread of AIDS Is Worrying Uganda," *The New York Times*, January 30, 1991, p. A11.

13. C. Dean Freudenberger, *Food for Tomorrow?* (Minneapolis: Augsburg Publishing House, 1984), pp. 15-16.

14. Philip Shakeroff, "Forests Disappear at One and One-Half Acres A Second," *The Denver Post*, June 8, 1990, p. 9a.

15. Cited in ibid., p. 26.

16. Quoted by O. C. Doelling, "Nakasone Apologizes for World War II," *The Oregonian*, October 24, 1985, p. A10.

17. Ibid.

18. Natalie Angier, "Gene Treatments For Human Illness May Be Tried Soon," *The New York Times*, August 1, 1990, p. 1.

19. See *Context*, vol. 22, no. 21, December 1, 1990, p. 1, and Ann Lammers and Ted Peters, "Genethics: Implications of the Human Genome Project," *The Christian Century*, October 3, 1990.

20. Guy Gugliotta, "Milking the Cow for All It's Worth," *The Washington Post National Weekly Edition*, July 2-8, 1990, p. 39.

21. Douglas John Hall, *The Steward: A Biblical Symbol Come of Age* (New York: Friendship Press, 1982), p. 7.

22. Ibid., p. 23.

23. Cited in *Context*, vol. 14, no. 5, March 1, 1983, p. 1.

24. Quoted in Tom Dorris, "Tambaram Jubilee," *One World*, May 1988, p. 9.

25. Ibid.

26. Kenneth Cracknell, *Towards a New Relationship: Christians and People of Other Faith* (London: Epworth Press, 1986).

27. Virginia Culver, "Evangelicals Trying to Convert U.S. Jews," *The Denver Post*, March 10, 1990, p. 6B.

28. Karl Barth, *Church Dogmatics*, vol. 4/3 (T. & T. Clark, 1962), p. 877.

29. John Hersey, *Hiroshima* (New York: Alfred A. Knopf, 1946), p. 61.

30. Krister Stendahl, "The Rainbow," in *Preaching on Peace*, ed. Ronald J. Sider and Darrel J. Brubaker (Philadelphia: Fortress Press, 1982), p. 52.

31. Arthur Waskow, "Noah and the Nuclear Rainbow," *Worldview* (October 1983), p. 18.

32. Charles Birch, unpublished address at the 1979 World Council of Churches' Conference on "Faith, Science and Technology," Massachusetts Institute of Technology, Cambridge, Mass.

33. Ibid.

34. Henri J. M. Nouwen, "A Spirituality of Peacemaking," *Harvard Divinity Bulletin*, October–November, 1985, pp. 6-7.

35. W. Gunther Plaut, *The Torah: A Modern Commentary: Genesis* (New York: Union of American Hebrew Congregations, 1974), p. 85.

36. Yuri Stscherbak, "A Fallen Star Named Wormwood," *Forum*, January 1989, p. 5.

37. See Tom Sine, "Moving Mission to Center Stage," *The Christian Ministry*, September 1985, pp. 12-13.

38. Richard M. Hunt, "No-Fault Guilt Free History," *The New York Times*, February 16, 1976, p. 19.

39. Grace Halsell, *Prophecy and Politics* (Westport, Conn.: Lawrence Hill & Company, 1986), pp. 21-27.

40. John H. Berthrong, "Interfaith Dialogue as Social Action," *Focus*, Boston University School of Theology, Spring/Summer 1989, pp. 1-2. See also "Liberian Government Offers Cease Fire," *The Denver Post*, June 9, 1990, p. 9A and "Buddhists and Christians Meet in Seoul," *Forum*, January 1989, p. 2.

3. The World as God's Body

1. McFague, *Models of God*, p. 13.

2. Dorothee Söelle, *The Strength of the Weak: Toward a Christian Feminist Identity*, trans. Robert and Rita Kimber (Philadelphia: Westminster Press, 1984), pp. 109-11.

3. Gordon Kaufman, *Theology for a Nuclear Age* (Philadelphia: Westminster Press, 1985), pp. 30-46.

4. McFague, *Models of God*, p. 52.

5. Ibid., p. 72.

6. Ibid., pp. 72-73.

7. Grace Jantzen, *God's World, God's Body* (Philadelphia: Westminster Press, 1984), p. 148.

8. Anastasios of Androussa, "Thy Will Be Done," Mission and Evangelism Conference, May 22–June 1, 1989, p. 11.

9. Hesselgrave, *Today's Choices for Tomorrow's Missions*, pp. 72-73.

10. Bosch, *Witness to the World*, pp. 239-40.

11. Eugene L. Stockwell, *Claimed By God For Mission* (New York: World Outlook Press, 1965), pp. 75-76.

12. H. H. Rosin, *Missio Dei* (Leiden: Interuniversity Institute for Missiological and Ecumenical Research, 1972), p. 20.

13. For a sharply critical evangelical assessment, see Arthur F. Glasser, "Conciliar Perspectives," in Glasser and McGavran, *Contemporary Theologies of Mission*, pp. 91-94.

14. Hesselgrave, *Today's Choices for Tomorrow's Missions*, p. 79. Reference is to John R. W. Stott, *Christian Mission in the Modern World: What the Church Should be Doing Now* (Downers Grove: InterVarsity, 1975); idem, "The Significance of Lausanne," *International Review of Mission* 64:299 (July 1975): 291.

15. McFague, *Models of God*, p. 106.

16. Ibid., p. 113.

17. Ibid., p. 119.

18. Norman Pittenger, *The Divine Trinity* (Philadelphia: United Church Press, 1977), p. 109. See also Norman Pittenger, *Love Looks Deep* (London: A. R. Mowbray & Company, 1969).

19. McFague, *Models of God*, p. 135.

20. Lovett H. Weems, Jr., "Toward Building a Passionate Ministry," *Circuit Rider*, July/August 1989, pp. 11-12.

21. Verkuyl, *Contemporary Missiology*, p. 97.

22. Bosch, *Witness to the World*, p. 53.

23. Thomas John Carlisle, *You! Jonah!* (Grand Rapids: William B. Eerdmans Publishing Company, 1968), p. 3.

24. See Messer, *Contemporary Images of Christian Ministry*, pp. 81-96.

25. See Bosch, *Witness to the World*, p. 203.

26. Louise L. Reiver, "A Day in the Life of a Volunteer at Mother Teresa's Missions to the Poor in Calcutta," *New Oxford Review*, July–August, 1989, p. 11.

27. Matthew Fox, *The Coming of the Cosmic Christ: the Healing of Mother Earth and the Birth of a Global Renaissance* (San Francisco: Harper & Row, 1988, p. 228. See also Matthew Fox, *A*

Spirituality Named Compassion and the Healing of the Global Village, Humpty Dumpty and Us (San Francisco: Harper & Row, 1979).

28. Sider, *Evangelism, Salvation and Social Justice*, p. 19.

29. Messer, *Contemporary Images of Christian Ministry*, pp. 19-32.

30. See Leslie Gerber and Margaret McFadden, *Loren Eiseley* (New York: Frederick Ungar Publishing Co., 1983), pp. 103-4.

4. A Covenant of Global Gardeners

1. Clodovis Boff quoted in Alex Shoumatoff, *The World Is Burning* (Boston: Little, Brown and Company, 1990), pp. 72-73. See also Andrew Revkin, *The Burning Season: The Murder of Chico Mendes and the Fight for the Amazon Rain Forest* (Boston: Houghton Mifflin Company, 1990).

2. Marta Benavides, "My Mother's Garden Is a New Creation," in *Inheriting Our Mother's Gardens: Feminist Theology in Third World Perspective*, ed. Letty M. Russell, Kwok Pui-lan, Ada Maria Isasi-Diaz, and Katie Geneva Cannon (Philadelphia: The Westminster Press, 1988), p. 136.

3. Wesley Granberg-Michaelson, *A Worldly Spirituality: The Call to Take Care of the Earth* (San Francisco: Harper & Row, 1984), p. 174.

4. Benavides, "My Mother's Garden," pp. 138-39.

5. McFague, *Models of God*, p. 120.

6. See Charles Seabrook, "Persian Gulf War Could Become Environmental Disaster," *The Atlanta Journal and Constitution*, Saturday, January 19, 1991, p. E-1.

7. Cited from "Tranet" and "World Press Review" in *The Other Side*, November/December, 1988, p. 5.

8. Ibid., " 'Garbage Imperialism' Hurts Poor."

9. Cited by Wesley Granberg-Michaelson, "Introduction: Identification or Mastery?" in *Tending the Garden: Essays on the Gospel and the Earth*, ed. Wesley Granberg-Michaelson (Grand Rapids: William B. Eerdmans Publishing Company, 1987), p. 1.

10. Ibid., pp. 3-4.

11. Walter A. Brueggemann, *Living Toward A Vision: Biblical Essay on Shalom* (New York: United Church Press, 1976), p. 15.

12. Mary Evelyn Jagen, "The Church's Role in Healing The Earth," in ibid., p. 112.

13. Glenn Leggett, "Savoring the Inseparable World of God and Nature," *The Grinnell Magazine*, Spring 1990, p. 22.

14. Eknath Easwaran, *Gandhi the Man* (Petaluma, Calif.: Nilgiri Press, 1978), pp. 170-71.

15. *Our Common Future*, World Commission on Environment and Development (New York: Oxford University Press, 1987), p. 27.

16. Ibid., pp. 3, 5, 7, 26, and 29.

17. Glenn Garelik, "It's Not Easy Being Green," *Time*, December 18, 1989, p. 65.

18. See Lori Woolpert, "Garbage" (periodical reviews) *Whole Earth Review*, Spring 1990, n66, p. 56.

19. Archibald MacLeish, quoted by James Reston, *International Herald Tribune*, June 21, 1982.

20. Fred Krueger cited in "The Environmental Crisis and the Church Response," *Sequoia*, October–November, 1988, p. 8.

21. George E. Tinker quoted in Marline Van Elderen, "Integrity of Creation," *One World*, May 1988, pp. 14-15.

22. Loren Eiseley cited by John Katzenberger, "Star Stuff and Stewardship," *The Windstar Journal*, Winter 1986.

23. G. K. Chesterton cited in Gerber and McFadden, *Loren Eiseley*, also in Eiseley's *All The Strange Hours*.

24. Ghillean T. Prance, "Missionaries as Earthkeepers," *Radix*, November–December, 1982, p. 23.

25. See Jim Castelli, "Worshipers Join Fight To Save the Earth," *USA Today*, February 28, 1990, p. 6D.

26. Alice Walker, *In Search of Mothers' Gardens* (New York: Harcourt Brace Jovanovich, 1983), p. 241.

27. Ibid.

5. A Collegiality of Bridge Builders

1. See Donald J. Shelby's sermon, "Thank God for Amateurs," First United Methodist Church, Santa Monica, California, May 17, 1987.

2. Halford Luccock, "A Bridge Costs a Life," *Halford Luccock Treasury*, ed. Robert E. Luccock (New York: Abingdon Press, 1950), p. 430.

3. The names and occupations are taken from "One Year in the Epidemic: The Faces of AIDS," *Newsweek*, August 10, 1987, pp. 24-31. By that time 22,548 persons in the United States had died of AIDS. By December 31, 1990, that number had increased to 100,777. In 1989 and 1990, 55,460 persons died—more than died in the first eight years after the disease was discovered.

4. Norman Cousins, *AGB Reports*, March/April, 1980, p. 38.

5. See Michael J. Christensen, *The Samaritan's Imperative: Compassionate Ministry to People Living with AIDS* (Nashville: Abingdon Press, 1991). See also *Embracing the Chaos: Theological Responses to AIDS*, ed. James Woodward (London: SPCK, 1990), John E. Fortunata, *AIDS—The Spiritual Dilemma* (New York: Harper & Row, 1987), Earl E. Shelp and Ronald H. Sunderland, *AIDS and the Church* (Philadelphia: Westminster Press, 1987), and John Codges, "Religious Groups Meet the San Francisco AIDS Challenge," *The Christian Century*, September 10-17, 1986, pp. 771-75. The United Methodist Church through its Board of Global Ministries operates an "AIDS Ministries Network Alert," which provides periodic updates on the AIDS epidemic globally and how churches are responding missionally.

6. Ellen Goodman, "North's Boffo Performance Masks Ugly Reality," *The Rocky Mountain News*, 1987.

7. Lindsay Gruson, "Remembering a Tortured Child Who Lives in the Streets of Guatamala City," *The New York Times International*, October 14, 1990, p. 3. Also Jose Zinner, ". . . Not Even the Children," *The New York Times*, October 27, 1990, p. 15.

8. See Níen Cheng, *Life and Death in Shanghai* (New York: Grove Press, 1987).

9. Thornton Wilder, *The Bridge of San Luis Rey* (A to C Boni, 1928), pp. 19, 23.

10. See Messer, *Christian Ethics and Political Action*, pp. 91-92.

11. Jonathan Kozol, *Rachel and Her Children: Homeless Families in America* (New York: Crown Publishing Company, 1988), pp. 69, 71.

12. Paul F. Knitter in "Toward a Liberation Theology of Religions," *The Myth of Christian Uniqueness: Toward a Pluralistic Theology of Religion*, ed. John Hick and Paul F. Knitter (Maryknoll, N.Y.: Orbis Books, 1987), p. 181, argues that ". . . . *a preferential option for the poor and the nonperson* constitutes both the *necessity* and the *primary* purpose of inter-religious dialogue."

13. Christopher Duraisingh cited in "New WCC Mission Director Notes Priorities Ahead," *Ecumenical Press Service*, June 16, 1989, p. 1.

14. John Sobrino, *Jesus in Latin America* (Maryknoll, N.Y.: Orbis Books, 1987), p. 143. Cited in Knitter, *The Drew Gateway*, p. 24.

15. Gustavo Gutierrez, *The Power of the Poor in History* (Maryknoll, N.Y.: Orbis Press, 1983), p. 13.

16. Frederick Herzog, "A New Spirituality: Shaping Doctrine at the Grass Roots," *The Christian Century*, July 30–August 6, 1986, p. 681.

17. Herzog, "A New Spirituality," p. 681.

18. Ibid.

19. "Salvador Wants Bishop Out: Clerics Who Side With Poor Must Go, Pope Told," *Rocky Mountain News*, November 19, 1989, pp. 1 and 3, and "Salvadoran Official Asks Pope to Withdraw Bishops from Nation," *The Denver Post*, p. 15A.

20. William McKinney, "Sidelined Protestantism: What Should Churches Do Now?" *In Trust*, Autumn, 1989, p. 18.

21. Stanley Hauerwas, *Suffering Presence* (New York: Harper & Row, 1986), p. 178. Quoted in *Context*, January 1, 1988, vol. 20, no. 1, p. 6.

22. Jacobo Timerman, *Prisoner Without a Name, Cell Without a Number* (New York: Alfred A. Knopf, 1981), Dedication. See also Robert Hirschfield, "Rabbi Marshall Myer: A Prophet's Agenda," *The Christian Century*, April 26, 1989, pp. 438-89.

23. V. H. H. Green, *John Wesley* (Lanham, Md.: University Press of America, Inc., 1987), p. 32.

24. Jesse Jackson quoted by Calvin Morris, "Does the Church Care?: A Challenge Confronts the Family of God," *Sojourners*, May 20, 1990, p. 21.

25. John Wesley sermon, "Salvation By Faith," *Wesley's Standard Sermons*, ed. Edward H. Snyder (London: The Epworth Press, 7th ed., 1968), p. 49.

26. See Hesselgrave, *Today's Choices for Tomorrow's Missions*, p. 52.

27. Noreen Towers, "Pastors After God's Own Heart," sermon at World Methodist Conference, Nairobi, Kenya, July 23-29, 1986, *Proceedings of the Fifteenth World Methodist Conference* (Waynesville, N.C.: World Methodist Council, 1987), pp. 70-71.

28. See A. Sung Park, "Theology of Han (the Abyss of Pain)," *Quarterly Review*, Spring 1989, and Daniel J. Adams, "The Sources of Minjung Theology," *Taiwan Journal of Theology*, March 1987, no. 9. For a critical assessment see Yong Wha Na, "A Theological Assessment of Korean Minjung Theology," *Concordia Journal*, April 1988.

29. George Mecklenburg, *The Last of the Old West* (Washington, D.C.: The Capital Book Company, 1927), p. 15. See also pp. 7 and 102.

30. Emilio Castro, "Your Will Be Done—Mission in Christ's Way," World Conference on Mission and Evangelism, San Antonio, Texas, May 22–June 1, 1989, p. 1.

31. Sergio Arce, *The Church and Socialism; Reflections from a Cuban Context* (New York: Circus Publications, 1985), p. 6.

32. This quotation is from the Constitution on the Church translated in J. Nuener and H. Roos, *The Teaching of the Catholic Church* (Staten Island, N.Y.: Alba House, 1967), no. 361, p. 369.

33. Avery Dulles, *Models of the Church* (Garden City, N.Y.: Image Books, Doubleday & Company, Inc., 1978), p. 47.

34. Emil Brunner, *The Misunderstanding of the Church* (London: Lutterworth, 1952), p. 17, and Yves Congar, *Lay People in the Church* (Westminster, Md.: Newman, 1965), pp. 28-58.

35. *Against Heresies*, 3, 24, 1 (PG 7, 966).

36. Dulles, *Models of the Church*, p. 64.

37. Parker J. Palmer, *The Company of Strangers: Christians and the Renewal of America's Public Life* (New York: The Crossroad Publishing Company, 1981), p. 67.

38. Jack Nelson-Pallmeyer, *The Politics of Compassion* (Maryknoll, N.Y.: Orbis Books, 1986), p. 4.

39. John Koenig, *New Testament Hospitality; Partnership with Strangers as Promise and Mission* (Philadelphia: Fortress Press, 1985), p. 67.

40. "The Third World Reaches to the Ends of the Earth," *Christianity Today*, December 13, 1985, pp. 63-64, and *The Futurist*, March-April, 1989.

41. Dana W. Wilbanks, "Historical and Theological Basis for Sanctuary," unpublished paper, p. 4.

42. Thomas W. Ogletree, *Hospitality to the Stranger: Dimensions of Moral Understanding* (Philadelphia: Fortress Press, 1985), pp. 7 and 8.

43. Luzbetak, *The Church and Cultures*, p. 76.

44. Cracknell, *Towards A New Relationship*, pp. 149-50.

45. Dwight D. Eisenhower cited by Cark Kreider, *The Rich and the Poor: A Christian Perspective on Global Economics* (Scottsdale, Pa.: The Herald Press, 1987), p. 145. The footnote had the specific reference to where Eisenhower made this statement.

6. A Company of Star Throwers

1. Loren Eiseley, *The Star Thrower*, ed. Kenneth Heuer (San Diego: Harcourt Brace Jovanovich, 1978), p. 171. This essay first appeared in Eiseley's *The Unexpected Universe* (New York: Harcourt Brace Jovanovich, 1969).

2. Ibid., p. 172.

3. Ibid., p. 182.

4. Gerber and McFadden, *Loren Eiseley*, pp. 114-25.

5. Parker J. Palmer, *The Promise of Paradox: A Celebration of Contradictions in the Christian Life* (Notre Dame, Ind.: Ave Maria Press, 1980), p. 47.

6. Eiseley, *The Star Thrower*, p. 184.

7. Ibid.

8. Gerber and McFadden, *Loren Eiseley*, p. 125. Citation from Eiseley, p. 185.

9. D. T. Niles, *That They May Have Life* (New York: Harper and Brothers, 1951), p. 96.

10. Emil Brunner, *The Word and the World* (London: SCM, 1931), p. 108.

11. E. F. Schumacher, *Small Is Beautiful: Economics as if People Mattered* (New York: Harper & Row, 1973), pp. 64-65.

12. General Omar Bradley, Chief of Staff of the United States Army, quoted in Boston, November, 1948. From his "Armistice Day Address" found in *The Morrow Book of Quotations in American History* (New York: Morrow Publications, 1984).

13. Schell, *The Fate of the Earth*, p. 65.

14. James Armstrong, *Mission: Middle America* (Nashville: Abingdon Press, 1971), pp. 89 and 94.

15. See David E. Rosenbaum, "Pentagon Spending Could Be Cut In Half, Ex-Defense Officials Say," *The New York Times*, December 13, 1989, p. 1, and Jesse Jackson, "It's Time for America to Reinvest Defense Dollars in Human Needs," *The Denver Post*, December 3, 1989, p. 4H.

16. Kurt Vonnegut, *Slaughterhouse Five* (New York: Dell Publishing Company, 1969), pp. 73-75.

17. Palmer, *The Promise of Paradox*, p. 47.

18. Cited by Wilfred Bockelman, "Eye of the Needle," *Context*, March 15, 1985, p. 3.

19. Dom Helder Camara cited in *Context*, March 15, 1985, p. 4.

20. Cited by Donald J. Shelby, sermon, "How's the World Treating You, Jesus?" First United Methodist Church, Santa Monica, California, October 25, 1987, pp. 6-7. Shelby's weekly sermons are rich with insights and illustrations.

21. By asserting the missional unity of evangelism and social justice, the author rejects the stance of those who give priority to evangelism over social action or vice versa. Likewise I do not accept mission and evangelism, as synonyms, but rather affirm mission as the more comprehensive term. See David J. Bosch, "Evangelism: Theological Currents and Cross-currents Today," *International Bulletin of Missionary Research*, vol. 11, no. 3 (July 1987): 98-103. No single definition of evangelism exists. Note the collection of definitions and interpretations in Richard Stoll Armstrong, *The Pastor as Evangelist* (Philadelphia: The Westminster Press, 1984), pp. 22-26.

22. See Gregory Baum, "Dialogue with Evangelicals," pp. 95-102, in *Justice as Mission: An Agenda for the Church*, ed. Terry Brown and Christopher Lind (Burlington, Ontario, Canada: Trinity Press, 1985), p. 30, and Arthur F. Glasser, "Mission in the 1990s: Two Views," *International Bulletin of Missionary Research*, (January 1989): 4. Robert Webber agrees that there are at least fourteen major evangelical subcultures and smaller groups within each of them!

23. See "Backsliding Born-Agains," *The Christian Century*, October 31, 1990, p. 990. "According to a recent Roper survey, while 4 percent of born-agains admitted to drunken driving before conversion, three times as many—12 percent—acknowledged doing so after. Similar slippage was discovered in the use of illegal drugs: 5 percent before, 9 percent after. And adultery more than doubled among the born-agains: 2 percent before, 5 percent after."

24. Hesselgrave, *Today's Choices for Tomorrow's Missions*, pp. 69-71.

25. Cited in a press release quoted by Leon Howell, "Summer Meetings," *Christianity and Crisis*, August 14, 1989, p. 229.

26. Waldron Scott, *Bring Forth Justice: A Contemporary Perspective On Mission* (Grand Rapids: William B. Eerdmans Publishing Company, 1980), p. 108.

27. See Richard J. Mouw, *Called to Holy Worldliness* (Philadelphia: Fortress Press, 1980).

28. See Bosch, *Witness to the World*, pp. 11-12 and 192-93. Emilio Castro, General Secretary of the World Council of Churches, tells how Mortimer Arias used to keep a list of the names of all the persons who were personally converted during evangelism events in Castro's church in Uraguay.

29. Mortimer Arias cited in A. James Armstrong, *From the Underside; Evangelism from a Third World Vantage Point* (Maryknoll, N.Y.: Orbis Books, 1981), pp. 35-36.

30. Carl F. H. Henry, "Evangelicals: Out of the Closet But Going Nowhere?," *Christianity Today*, January 4, 1980, p. 22.

31. Virginia Ramey Mollenkott, "New Age Evangelism," *Perkins Journal* (Winter-Spring 1982): 1-2.

32. John B. Cobb, Jr., "Whither the UMC?" *Circuit Rider* (May 1985), p. 11.

33. Graeme Murray, "Renewal of the Local Congregation for Mission," *International Review of Mission*, vol. LXXX, no. 317 (January 1991): 46-47, 54.

34. Raymond Fung, "A Monthly Letter on Evangelism," (Geneva: World Council of Churches, June/July, 1989), p. 3.

35. Castro, "Your Will Be Done—Mission in Christ's Way," p. 7.

36. See Walter Wink, "My Enemy: the Transforming Power of Non-Violence," *Sojourners*, February, 1987, pp. 31. Thanks is expressed to Donald J. Shelby for this illustration.

7. A Community of Fence Movers

1. Douglas V. Steere, *Mutual Irradiation* (Pendle Hill: Sowers Printing Company, 1971), p. 7.

2. See Dulles, *Models of the Church*, pp. 39-66.

3. Dietrich Bonhoeffer, *Life Together*, trans. John W. Doberstein (New York: Harper & Row, 1954), p. 17.

4. See Dietrich Bonhoeffer, *The Cost of Discipleship* (New York: The Macmillan Company, 1963).

5. See James M. Gustafson, *Treasure in Earthen Vessels: The Church as a Human Community* (New York: Harper & Row, 1961).

6. H. Richard Niebuhr, *The Social Sources of Denominationalism* (Cleveland: The World Publishing Company, 1957), pp. 3-25.

7. Larry L. Rasmussen, "Creation, Church, and Christian Responsibility," in *Tending The Garden: Essays on the Gospel and the Earth*, ed. Wesley Granberg-Michaelson (Grand Rapids: William B. Eerdmans Publishing Company, 1987), p. 116.

8. Lawrence Elliott, *I Will Be Called John* (New York: Reader's Digest Press, E. P. Dutton & Co., Inc., 1973), p. 146.

9. Robert Frost, "Mending Wall," in *The Poetry of Robert Frost*, ed. Edward Connery Lathem (New York: H. H. Rinehart & Winston, 1969), p. 33.

10. See Ruth A Tucker, *Guardians of the Great Commission: The Story of Women in Modern Missions* (Grand Rapids: Zondervan Publishing House, 1988), p. 35.

11. "No Divorced Missionaries," *The Christian Century*, October 11, 1989, p. 904.

12. See Hesselgrave, *Today's Choices for Tomorrow's Missions*, pp. 188-89.

13. Cited in "The Dispossessed Are Inheriting the Faith," *Context*, May 1, 1989, pp. 4-5.

14. See Betty Thompson, "Encountering the World Church in Mission," *Response*, October 1989, p. 12.

15. Donald H. Treese, "Church and Academy," *Occasional Paper*, May 1, 1990, pp. 10-11.

16. See John B. Cobb, Jr., Monika K. Hellwig, Paul F. Knitter, Leonard Swidler, *Death or Dialogue? From the Age of Monologue to the Age of Dialogue* (Philadelphia: Trinity Press International, 1991).

17. Aaron T. Beck and Gary Emery with Ruth L. Greenberg *Anxiety, Disorders and Phobias: A Cognitive Perspective* (New York: Basic Books, Inc. 1985), pp. 8-9.

18. See S. Wesley Ariarajah, "Christian Minorities Amidst Other Faith Traditions: A Third World Contribution," *The Ecumenical Review*, vol. 41, no. 1 (January 1989): 21.

19. Appreciation is expressed to Dennis R. MacDonald, Charles S. Milligan, and Bonnie J. Messer for their insights and ideas about phobias and possible terms to describe this phenomena.

20. See Paul F. Knitter, "Preface," Rosemary Radford Ruether, "Feminism and Jewish-Christian Dialogue," and Marjorie Hewitt Suchocki, "In Search of Justice," in Hick and Knitter, eds., *The Myth of Christian Uniqueness*. Also see Karl Barth, "The Revelation of God as the Abolition of Religion," Karl Rahner, "Christianity and the Non-Christian Religions," Wilfred Cantwell Smith, "The Christian in a Religiously Plural World," and John Hick, "Whatever Path Men Choose Is Mine," in *Christianity and Other Religions*, ed. John Hick and Brian Hebblethwaite (Philadelphia: Fortress Press, 1981).

21. James M. Wall, "Jimmy Carter: Doing Work That Speaks For Itself," *The Christian Century*, May 16-23, 1990, pp. 515-16.

22. This section and quotations from John Wesley are cited from Cracknell, *Towards A New Relationship*, pp. 131-33.

23. Paul F. Knitter, "Dialogue and Liberation: Foundations for a Pluralistic Theology of Religions," *The Drew Gateway*, vol. 58, no. 1 (Spring 1988): 8.

24. Wesley Ariarajah, *The Bible and People of Other Faiths* (Geneva: World Council of Churches, 1987), p. 26.

25. Cracknell, *Towards A New Relationship*, pp. 110-27.

26. Cited by Grant Colin, "The Threat and Prospect in Religious Pluralism," *The Ecumenical Review*, vol. 41, no. 1 (January 1989): 50-51.

27. Lesslie Newbigin, *The Open Secret* (London: SPCK, 1978), p. 211.

28. See Hesselgrave, *Today's Choices for Tomorrow's Missions*, pp. 83-84.

29. Cited from Samuel Wilson and John Siewert, eds., *Mission Handbook: North American Protestant Ministries Overseas*, 13th ed., (Monrovia, Ca.: MARC, 1986), p. 564.

30. See Hesselgrave, *Today's Choice for Tomorrow's Missions*, pp. 52-53.

31. Esther and Mortimer Arias, *The Cry of My People* (Friendship Press, 1980), p. 7. See also, David Stoll, *Is Latin America Turning Protestant? The Politics of Evangelical Growth* (University of California Press, 1990).

32. K. P. Yohanna, *The Coming Revolution in World Missions* (Wheaton: Creation, 1986), p. 15.

33. *International Review of Mission*, The San Antonio Conference, vol. LXXVIII, nos. 311/312 (July/October 1989): 457.

8. A Conspiracy of Goodness

1. Philip P. Hallie, *Lest Innocent Blood Be Shed: The Story of the Village of Le Chambon and How Goodness Happened There* (New York: Harper & Row, 1979), p. 108.

2. Harold M. Schulweis, "Remembering the Rescuers: The Post-Holocaust Agenda," *The Christian Century*, December 7, 1988, p. 1127. See also Peter Steinfels, "Beliefs," *The New York Times*, May 12, 1990, p. 9, and Virginia Culver, "Denver Doctor, Priest-Uncle Rescued Jews," *The Denver Post*, p. C1.

3. Quoted from "The Miracle of Denmark," a Christian service of commemoration and celebration of the rescue of the Danish Jews (New York: National Conference of Christians and Jews), p. 5.

4. Schulweis, "Remembering the Rescuers," pp. 1127-28.

5. Ibid., p. 1128.

6. See Nikos Kazantzakis, *Saviors of God* (New York: Touchstone Books, 1969).

7. Pierre Teilhard de Chardin, cited by Canadian Prime Minister Pierre Trudeau at a United Nations Habitat Conference in Vancouver, and quoted in Marilyn Ferguson, *The Aquarian Conspiracy: Personal and Social Transformation in the 1980s* (Boston: Houghton Mifflin Company, 1980), p. 19. See also Pierre de Chardin, essay on "The Spirit of the Earth," Beijing, China, 1936, in the Yale Divinity Library, New Haven, Conn.

8. "Notes from Underground: the Journal of a Family with Hostages in Kuwait," *Newsweek*, November 12, 1990, p. 12.

9. Hallie, *Lest Innocent Blood Be Shed*, p. 183.

10. Philip Hallie, "From Cruelty to Goodness," *The Hastings Center Report* 11 (1981), pp. 26-27.

11. Koenig, *New Testament Hospitality*, p. 143.

12. Hallie, "From Cruelty to Goodness," p. 27.

13. "1993 is the Year," *One World*, July 1990, p. 17.

14. Samuel P. and Pearl M. Oliner, *The Altruistic Personality: Rescuers of Jews in Nazi Europe* (New York: The Free Press, 1988), p. 6. Their study is based on a social psychological orientation, which posits that human behavior is best explained as a decision-making consequence of an interaction between personal and external social, or situational, factors. They dissent from sociobiologists who view genes as the primary source of altruism, from psychoanalysts who emphasize learning, from cognitive developmental theorists who believe that individuals progress through stages of moral reasoning, and social learning theorists who emphasize the reward nature of altruism through reinforcement and modeling.

15. Samuel P. and Pearl M. Oliner report that 87 percent of the rescuers of Jews were motivated by concerns of equity and care. They note that 83 percent of rescued survivors also believed the rescuers were so motivated. See pp. 163 and 170.

16. Ibid., pp. 187 and 222.

17. Iris Murdoch, *The Sovereignty of Good* (London: Routledge and Kegan Paul, 1970), p. 37.

18. Hallie, *Lest Innocent Blood Be Shed*, p. 46.

19. Ibid., pp. 126-27. See also Samuel P. Oliner and Pearl M. Oliner, p. 112.

20. Ibid., pp. 54-55.

21. Ibid., p. 173.

22. A similar story is told by Hallie as happening in Le Chambon, France, in *Lest Innocent Blood Be Shed*, p. 24.

23. See *The Journal of John Woolman* (New York: Corinth Books, 1961).

24. Joseph Tson, "God's Miracle in Romania," *Challenge to Evangelism Today*, 1990, p. 6. See also Jill Schaeffer, "Romania: The Eighth Circle of Hell," *Perspectives*, May 1990, p. 6.

25. Daniel Buttrey, *Bringing Your Church Back to Life: Beyond Survival Mentality* (Valley Forge, Pa.: Judson Press, 1988), p. 42.

26. Ibid., p. 84.

27. Ibid., p. 86.

Index